2008

D1709895

Confessions of a Train-Watcher

Four decades of railroad writing by David P. Morgan

From the pages of **TRAINS** Magazine

Edited by George H. Drury

Confessions of a Train-Watcher

Four decades of railroad writing by David P. Morgan

From the pages of **TRAINS** Magazine

Edited by George H. Drury

KALMBACH BOOKS

On the cover: *Only Yesterday — NY Central 4-6-4 5403.* Watercolor by
Ted Rose in tribute to David P. Morgan. TRAINS 50th anniversary,
November 1990

Printed in Hong Kong

97 98 99 00 01 02 03 04 05 06   10 9 8 7 6 5 4 3 2 1

For more information, visit our website at
http://www.kalmbach.com

Book design: Kristi Ludwig

Publisher's Cataloging in Publication
(Prepared by Quality Books Inc.)

Morgan, David Page, 1927–1990
   Confessions of a train-watcher : four decades of railroad
 writing / by David P. Morgan ; edited by George H. Drury.
   p. cm.
   ISBN 0-89024-306-9

   1. Railroads. I. Drury, George H. II. Title.

TF145.M67 1997   625.1
                            QBI96-40834

Contents

Foreword

The man with the notebook

DAVID P. MORGAN whispered in my ear as I gazed out over a vast gymnasium at Michigan State University and suddenly realized I had to do something with my life. It was the spring of 1971, and as a sophomore, I was required to declare a major. Confronted by the mass frenzy called "registration," I knew I had to make a decision before I could sign up for any classes. I thought of how much I loved TRAINS Magazine, looked down at the registration form, and instinctively put a check mark in the box marked "Journalism."

David could have that effect on you. As the editor of TRAINS, his influence was pervasive among thousands of people interested in railroading — railfans, certainly, but also professional railroaders and journalists. Especially journalists. Reflecting on David's death in January 1990, veteran railroad reporter Fred W. Frailey proudly asserted: "I studied at the David Morgan School of Journalism."

Many readers of this wondrous anthology will know immediately what Frailey meant. For you, this book will be a homecoming, a chance to renew your acquaintance with the man known as D.P.M. You'll find many of your favorite Morgan pieces here, expertly assembled by George H. Drury from hundreds of possible entries from David's 39-year career at TRAINS. There are many others of you, though, who have been drawn to railroading since 1990, readers who have yet to discover the magic of David's writing. Shocking as it is, around the TRAINS offices we have gotten used to the occasional inquiry: "Who was D.P.M.?"

First of all, he was an editor. A great editor. From the moment he assumed the top job at TRAINS in 1953, David began making uncannily "right" decisions. The essence of a magazine editor's job is to have a feel for what readers want and what readers need. The trick is in finding the right combination. David nailed it almost every time. From his embrace of the diesel revolution in the mid-1950's to his landmark "Who Shot the Passenger Train?" issue of April 1959 to his unwavering support of controversial columnist John G. Kneiling, David showed he was willing to take risks and challenge his readers. Then he rewarded them with copious amounts of the sorts of photography, history, romance, and good humor that made TRAINS unique among railroad publications.

David's instincts paid off. When he took over as editor in 1953 (he hired out in 1948, with time out for the Air Force), the magazine was losing money on a circulation of 39,000 and trying to come to grips with a readership that was deserting the railroad hobby — and the magazine — with the passing of the steam locomotive. With the support of a patient publisher, Al Kalmbach, David boldly refocused TRAINS on exciting new things, infusing them with a fresh allure. Diesels, mergers, new technology — all were candidates for a style of active, lively journalism that helped make up for the loss of steam. Readers rewarded him: circulation began to grow, and gradually the magazine became strong. Years later, when the traditional passenger train gave way to Amtrak, there was no commensurate loss of readers. By the time David retired in May 1987, TRAINS had become a profitable magazine, with a devoted audience of 88,000 readers, most of them subscribers.

That's what David the editor could do.

But this book celebrates the writer, not so much the editor. And as a writer David was a triple threat — part poet, part historian, part reporter. The poetry was evident in nearly everything he wrote. His lyrical style evolved in the early 1950's, as a confident young talent matured and began to view his subject with some perspective. Of course, David had a natural gift for the language, as all poets do. But there were outside influences, too: his native South, perhaps, with its traditional reverence for language, and certainly his father, Rev. Kingsley J. Morgan, a Presbyterian minister from whom David inherited a love for the sonorous, measured cadences of the church.

As a student of history, David had few peers, although he never thought of himself as a historian. But he knew that context is critical in good journalism, especially in a hidebound field like railroading. And David provided context every chance he got.

Thus, any analysis of Al Perlman's lean, retooled New York Central of the 1960's had to be made against the backdrop of the four-track, passenger-oriented NYC of a previous era. Any reporting on Electro-Motive's second generation of diesels had to take into account EMD's pioneer days with the FT. Because he was a master researcher, he built the TRAINS library into a formidable resource, then exploited it for all it was worth. Today, the shelves of Kalmbach's David P. Morgan Library are lined with a wide range of books and reference materials, their pages worn from D.P.M.'s attempts to find the one departure time or builder's number or driving-wheel diameter that would make a story airtight.

More than anything else, though, David was a reporter, an old-fashioned pro with a complete command of craft. He lived for the deadline, learning over the years how to make it a motivator rather than a curse. Some of it came from his first job, a short stint with the *Taft Tribune* on the Texas Gulf Coast. David hired out on the small weekly in 1947 and stayed only a year. There he cut his teeth in a gritty small-town newsroom, learning the ropes as he wrote obituaries and reported on car crashes, school board meetings, and local politics. He must have figured out that the best journalism comes from doggedly pursuing the details, every time, for every story. (How lucky we are that Al Kalmbach hired

David before the *Houston Chronicle* or the *Dallas Morning News* could send him soaring off on another career.)

For David the reporter, the tool of choice was the pocket-size, spiral-bound notebook. Even before he entered professional life, David carried a notebook wherever he went on the railroad. In it he would record just about any pertinent detail. Locomotive numbers, car builders, the names of engineers and porters, timetable entries, lengths of sidings, milepost numbers, dates (always dates) — all were important, all were interesting. David didn't keep track of this stuff only out of an obsession for detail, although he certainly was obsessed with detail, like any good fan. No, even as his career was barely beginning, David knew that someday, somehow, all these little scribblings could be useful.

And useful they were. TRAINS Senior Editor Dave Ingles recalls a day in the office when he and David were discussing plans for an upcoming tribute to E7 diesels, published in January 1979 as "The Essence of the E7." Morgan mentioned that he'd seen what turned out to be Burlington Route's first E7's. A possibly skeptical Ingles wanted more detail, so David reached down into a desk drawer, pawed through a pile of notebooks, and yanked out a little dog-eared number held tight with a rubber band. It was a notebook David had with him on a trip out of Denver in 1945. More than three decades later it gave him the lead he needed: "Sunday morning, November 25, 1945, was the final, climactic act of a railroad drama. Not for my fellow GI's fitfully dozing on the walkover plush seats of the 1910 Barney & Smith 12-wheel composite coach hung on the rear of Burlington No. 12, but certainly for me. All night the great O-5 Northern on the head end of our train had played with the 17-car consist as a circus ringmaster cracks his whip. Why, out of Denver the evening before, 4-8-4 5617 had covered the first 78 miles to Fort Morgan, Colo., in 77 minutes, start to stop, per schedule; and come morning I was clocking her at 82 mph. We went into Lincoln, Nebr., dead on time." Later on in the story, David reports on his encounter with EMD cab units 9916A&B, parked in the Lincoln station. "Unbeknownst to me, the E's were brand new, delivered that month," he wrote. "But a glance told me that these E's were different. My notes read: 'dull paint, and 'no names.'"

Think of the details this 18-year-old GI recorded — the number of his 4-8-4, the interior of his coach, the length of the train, the timing to Fort Morgan — and notice how, in the company of a good story, they become much more than a hobbyist's ephemera. David used the details like a rich glue, holding the prose together, giving it irreproachable authority.

I was lucky to learn something of David's methods firsthand in the mid-1970's, when, as a young advertising copy writer at Kalmbach, I wrote the dust-jacket and promotional copy for his most famous book, *The Mohawk That Refused to Abdicate, and Other Tales.* The book was a reprise of David's and photographer Philip R. Hastings' landmark 1950's TRAINS series about the last days of steam. Over the years it had acquired the status of legend, and I was intimidated by my assignment. Of course, David would have none of that. Amused by my nervousness, he took me under his wing and did a great job of editing my very rough copy. "Look for the details," he would say. I can't vouch for the finished product, but I do know that David said he liked it, and that was enough for me.

I had first met David a couple of years earlier, in May 1973, when he and Margaret came to MSU. I was a senior then, and president of the campus railroad club. We had taken it upon ourselves to restore the MSU Museum's largest artifact — Pere Marquette 2-8-4 No. 1225 — and to our great surprise David accepted our invitation to come and speak at our annual spring banquet.

I don't remember much about that day. I was the Morgans' host, and much too nervous about taking care of my guests to keep track of everything else that was going on. But I do recall what happened when we stopped by the engine, which was in a state of substantial dismemberment at a display site near the football team's practice field. As we walked around the locomotive, members of the club couldn't help fawning all over the great editor. But David was a shy man, uncomfortable with his own celebrity, and he tried to shift the focus away from himself. He reverted to the old reporter in him and peppered us with questions. "When was she shopped last before retirement? How good are the flues? How is she different from Nickel Plate's 700's? Who's going to run her?" Always the reporter, always the TRAINS staffer, David couldn't help treating it like an assignment.

And he was taking notes.

Kevin P. Keefe, Editor, TRAINS
Waukesha, Wisconsin
November 1996

9

When the train left, the fun paled

AN alligator crosshead moving back and forth on its greased guides to the dictates of a hot piston rod; the hurried, hollow sighs up the stack as a pair of air pumps breathe life back into the train line; coupled, flanged driving wheels with an overlay of Walschaert beginning their counterweighted, spoked revolutions: these are beautiful things. I first saw and heard them in a little county seat in the heart of Georgia through which four mixed trains passed a day. The town was Monticello, the railroad was the Central of Georgia, the engines were 500-series Baldwin Consolidations, the time was Franklin D. Roosevelt's first term.

Small boys, alas for them, don't grow up in Monticellos anymore. The nation has civilized and urbanized its way up and away from what we called fun. Like digging your toes into the hot, bubbly, black stuff laid down by the jets on the rear of the Mack chain-drive tar truck, or running alongside the yellow road-scraper or watching the hogs being slopped behind the Jordan place. Fun was a rubber gun (i.e., a revolver-shaped piece of wood with a clothes pin on the butt and a knotted slice of inner tube for a bullet) and an American LaFrance fire pumper in full, unmuffled cry and an afternoon of John Wayne for 15 cents.

The most fun, for me anyway, was the railroad. Even a small boy knew instinctively that the railroad was not local, not a resident. The rails came over the hill from Athens, and they curved through town and vanished toward Macon. Monticello was simply a black dot on a map, a 6-point line in the *Official Guide*, a depot, and sidings. We had the courthouse, a Confederate monument, the bobbin mill factory, a sawmill, a cotton warehouse — they were ours. But not the railroad. The 2-8-0 and its mixed train paused, yes — but they did not linger.

The mixed train made an enormous impression upon a sensitive 8-year-old in swishy corduroy knee pants and silent tennis shoes. The 10:30 appearance of the southbound run on Saturday morning was, without question, the biggest event of the best day of the week. I suppose a whistle or the sight of smoke alerted me to its arrival — it's been so many years ago now that I can't quite recall. One tends to remember instants rather than the entire sequence. What I recollect is how suddenly the locomotive was rounding the mountain of sawdust at the mill, loping downgrade to the tangent that began at the stock chute, then rolling straight for me as I stood beside the bay window of the rambling frame station. It seemed to me that the elderly, white-haired, bespectacled operator always waited until the last possible second before picking up his bamboo hoop with the green tissue orders and walking out to the approaching engine. Then, too suddenly and too enormously for a small boy to digest it all, the 2-8-0 was upon us.

It took place all at once — the big, high boiler thrusting by on clanking rods; the Negro fireman down in the gangway thrusting his clenched fist through the proffered order hoop (one of my "jobs" was to retrieve it for the agent); the lurching, complaining freight cars behind perceptibly slowing as determined brake shoes grabbed at the shiny steel treads of their wheels; and finally a confounding noise, total silence, then an explosion of air. The mixed had arrived.

You could almost touch the tension in Monticello. For the town waited on the train and not the other way around. Monticello had all day to pack peaches and bale cotton and sort letters and talk about *Gone with the Wind* and get a haircut — but the mixed train only tarried 20 minutes to a half hour, and if you were riding down the line to Round Oak or picking up the mail and express or meeting your cousin, why, you'd best be down at the depot at half past the hour. The obligation was doubly important for a small boy. I remember peering into ventilated box cars at watermelons stacked double on straw, being delighted when the engine lost her feet on some weed-obscured siding, staring in wonder at the engineer, and trying to see my face in the varnished wood of the coach.

Then all too soon the Consolidation had her train together and was moving off to Macon.

The bystanders vanished uptown, the depot went back to sleep, the rails became still and empty.

When the train left, the fun paled. Oh, the agent might translate the mysterious clicks that occasionally erupted from the sounder next his telegraph key or let you help him unload l.c.l. or allow you to accompany him uptown to collect on waybills. But the mixed was the living thing, and once it had gone you might as well head home for dinner and contemplate whether you should spend your pocket money on John Wayne or jawbreakers and a Butterfinger candy bar.

Even then, deep in a depression and remote in the red-clay interior of Georgia, I was aware that other and grander locomotives than our 500's existed. The engine in the awesome Association of American Railroads grade-crossing poster tacked on the waiting-room wall bore down on a foolhardy motorist so rapidly that the spokes in its drivers were blurred. And the older boys whose fathers drove them over to Jackson to pick up the Atlanta newspapers flung off the Southern Railway told of huge green engines making incredibly fast speeds through the night. My Dad, though, was the highest authority and the most respected. He, too, had loved engines as a boy — strange engines painted crimson and blue and yellow and "black with red lining," engines with inside cylinders and no bells or headlights — English engines. He'd even been an apprentice at the Crewe Works of the London & North Western before entering the ministry. He bought *Railroad Man's Magazine* each month and helped us spike home American Flyer empires all over the attic and told us of other locomotives — Central Hudsons, Pennsylvania K4's, and Seaboard 4-6-2's.

Dad tolerated my Central of Georgia. On the face of its red and blue timetable was a system map in the palm of a hand and beneath it the caption, "A Handful of Strong Lines." That amused my Dad; he'd laugh and say, "That's just about it, too — a handful." I was told that the 500's were all right in their way, though not nearly so sharp as the 400-series Ten-Wheelers beyond my memory which had pulled regular passenger trains through Monticello when he'd first come over from Athens as a guest pastor. That was in pre-depression days, before the banks closed and the CCC crews showed up and the NRA stickers appeared and the CofG acquired a receiver.

Still, for years, the only locomotives of my acquaintance that weren't in his conversation or on a printed page were CofG 500's — the only exception being when a Mikado showed up, which was seldom (indeed, only once in my recall). In retrospect, I suppose a 500 was a reasonable machine to first impress the image of steam upon the mind of a sensitive youngster. She wasn't an eccentric like a Shay or stamped in a singular cast like a Pennsy H10 or ugly because of some deformity like inverted cylinders. Instead, a 500 possessed good lines accented by interesting detail: visored headlight, capped stack, serif numerals, striped sandbox, generous cab. You couldn't ask much more of an example of America's most prolific wheel arrangement.

Not, as I say, that it made much difference, because 500's were all that our branch saw anyway. On the exciting day in peach season when the two morning mixeds had a meet in Monticello with an extra — why, all three engines were 500's. And when an engine spread the rail on the house track behind the station, she was a 500. (She looked big enough that day with her rear drivers dug down in the dirt, and you should have seen her rock perilously back and forth when the hogger eased her back over the frog onto rail again. There was no John Wayne on that Saturday.) Why, we even had a man who was to the 500's what Bob Butterfield was to the faraway Hudsons on Lionel's radio program. The depot loungers called him Whistlin' Dick, said you could hear him rolling clear out across the swamp. He was running a 500 the night a brakeman was crushed between two cars in our town, an event which in some strange way enhanced his esteem among the younger generation.

They say that once you leave a town like Monticello, as my family did at the start of F.D.R.'s second term, you should never go back. I say horsefeathers to that. I've been back — more than

Central of Georgia 2-8-0 No. 500 (Baldwin, 1906) at Birmingham, Alabama, April 23, 1949. Photo by F. E. Ardrey, Jr.

once, too. Once a trio of tired FM H1544's were switching around the boarded-up depot; then — after Southern had taken over the Central — a pair of brand-new little U23B's were coming to grips with a mile of huge woodchip hoppers. And uptown, the monument's still standing tall: TO THE CONFEDERATE SOLDIERS OF JASPER COUNTY, THE RECORD OF WHOSE SUBLIME SELF-SACRIFICE AND UNDYING DEVOTION TO DUTY, IN THE SERVICE OF THEIR COUNTRY, IS THE PROUD HERITAGE OF A LOYAL POSTERITY. "IN LEGEND AND LAY, OUR HEROES IN GRAY, SHALL FOREVER LIVE, OVER AGAIN FOR US"

I like that last line in the inscription on the stone flanked by the statues of CSA infantrymen. " . . . shall forever live, over again for us." I have an accord like that with my 2-8-0's, the 500's. I

Dad said we were doing a mile a minute

THIS is one reason they call 'em the "good old days." The open-platform observation car. Mother would settle in the lounge with the *Ladies' Home Journal* but Dad would accompany my brothers and me "outside" to the rubber-tile floor, brass railing, and campstools, to where the railroading was unmuffled. We'd stare back enthralled as the many tracks of the yard dwindled into the pair of rails of the main, as the horizontal semaphores rose to a 45-degree angle in the distance, as the clickety-clack grew louder and the car cracked the whip on the curves. And Dad would study his Hamilton intently and announce that we were doing a mile a minute. You know, a 707 doesn't fly that fast today. ⌶

Illinois Central's *Seminole,* northbound at Brush Creek, Alabama. IC photo.

A place to watch trains

The station that was God's gift to people who like railroading

THERE are splendid railroad stations and there are places to watch trains, but the two are infrequently synonymous, at least in America. New York's Grand Central is a beautiful terminal, but the intricacies of its levels and loops are remote from the eye and, anyway, too many of its trains are lookalike M.U.'s. Chicago's Dearborn is admittedly rich in atmosphere, for the trundling of baggage trucks and the throb of diesels are close and hi-fi, yet the necessarily great distance to the engine of an outgoing train (inherent in a stub-end depot) as well as the gloom and close quarters beneath the trainshed limit the viewing. On the other hand, L&N's old eyesore on Canal Street, New Orleans, is warm in the memory of many a train-watcher; and although it's no shakes as an edifice, North Philadelphia is one place to watch trains that run on the proverbial headway of streetcars.

Now and then, as in Jacksonville, architecture complements train visibility with happy results.

Ultimately, the fortunate train-watcher arrives at the right station . . . and at the right time. I increasingly suspect that for me this meant Denver Union Station in the fall of 1945.

To begin with, Denver itself is geographically correct to ensure a variety of railroading. The granger roads, Burlington and Rock Island, come bounding over the prairies and through the Colorado uplands, take a look at the Rockies glowering in the distance, and turn their engines around. Union Pacific, too, rolls in from the wheatfields, stays in town just long enough to change power, then heads due north to seek the easier ascent that is Sherman Hill. The Q's Colorado & Southern plays footsie with the Rockies all the way from New Mexico to Wyoming, but it doesn't

Union Pacific 7018, a 4-8-2, is ready to depart Denver with a morning local to Cheyenne. TRAINS Magazine photo by Wallace W. Abbey.

14

dare cross 'em — at least, it hasn't since it quit running narrow gauge to Leadville. For Santa Fe, Denver is an end-of-track town; after all, Atchison has its own altitudes down at Raton.

So that leaves Denver & Rio Grande Western which climbs right up and over the mountains on a continuous 2 per cent grade that plunges through 29 tunnels before it enters America's second longest, the 6.2-mile Moffat.

Denver Union Station, where the passenger trains of all these roads terminate, begin, or pause en route is a through-type affair built in 1880 and drastically revamped and enlarged during 1914–1916. Between each two tracks, which range from 1200 feet to approximately four blocks in length, there is a platform of generous width (17½ feet) protected by concrete umbrella sheds. The structure is owned jointly by all the roads in the name of the Denver Union Terminal Company, but each line handles its own switching and maintains independent coach yards. In regard to train-watching, the station — which stands at the foot of 17th Street — is flanked by viaducts at 16th and at 20th, and I encountered little trouble in getting into the passenger subway which offers access to all platforms.

So much for the mechanics. Why 1945? In a sense I was too late . . . too late to see the C&S narrow gauge trains that once departed on the third-rail outside tracks for Leadville and Georgetown, too late to witness pre-automobile summer traffic (there was an average of 200 trains a day handled in July and August of 1915, up to 45 in less than 2 hours!), too late to see the first *Zephyr* snarl off on its dawn-to-dusk flight to Chicago. Yes, and too late to see them pick up the pieces of the Rio Grande 4-8-4 that blew up in the station area.

And yet 1945 was precisely right. Weary railroads and engines were winding up the herculean work of war in the last stand of big-time steam railroading. But in Denver Union Station the main trains and Mallets rubbed shoulders with two other elements of the railroad scene: the modernism of the 1930's symbolized by articulated streamliners; and the looming future, keynoted by freight diesels and an experimental dome car. In Denver, in 1945, all this lay side by side — great to behold, wondrous to recall.

Let's go back, more than a dozen years back, to a crisp November afternoon . . . back to a few minutes before two o'clock.

No. 5, the *Exposition Flyer*, went west on Rio Grande at 2 p.m. Ancestor of today's *California Zephyr*, she was quite a train. She raced out of Chicago on the Q shortly after noon, got to Denver next day at breakfast — then lay dead for almost 6 hours! (I wondered if perhaps it took D&RGW that long to gather the courage and motive power to tackle the grades ahead.) At length power did appear, infrequently a 5400-horsepower diesel freighter, often a compound 2-8-8-2 piloting a 1700-series Northern. They were unkempt, dirty, tired-looking locomotives that showed their upgrade miles through tunnels, and the white paint on their tires and running boards only called attention to their filth. Air pumps would talk up, then sigh occasionally when the trainline was filled; the communication whistle would beep twice; and No. 5 would move with an assortment of standard cars moistened in the steam of open cylinder cocks and tailed by a 10-section observation car.

Now, Mallets on varnish are unusual enough, but later in the same afternoon from the same station the streamliners whined off across the prairies to Chicago — Q's *Denver Zephyr* at 4 p.m., UP's *City of Denver* at 5. Then, in 1945, they were the true article:

Burlington's *Denver Zephyr* and Union Pacific's *City of Denver*, both in their original form, are ready for their overnight dashes to Chicago. Photo by William C. Moore.

15

lightweight, articulated, custom, fast. Shovelnose units, perhaps the marriage of *Silver King* and *Silver Queen,* powered the Q's entry, and a grille-nosed creature with a streamlined cupola of a cab (that anticipated both *Aerotrain* and the Italians' *ETR 300*) fronted UP's train. Modernists? Odd, but even in 1945 they both were as dated in a sense as Rio Grande No. 5.

There were other diesels, standardized EMD's; but except for Rio Grande's oddly disturbing freighters, I didn't for one moment think of them as forerunners of a revolution. They were just the icing, not the cake, and their presence on such trains as the *Colorado Eagle* and *Rocky Mountain Rocket* only underlined the majority rank of steam.

I, for one, associated engines with trains in Denver. Burlington No. 12, for instance, was a nameless job that left town at 9 p.m. (eventually wandering into Chicago almost 24 hours later) with the cleanest steam power Denver afforded the train-watcher. You could comb your hair looking in the polished, waxy flanks of its 4-6-4 or 4-8-4, high-drivered Baldwin or homemade engines that contrived to look as trim and confident as the day they left the erecting floor. (When I finally left Denver in 1945 it was on No. 12, and next morning the Northern up front was rolling the 80 miles per hour that my train-watching in Denver had led me to suspect.)

There was also Santa Fe 101, the *Centennial State.* It usually rated a 4-8-2, a tall engine of complex valve motion that bespoke faraway places as did no other locomotives I saw. And she could run, too, as I discovered that fall when the 3745 dropped down those 2000 feet from Palmer Lake into Denver in 52 of the fastest miles I ever care to ride — at least around curves.

Finally there was Union Pacific 38 — the *Pony Express* to Kansas City. Or to be exact, Second 38. The first section ordinarily rated diesels with odd numbers such as 7M1 and 7M2 but the second had steam and departed after dark.

I remember the night of November 10, 1945, when I found a train of 13 cars running as Second 38. I walked from the markers' end forward, fully expecting a 4-8-2, instead finding a light Pacific — the 2874 — trailing a ridiculously tiny Vanderbilt tender. (Perhaps it was meant to carry the crew's drinking water, I thought half seriously.)

"Will you make it, with this engine?" I asked the oldster on the right-hand side of the cab. He slid his window open a bit more and contemplated the issue. Then: "Yep, she'll make it." No exclamation, no cursing over the fact that First 38 had had 4000 horsepower worth of diesels with fewer cars, no jesting.

I tended to discount his confidence, especially when the skipper echoed my doubts as he compared Hamiltons with the engineer. Thirteen standard cars were a load and Limon, Colo., the engine change point, seemed worlds removed.

The highball came, my friend released the air, made a cutoff adjustment and hiked back the throttle, and the 2874 left without taking so much as an inch of slack!

That was Denver, 1945.

Editor's note: In 1945 Morgan enlisted in the U. S. Army Air Forces, as it was then called. He did his basic training at Sheppard Field in Wichita Falls, Texas, then was stationed at Lowry Air Force Base in Denver. Denver Union Station wasn't Morgan's first big-league train-watching place, but it was likely his first encounter with Western railroading.

Where the West began

According to whose word you accept on the subject, the American West begins at the Mississippi River, or the banks of the Missouri, or even at the foot of the Rockies. Which may be true in geography or history. But Western railroading begins at the bumper posts in Dearborn Station, Chicago, where the drumhead signatures of Atchison, Topeka & Santa Fe limiteds glow in the perpetual dusk. And the West unrolls across the Illinois Division. You see as much in the desert-yellow agencies, the big bridges, most of all in the trains. Look here now as No. 23, the *Grand Canyon Limited*, comes thundering down upon Chillicothe, Ill., behind a Hudson so huge she dwarfs the 16 or so standard cars behind. The locale, the site are Illinois in name only; the implication, indeed the substance, is of endless space and red men and canyons to come. Yes, the 3460's and the red-and-yellow diesels that supplanted them prove that man is master of his environment, for otherwise how could the Santa Fe Trail begin at Dearborn and Polk streets?

Photo by Wallace W. Abbey.

Confessions of a train-watcher

I THIS MUCH is personal but pertinent. Ten years ago I had a choice to make about this lonely, frustrating, misunderstood, and immensely satisfying matter of train-watching.* Either I had to sharply curtail my interest in railroading in order to seek and hold employment in some unrelated field like insurance or education or I could try to get my paycheck as well as my kicks out of locomotives and such. I was reluctant to cast my lot with any one particular railroad (after all, aren't they almost as intriguing for their differences as for their similarities?), and besides, I didn't have an engineering degree, which comes in handy if one wants upstairs eventually.

No, the gamble was more complex than that. I not only wanted to stick with railroading round-the-clock, but I wanted, as much as my one-fingered typing talent would permit, to explain and to share this preoccupation with others. Which provoked questions: Was railroading just an adolescent whim? Was it worth investing a life in? And who else really cared anyway?

Deliberate train-watching, on either an amateur basis or professional, is a sometimes thankless pastime, of course. Unlike stamp collecting or golf, it has never received Presidential endorsement. The urge is not easily explained, either, as is the love of flight, nor is it a fashionable lunacy like indulging in hi-fi or sport cars or a figure 8 on ice. People in the mass think of trains as things to ride on or things that carry coal and scrap iron and oranges, never as art and fun, drama and tragedy. Well, almost

never, because I seem to recall a musical score on "Pacific 2-3-1," and Christopher Morley has written verse on the subject for *Atlantic Monthly*. As a rule, though, friends, family, and the general John Q. do not comprehend. It is even better for the train-watcher when they ignore him altogether. Otherwise he is the butt of ridicule ("Come again . . . you went a thousand miles to see a *steam* engine?") or the object of well-meaning sympathy ("This is a beautiful photo, honey — just look at all the trains in the roundhouse!").

As for the object of love, the railroads themselves, why, they now have what might be described as a controlled puzzlement about train-watchers. At first, way back in the early 1930's, most roads made the understandable but colossal blunder of rejecting their only genuine suitor: the man who liked them, not for what they could do for him, but just for being railroads. Then, gradually, the industry realized that here was something unique, a ready-made ambassador to whom pay would have been an insult and removal of a treasured amateur standing. So railroading accepted the fan, scheduled excursions for him, sold him engine bells, told him how much a 2-10-4 weighed. I do not think that railroading understands him, though, that it has really convinced itself that the business might just be so engrossing that normal people would pay good money just to ride, and hang the destination.

By its very nature, railroading does not lend itself to armchair enjoyment. Somebody has called it the industry without a roof. Certainly anybody who has seriously watched trains has also made himself cold, dirty, tired, and miserable on their account. Enjoying a cocktail under the tinted glass of a dome is

---

Train-watcher has an English flavor to it; *railfan* is the stock American equivalent. But you can use *enthusiast, student, historian, aficionado,* even *ferroequinologist,* and get the idea across. Anything, indeed, but *hobbyist* — which is a bit weak in view of railroading's appeal.

Mikados of heavy USRA design — led by 1824, L&N's only locomotive to carry a Worthington BL feedwater heater — accelerate a Cincinnati-bound freight through St. Matthews, Kentucky, in May 1943. Photo by Howard Blackburn.

the exception; more typical is listening to the profanity of a switch crew which has just put a gondola on the ground in knee-deep snow, or contemplating one's trousers after open cylinder cocks unexpectedly scoured the top layer of cinders off the station platform. I recall the very day that this aspect of the game was impressed upon me. It was a bleak, wintry afternoon in Louisville & Nashville's South Louisville Yard, and I was watching an 0-8-0 kicking cars. I remember thinking that this was a rough, cold, dirty business, and not one for flower pickers. Not being the outdoor type by nature, I reluctantly concluded that my enthusi-asm for engines and such, if continued, might lead into paths not all hearts and flowers. Once, at least, I was wise beyond my years.

It follows that the more difficult railroading is to behold and admire, the more of a public curiosity is the train-watcher. And it burns us up to receive the label "crank" (of course a minority of fans are nuts; what assembly of human beings ever lacked 'em?), even in its more subtle forms, such as the arched eyebrow and the bemused expression. It is natural for anyone obsessed with the drama of an avocation to want to share his love or, at the least, to have both it and him treated with dignity. Thank God, I say, that Lucius Beebe caught the disease so that at least the book trade could get a few $10 volumes of erudite prose as evidence that, to some people at least, railroading is art and that one need not be odd as a prerequisite to sense same.

I do not mean to stress this persecution complex business too much because, in his turn, the true train-watcher regards The Great Unwashed with that most cruel of human emotions . . . pity. Pity for a soul so drugged with the conventional that it does not respond to the sigh of air brake cylinders or the wallop of a crossing taken at 85. Pity for eyes that see not the beauty of a smoke plume, ears that hear noise instead of stack music, hands that grip Pullman handrails without touching.

So I had a choice to make 10 years ago, and in another sense the choice had already been made. I think it was made when I saw my first steam locomotive, that most awesome of all man's creations. The love of steam is something akin to the love for a woman: no explanation is really necessary, it is just there. And it can be carried to great extremes. Years after the graveside funeral service for steam has been completed and the body is all but in the ground, this magazine continues to receive an occasional letter from some suitor who deems the diesel a farce, who tells me that the railroads are variously wasting precious oil resources, shamefully scrapping good engines, indebting themselves to the bankers for generations, throwing honest men out of work, and losing their grip on the public consciousness — all because of dieseldom. What he argues on factual ground, though, is nothing more or less than his expression of horror and helplessness at the prospect of losing his love. And I sympathize. It is cruel to see steam go, and even the sure knowledge that its passage is a great economic blessing does not ease the pain.

Oh, yes, we train-watchers can be extremists about steam. Without apology, too. I recall forgetting play as a boy in Louisville and running to the end of the street at the first sound of slogging exhaust, and there standing enthralled as a heavy 2-8-2 came fighting up the 1 per cent to Cincinnati with too much tonnage, the whole engine thrusting from side to side with the beat of the pistons, black smoke boiling skyward, and the stack deafening the ears with the old, old, ever-new talk of "I think I can, think I can." Yes, and the goggled, overalled engineer raising his right arm to me as if to say, "It's all right, son; we've got her by the tail."

Hard, mean, tough work, and steam let you know about it, let you know all about the job at hand, let you know she had the tonnage in her teeth and was writing home about it.

Glory! . . . and yet, the urge for me was more than steam, else I should have turned down TRAINS because 10 years ago the handwriting was on the wall. Back then you could (and I did) allay your fears all you wanted with endless discussion of Norfolk & Western and poppet valves and Lima advertising, but the plain fact of the impending funeral was uncomfortably apparent. So the other virtues of the industry, some esthetic and some not, made it seem inviting, steam or no.

Like what? Well, like the inherent nature, flexibility, and productivity of the railroad, particularly on this continent. For example, the Milwaukee Road has a freighthouse only a few hundred feet from the back door of my apartment. It looks local, suburban, small time; to most people it is local. Yet Milwaukee Road could spot virtually any one of the nation's 1,700,000 freight cars at that house; it could be loaded with virtually any material or product known; and that car could move without restriction to virtually any of 56,700 freight stations strung out along 222,000 route-miles of railroad in the U.S. as well as thousands of other sidings in Canada, Mexico and Cuba. The railroads have a very mild word for this transport phenomenon; they call it simply "interchange." It means a common 4-foot 8½-inch gauge and standardized dimensions, air brakes, safety appliances, couplers, etc., not to mention rules and regulations covering all the paperwork involved — the waybill, per diem, switch lists, etc.

In a sense, all of the physical plant of railroading is connected to and at the disposal of the shipper who uses that freighthouse behind my apartment. Cascade Tunnel, Conway Yard, Dotsero Cutoff, the energy of 26,000 diesel units, the talents and muscle of more than a million men and women — all right there in my back yard, as near as my phone. And I find this interesting and vital and praiseworthy. The other night as I was driving out to that apartment, I paced a westbound Milwaukee Road time freight — three F7's leading 70 or more cars along at a sprightly 35 miles per hour. Naturally the raw, bold drama was present, the chanting V-16's, the solid roll and sway of train tonnage following obediently along — coupler locked in coupler, flanges held in check by rail width of precise dimension. Yet there was more. The big mechanical reefer of Northern Pacific — heading back empty to home rails at St. Paul? And the vivid blue Boston & Maine box on roller bearings — cloth from a New England mill for Seattle or Harlowton or Superior?

Skip the importance for the moment; what is essential need not be exciting. And yet I *do* find this exciting, far more thrilling in fact than the Braves in the ninth or Mr. Greco's dancers or even — no, no, not music, for it has too much in common with the logic and harmony of railroading to bear comparison.

I find the railroad stimulating to watch even when action is absent, before and after the trains have rolled. Its buildings and men and geography and history are worth-while cause for study.

Stations alone have recently been the sole subject of a scholarly, book-length examination (*The Railroad Station,* Yale University Press, $7.50), and well they might be. I like to poke around the big, rambling wooden junction depots where the crowds of drummers and picnickers of yesteryear have diminished in sound to the lonely clatter of a veteran L. C. Smith as the agent bills a car of feed from B. J. Jones & Sons. And Union Station, Chicago, at 1:30 a.m., when a handful of weary stragglers and deadheads go through the gate for Milwaukee Road No. 55, when the bar and newsstands are locked up and the last train out doesn't even rate a call on the loudspeakers. Plant City, Sioux City, San Rafael, 30th Street, Englewood, Taft . . . each a building, each an experience, each a few bricks and boards in the vast structure of railroading.

Or the men. Because of the moving about, either aboard train or from one office to another, most railroaders bear a certain stamp that identifies them in their walk and look and dry, caustic, well-intentioned humor. Because railroading is big, so it produces big men, men who can speak of the almost incredible fact of moving 14,000 tons in a single train with the ease of selling a shirt in Sears Roebuck. Also it produced the steward, say, on the *St. Louisan* who seated and fed a dinerful of giggling but prim coeds, saw to it that the expense-account man's steak was medium-rare, mixed a pair of highballs for the coach passengers not allowed in the Pullman lounge, and still found time to smile at and cajole a mentally retarded little girl traveling to a special school. I watched him and I was proud that he was a railroader and not (as he easily could have been) a bank clerk or a librarian.

I suppose, on balance, a railroad man is no better or no worse than any other. Certainly I have encountered my quota of crass, conceited individuals, one or two in the president's chair and, by the mathematical odds, a great many more behind the ticket counter and in the caboose. I recall an agent in L. A. who not only refused to switch my return ticket from one transcontinental to another but took positive delight in impugning my motives, at least until I threatened to dial either Mr. Gurley or Mr. Stoddard (I knew neither gentleman at the time) for satisfaction. Such events are reasonably rare, though, and even then I have at least been on home ground — talking to a railroader about a railroad. Anyway, I must equate such experiences with the countless officials who have trusted my editorial intelligence, with the North Western brakeman who patiently and perchance too simply explained to a lady that the train was delayed picking up mail because "you might say, we're Santa Claus's helpers," and with the Western Maryland fireman who let me run the stoker on his Pacific clear into Elkins.

The geography is good, too. The layman thinks of the Canadian Rockies; I muse over the Spiral Tunnels. He waxes eloquent over the fishing in the Atlantic surf; I recollect Florida East Coast's 800's on the night perishable through Boca Raton. Man can build a highway across any manner of terrain because the automobile is — let's face it — an almost inexcusably inefficient, grossly overpowered thing that eats up grades and curves like an elephant steps on anthills. Yet where the highway can go, so can the railroad — and usually it got there first. I find it marvelous to look from the cupola of a caboose trailing tonnage over Tehachapi — to look up and discover one's road locomotive immediately overhead and at right angles. It is similarly remarkable to witness, say, Chesapeake & Ohio lift 8000 tons of coal 700 feet up and 50 miles forward in just 2½ hours and with only 4500 horses with which to work. Rio Grande Southern's Ophir Trestles, Horse Shoe Curve, those tunnels under the Hudson — all fine and wondrous, and my only regret to date is that time and finance have not yet allowed railroading down the Riviera and up the Andes.

History, too, is within the realm of railroading. It is dramatic history, full of Casey Joneses and Stampede Passes and *Pioneer Zephyrs* (Hollywood, where art thou?), and it is also good. It is an

Four Pennsylvania Railroad I1 Decapods — two here on the head end and two more pushing on the rear — struggle to lift 90 cars of iron ore through Shamokin, Pennsylvania. Photo by Philip R. Hastings.

exclusive story, for what other industry has used so little of our resources and produced so much in return for our economy? Did the steel barons anticipate demand, as Jim Hill did when he threw Great Northern across a wilderness that couldn't support a wagon, much less an iron horse? And how many men of history, no matter what their trade, possessed the corporate courage of Harriman as he gazed across Salt Lake, spurned his engineers' dubiousness, and ordered them to lay a railroad over the waters whether it was possible or not?

Oh, yes, this history has its scalawags, its Daniel Drews and Jay Goulds, but then so has the White House. Moreover, railroading's rogues have generally been aboveboard about it. When they fleeced the suckers they didn't write it off as social progress or as a defense of free enterprise: All of which brings up the basic railroad position of 1957 and a fundamental reason why I, for one, stay close to the rails and have faith in them.

Railroading remains one of the few institutions of the once-popular do-it-yourself school. Railroads ask no Federal or state handout; they get none. For the railroad there are no rivers and harbors bills, no soil banks, no Washington-sponsored public relations agencies of the stripe of the C.A.B., no depletion tax allowances, no "round-trip" gasoline taxes, no nothing that doesn't come out of what the ticket or the cargo calls for. This is unusual. It is so unusual that people flatly refuse to believe it. Those of my acquaintance mutter something about that most ancient of debates, the land grants, and even when I have convinced them that these were loans, not gifts, they still manage to resolve their thinking with some meaningless platitudes about Government and its obligation to help pay parity crop prices, drill oil, dredge the Missouri, widen highways, to do virtually anything for anybody. Excluding railroads. Me? I'm no Old Guard Republican. I just like people and industry to mean what they say, and when railroading says it's self-supporting, you can believe it.

So my acquaintances tell me that a brakeman was surly or No. 23 came in late or they paid $1.25 for a ham sandwich and potato chips, and I think, "Yeah, the railroads do a lot of things wrong — but every last tie and wheel and gallon of diesel oil they own is what *they* paid for, not you or I or us." And I admire this old-fashioned way of doing business. For one thing, it makes the life of an editorial writer easier and his conscience cleaner.

So I took railroading round the clock, as vocation as well as avocation, first as a free-lancer, then for TRAINS. Ten years later I'm here to say the choice was correct. Just the travel would have been worth it — making 2224 miles on an *Aerotrain* . . . accompanying a pair of hoppers from West Virginia to seaboard . . . riding a Camelback (and a turbine and a narrow-gauge 2-8-0) . . . seeing the speedometer of a Hudson on 94 and of a diesel on 98 . . . yes, and lying in the upper berth in a Pacific Great Eastern drawing room high above the Fraser River Canyon, oddly thinking that my fall would be a bit more than most if a wheel got on the ground and we went down the slope.

Also the sights: A big cab-forward 4-8-8-2 standing in the rain at night in Reno, waiting to be off with a Sacramento local — a mountain battler sniffing through her compound air pumps . . . four Pennsy 2-10-0's attempting to restart 90 cars of ore on the steepest part of the grade — also in the rain . . . Electro-Motive's production line . . . Cincinnati Union Terminal's vast arch . . . Tower A down in the third-railed blackness beyond the ends of the platforms in Grand Central Terminal.

And the experiences! *Drinking* maple syrup at the skipper's urging on a Central Vermont caboose. Riding box-car tops through a mild sandstorm on Espee's narrow gauge. Watching the railroad flow through the hands of countless dispatchers and ops and towermen (always finding it difficult to believe that those pen scratches and buttons and push-pull levers actually put trains in the hole, around each other, safely through interlockings). Talking to the brass, thereby getting a fresh perspective on a business, discovering why it frowns upon doubleheaders (labor costs), how long it takes to pick up a typical wreck (30 minutes per car), where it disagrees ("UP may cut the helpers off on the fly, but *we* don't!). Talking to the worthy Brothers — listening to what it was to buck an extra board in 1934, survive aboard a 2-8-8-2 inside Moffat Tunnel, and find one's job of boilermaker had suddenly been eliminated by an engine that didn't have any stay-bolts or crown sheet.

You could call me a professional train-watcher, someone paid to do it — otherwise no different from thousands of other enthusiasts, like my Dad, like you. It's like one of the automobile makers blurbed last fall: "No one can enjoy a new Ford more than you can." So it is with this wonderful world of trains.

The particular payoff of the work I do is that it allows me to see more of railroading than some and to explain and/or share the experience. This can be a rewarding thing, too, this conversing each month in print with 37,000 other train-watchers. It is fine to get a kick out of railroading; it is better to know that you're not the only one. Just the other issue I threw caution to the wind and exclaimed out loud that the most beautiful thing in steam was a Southern Railway Ps-4, and soon a kindred soul in Mississippi — an engineer, in fact — replied amen to that. And now and then some couple stores the sedan, takes me at my word, and domes westward on *California Zephyr;* and the result is invariably the same, "You're right, it is a resort on wheels." The critics are stimulating, too — the firemen who tell me diesels do need firemen and if I'd get out from behind a desk I'd find out why . . . the readers who declare the passenger business is going to pot because the rails don't give a damn and the readers who say I've got on rose-colored glasses if I think passenger trains aren't losing a small fortune . . . and those who tell me I'm losing my touch if a Geep sounds enchanting (or displaying signs of hardening arteries because of certain nostalgic copy on steam).

The disturbing question a few of them ask is this: "Look, Dave, you're closer to the business than I am. Is it really on the rocks? How much longer can an impoverished industry like that stand the gaff?"

A solemn, serious query, that is. And even if I possessed a dogmatic, conclusive answer (which I do not), this would not be the place to print it. It is the place, though, to advance this thought. Even if railroading ended tonight at 11:59, you and I would have been the fortunate ones — those who experienced the great drama, who were close by during one of those rare seasons when man's genius produced something at once useful and beautiful.

Me? I'll remain a train-watcher. ⅂

Super-Power

How the youngest builder in the nation turned out the most important steam locomotive of the century

IF you hail a cab in Lima, O., today and give the driver the most famous address in town, she'll lift the radio mike off the dash and report to the fleet dispatcher:

"Going out to the 'Loco.'"

Only it isn't the "Loco" any more. Nor is it The Lima Locomotive Works, as the engraved stone over the doors of the office building announces. It's just a factory where they manufacture cranes and shovels and work on military contracts behind doors marked "Restricted." No cast steel engine beds are spotted on the production line and no boilers are being swathed in white magnesia blocks. The overhead cranes are not lowering any diesel engines onto the frames of road-switchers nor are any freshly painted traction motors awaiting truck assembly. There are just cranes and shovels and products the Defense Department won't let you write about.

But here and there on the walls of the drafting offices at the "Loco" you find framed pictures of locomotives: a diesel yard engine, a 2-8-4, a streamlined Northern. Eventually someone locates a key and unlocks the door of the board room on the first floor. On the wall at the foot of the chair-lined oak table is a huge photograph of a Chesapeake & Ohio 2-6-6-6 simple articulated. The 549-ton locomotive (and tender) was the largest single product ever constructed by the "Loco." There is a dinosaurian quality about the picture in the board room today: the Allegheny type is a member of a race slated for extinction and the corporation that designed and built her no longer has its shares listed on the big board of the New York Stock Exchange. Lima is just an outlying factory of a company with headquarters in Philadelphia, and the board room table and chairs have a film of dust upon them.

The firm which engineered C&O's H-8 articulated got into the locomotive business as unobtrusively as Electro-Motive, the GM division that was actually responsible for Lima's getting out of the same trade. In 1879 it was a Lima machine shop doing a lucrative business in "direct-acting circular saws" for the lumber industry, with an agricultural sideline of mowers, reapers, threshers and plows. In 1879 the buzz saw of the Lima Machine Works was the loggers' best friend, but it only felled the trees — it could not drag them out of the forests. Teams of mules and horses did that and they also swallowed up the lumberman's profit. Crude railways with wooden rails helped out in the cold mud of winter, but on a descending grade the trucks of logs, with no braking power, would break away and maim or kill the animals. Small steam locomotives were a poor solution because they derailed too easily on the homemade track.

The machine shop built three locomotives that year for the J. Alley Company, presumably a logging outfit. Earle Davis, writing in *Railroad Magazine,* called the first of this trio a Shay while Lima itself thinks all of them were direct-drive engines. The big green record book of the plant identifies No. 1 as a Shay of the "Fontaine type." The historian of today can assume that both Davis and Lima are partially correct, that No. 1 was a half-breed, a cross between a rod and a geared engine. It is known definitely, however, that a genuine Shay type locomotive was built by Lima in 1880 to the patented plans of Ephraim Shay, a white-haired old Michigan lumberman with a flowing mustache and an undisciplined beard.

E. Shay, as he signed himself, was quite an inventor. Prior to the geared locomotive he had figured out a propeller that could steer a boat and eliminate its rudder and he had done some heavy thinking about submarines. The idea of a geared engine came to him almost accidentally. With the help of a local foundry he had built a little locomotive to haul his lumber and save the expense of teams. But he quickly discovered that his motive power destroyed the track even though it weighed only half as much as a loaded log flat. It struck him that if he could substitute *trucks* for *driving wheels* his engine would ride as smoothly as his cars.

During seven winters, when the snow made the wooden rails too slippery for log hauling, Shay kept rebuilding his locomotive until only the cylinders were original. "My friends remonstrated with me," he explained later, "for spending so much time and money on such a crazy idea, and, in fact, they really thought I was a little cracked, and did not hesitate to say so. Actually, I was tired of it myself and would have been pleased to give it up, but the constant ridicule to which I was subjected angered me and I was obliged to continue in self defense to make it a success."

Once Shay thought his "crazy idea" had jelled, he sketched his plan for a geared engine for the proprietors of the Lima Machine Works, who knew him as an old-line customer. They forthwith built one for sale at $1700. It was basically a flat car with a pair of four-wheel trucks; an upright boiler which fed steam to a pair of vertical 7 x 7-inch cylinders was mounted in its middle. These cylinders, in turn, powered a longitudinal shaft

which turned the four axles through bevel gears. The shaft was fitted with universal joints of Shay's own patent to get the locomotive around curves.

The Shay was a logger's dream. Its geared drive supplied high tractive effort at low speed and made that power almost constant torque as compared with a rod-connected engine. Its trucks swiveled around the tightest curves without a squeal and gave a bear hug to the bumpiest rail. The Shay's entire weight was available for adhesion, yet it was well distributed over several axles. The engine machinery was tough and accessible.

Lima's people received Ephraim Shay's blessing to build his geared logger in volume because, as he told a friend, "they put more brains in their work than any firm I [am] acquainted with." Acclaim for the Shay spread through the lumber camps like a forest fire. By 1882 Lima was advertising it for any gauge, wood or steel rails, and any fuel that was handy. The cheapest model retailed for $1700 while the heaviest and most de luxe version sold for $3500. Business was so good that Lima striped up its 450th Shay for special display at the Chicago World's Fair of 1893. By that date the typical Shay had been refined with an offset horizontal boiler, a steel fishbelly frame, and three cylinders. It was possible to buy a three-truck engine, and shortly after 1900 a four-trucker appeared. E. Shay's "crazy idea" finally evolved into a 150-ton locomotive with a boiler pressure of 225

KL&D No. 3, a 42-inch-gauge, two-truck, three-cylinder Shay built for Millars Timber & Trading Co., Ltd., in 1923, is typical of the machines that put Lima into the locomotive business. Lima photo.

pounds and the tractive effort of a heavy Mikado. It was equipped with a superheater and often a feedwater heater. Lima's last Shay, a Western Maryland three-trucker turned out in 1944, was its 2771st.

Both the Climax and the Heisler invaded the geared engine field but neither could match the popularity of the Shay. She was a rough, tough backwoods baby that thrived on 10 per cent grades and practically no maintenance. When winter halted lumber camp operations, the crew simply drained her boiler and greased her rods; next spring she pulled as hard as ever. Hundreds upon hundreds of Shays have completed their labors and been melted into scrap today. The underbrush of swamps and cutover timberland grows deep around the bevel-geared drivers of many others. But even in 1952 a few old veterans are still very much alive. Out in the Mother Lode Country of California on a late afternoon you can hear a lonesome call echoing through the Sierra as a Shay comes down off the mountain with a load of log flats. It would be good to know that somewhere old man Shay hears that awesome whistle and listens to the incredibly rapid exhaust that always betrays the approach of one of his engines.

During the early years of the 20th century the Lima Locomotive & Machinery Company (the more informative name it had adopted in 1892) began to pad its business with orders for rod engines, mostly little lawnmower Consolidations for short lines and class 1 road six-coupled switchers. It was becoming clear that the peak of the Shay boom had passed. In 1912 the firm spent two million dollars for more buildings and new tools, then started soliciting heavy-power orders with a vengeance. In the following year it printed up a new letterhead with the name "Lima Locomotive Corporation" on it and outshopped its first big road engines: five class K-2 Pacifics for the Erie. Erie had purchased No. 50000, the famous Alco experimental Pacific. Its K-2 was approximately the same size as the graceful Alco but it did not measure up to it in performance and Lima received no repeat orders.

The locomotives that Lima built throughout the First World War and its aftermath were long, lanky machines and anything but spectacular in design. The only quality which distinguished them from any others was their uniformly high craftsmanship.

The pride and care of Lima's draftsmen and machinists was a holdover from Shay times. No Lima ever got an inspector's O.K. with slipshod work on it. Otherwise they were conventional and typical. In those years the builders were almost feverishly preoccupied with tractive effort; the stock formula was to add another pair of drivers; and the Mallet, therefore, was in its element. Alco went on record as believing three-cylinder power should be exploited while a Baldwin designer thought that Quadruplexes could be built with 300,000 pounds tractive effort.

Lima was too wet behind the ears in the big engine business to think much about these ideas or do much except duplicate. But in 1916 it attained a new stature overnight when Joel Coffin and Samuel G. Allen and their associates bought up control of the plant, reincorporated it as the Lima Locomotive Works, and adopted a diamond data plate. The Coffin-Allen interests had already played a hand in the hard game of the supply trade by organizing the Franklin Railway Supply Company and the American Arch Company. Big, aggressive Joel Coffin and "lawyer" Allen naturally figured that Lima was a handy market for their wares; they also reasoned that they could bring home a bigger share of the bacon, which at that time was almost entirely divided between Alco and Baldwin. To that end they "stole" the best engineering talent available from the big builders and rolled up their sleeves.

When Coffin and Allen blew into town, Lima was in the midst of its biggest job yet — construction of 25 Western Maryland 2-8-8-2 Mallet compounds. They were ungainly creatures but they did a piece of work out on the road and Western Maryland was quite pleased. The advent of Government control and the United States Railroad Administration in 1918 blocked any immediate design changes at Lima; the erection floor was busy with 130 light U.S.R.A. Mikes and 30 "standard" 0-8-0's. Once the railroads were returned to private ownership Lima kept its forges hot building Pacifics for the Missouri-Kansas-Texas, switchers for the New York Central, a hundred 2-10-2's for the Illinois Central, 4-8-2's for the Burlington. Gradually the diamond crest was finding its way into more and more roundhouses.

Upstairs in Lima Locomotive's brick office building during those years a thin little man bent over a drafting table and peered through silver-rimmed spectacles at an extraordinary blueprint. He was W. E. Woodard, a Cornell graduate who had learned about locomotives on the payrolls of Baldwin, Dickson, Schenectady and Alco; he was one of the designers imported by Coffin and Allen. The plan on the desk before him detailed a 2-8-2 with a fat boiler. It was unlike any engine taking shape in the shops behind Woodard's office. In point of fact, it was unlike any other engine anywhere.

Once Will Woodard had completed his blueprints, the cost of the Mike was budgeted on the company's own expense account and work was begun. The last jacket sheet was secure in May 1922, and the company photographer was called in for a picture. The locomotive he saw had, as *Railway Age* phrased it, "a striking appearance." She had a fierce, almost ugly look suggested by an Elesco feedwater heater hung ahead of the stack and an outside dry pipe along the boiler top that took steam from the dome to the front-end throttle. The Delta trailing truck that supported the extra-big firebox mounted a booster. And there was a lip on her stack.

Even more startling than her enormous look were her statistics. Woodard had purposely designed the 2-8-2 so that she would not exceed the axle loadings of a Michigan Central H-7e, the NYC subsidiary's newest and finest Mikado. He had also engineered her to (1) deliver more power for her weight than any other engine ever built and (2) to do it on less coal. No. 8000, as the Woodard engine was numbered, was slated to go into immediate service on the Michigan Central. It is understandable that President Alfred H. Smith of the New York Central took a personal interest in the 8000's progress and was on hand to give her a pre-service inspection.

Few, if any, new locomotives ever sold themselves more quickly. No. 8000 had been on the road little more than a month when the New York Central ordered 150 duplicates. The H-7e, with which she was compared, was considered a "very well designed Mikado." The 8000 outperformed the H-7e in every department. Notwithstanding an increased weight of less than 2 per cent, the Lima locomotive developed 17 per cent more indicated cylinder horsepower and reduced rail pound by over 42 per cent. *Railway Review* considered her coal and water economy "phenomenal." In tests between Detroit and Toledo the MC kept adding cars until one day the 8000 walked across the division with 10,039 tons behind her tank. New York Central classified the 8000 as its H-10 and by the end of 1924 had over 300.

Woodard's fat 2-8-2 was a demarcation point in American locomotive design. Instead of merely adding more drivers and more weight, he added a booster to obtain more starting power. That left him free to concentrate on horsepower. Woodard had sought an engine that would not run out of steam at 35 or 40 miles an hour (as 2-10-2's had an unhappy habit of doing) or require excessive rates of firing. Subordinate to these aims was a sheaf of minor refinements that added up to more engine and less bulk, improvements like the use of superheated steam for all auxiliaries, hollow axles to save weight, lighter rods to cut down on dynamic augment, and stack exhaust for the booster engine to improve boiler draft at low speeds.

Woodard was pleased with the way the 8000 handled herself on the Michigan Central. But he was not satisfied. He never was.

New York Central cooperated by running a series of starting and acceleration tests at Ashtabula, O., in 1923 and also supplied the results of its invaluable boiler tests conducted at Gardenville, N. Y. Woodard then obtained the bulletins of the Pennsylvania Railroad's Altoona test plant. Thus armed, he sat down at his desk and set himself a problem. Could a locomotive be designed that burned 20 per cent less coal than the 8000 in drag service and 12 per cent less in fast freight operation? Or an engine that developed 10 per cent more drawbar pull for the same fuel?

By late 1924 Will Woodard had his super locomotive down on paper and the forges and lathes were hammering and cutting it out of new steel — again at company expense. Early the next year the A-1, as she'd been dubbed by the works, poked her nose outside the paint shop. She looked like an 8000 that had gone to college, for in addition to an Elesco feedwater heater mounted up front she wore shield air pumps on her pilot, footboards, and a bell on her left cheek. She had a long, large smokebox and a sizable boiler — but behind it all was an enormous firebox supported by a four-wheel trailer truck equipped with a booster. Indeed, as the spectators noted, she was a 2-8-4, a brand-new wheel arrangement.

The A-1 was Woodard's horsepower freight hauler with no holds barred.

A cross-check of her dimensions with those of the 8000 clearly indicated the basic philosophy of Woodard's engineering. Weight on drivers exceeded that of the Mike by a mere 200 pounds while the weight on the rear truck was nearly doubled. Size of cylinders and drivers was identical. The A-1, without her booster cut in, had only slightly more tractive effort, while her factor of adhesion was actually a trifle less. But while the 2-8-2 had 291 square feet of firebox heating surface (including arch tubes), the 2-8-4 had 337. The A-1's 100 square feet of grate area was unmatched by any conventional nonarticulated of that period; even the Virginian's 2-10-10-2 could boast of only 108.7 square feet. The result was a locomotive that delivered her power to the rail in approximately the same manner as the Mike of 1922 — except that the new engine could produce far more of that power.

The painstaking refinement of subordinate parts — rapidly becoming a trademark of Lima — was exemplified all over the A-1. The use of cast steel cylinders (an idea first employed on Alco's 50000 by Francis J. Cole, Woodard's old tutor) saved 4000 pounds of dead weight. To absorb the increased thrust of more horsepower there were tandem rods which placed their load on two axles and four crank pins. An articulated rear truck permitted a bigger ash pan. And there was a gimmick labeled "limited compensated cutoff." This meant that instead of working full stroke when starting (with the reverse all the way over into the front or "company" notch), the A-1 worked at 60 per cent cutoff. The idea has since been described as "an insurance against the engineer working at full stroke without necessity and thereby burning excessive coal." To compensate for a certain drop in starting power, the A-1 steamed at 240 pounds pressure instead of 210 as on the 8000. The design of the cylinders was also adjusted to provide slightly larger intake ports on the front end at low speeds.

On February 18, 1925, the 2-8-4 showed up at the Selkirk (N. Y.) roundhouse of the Boston & Albany and was promptly broken in on a few freight trains. Then the West Springfield Shops mounted a wooden wind screen on her pilot (to protect technicians taking cylinder readings at speed), coupled her up to NYC dynamometer car No. X-8006, and sent her out into the

Lima demonstrator No. 1 was the most successful steam demonstrator ever built. Lima photos.

28

Six Boston & Albany 2-8-4s are shown on the production line in 1926. Lima photo.

Berkshires. For a month and a half the one-spot's performance through New York and Massachusetts was translated into a mass of cylinder cards, tapes and graphs. Then on April 18 she made a run that caused immediate and wide-eyed comment in the pages of the trade press.

At 10:57 that morning B&A Mikado No. 190, an H-10 sister of the 8000, cleared Selkirk Yard eastbound with 1691 tons. At 11:44 the A-1 departed with 2296 tons in tow and began to steadily narrow the gap between the two freights. Out of Chatham both trains were running on multiple track, and at approximately 1 p. m. the 2-8-4 gradually overhauled the laboring Mike and left her behind. She was into North Adams Junction at 2:02, just 10 minutes ahead of the Mike and after 46 miles on the road since Selkirk. Horsepower had paid off.

After her B&A trials were completed, the A-1 piled up more mileage on seven other roads, including the New York Central, Missouri Pacific and Illinois Central. She even hauled the Milwaukee Road's *Pioneer Limited* into Chicago.

As a wheel arrangement, the A-1 was both a pioneer and a salesman. More than 600 Berkshires were turned out for service in the U. S. and Canada; of that number Lima built 355 while Alco, Baldwin and Montreal divided up the remaining 253.

As a flagbearer of the horsepower age, the A-1 had an even greater impact upon the American railroad scene. It is necessary to recall that when she was running road tests, Alco was busy peddling three-cylinder engines and Baldwin was building a watertube-boilered compound 4-10-2, also with three cylinders. Elsewhere, Delaware & Hudson's high-pressure drag engines were raising eyebrows. There was admittedly much of boiler and machinery merit in all of these locomotives, but there was not a true horsepower engine among the lot. In 1925 Lima was the only spokesman for what it termed "Super-Power" locomotives — locomotives with great steaming capacity at speed. Eventually the railroads themselves gave the decision to Super-Power. Baldwin's 4-10-2 was parked in a museum, D&H's ponderous experimentals were scrapped, and orders for three-cylinder power played out. The engines that pulled the roads out of the depression were Hudsons and Berkshires and 4-8-4's and 2-10-4's — engines built upon the Super-Power principles laid down by the A-1 in 1925. No other steam locomotive since the First World War had a comparable effect upon the industry. It is significant to observe that the last new steam engines produced by both Alco and Lima were 2-8-4's.

And the engine that put Lima in the big time? Today the A-1 is No. 8049 on the roster of the Illinois Central, working in a freight pool out of Memphis to Bluford, Ill., and Paducah, Ky.

The A-1 was not the only achievement that Lima Locomotive crowded into that momentous year of 1925. It also built the first engines of a fleet of 70 Texas & Pacific 2-10-4's. The Texas type was the first ten-coupled locomotive with a firebox so large that it required a four-wheel trailing truck, and it thoroughly outperformed T&P's 2-10-2 in tonnage, speed and economy. The fame of Super-Power spread from railroad to railroad and it became a standard topic of discussion at all mechanical conventions. Page after page of feature space was devoted to it in the trade journals and not a few editorials were written in its favor.

Among the railroads which had been impressed by all this

beating of drums was the Chesapeake & Ohio. At that time it was working 10,500-ton coal trains north from Russell, Ky., to Columbus, O., behind large 2-8-8-2 simple articulateds. The trains were broken up in Columbus and dispatched beyond to Toledo behind either Mallets or 2-10-2's. C&O wondered if a Super-Power locomotive could eliminate the engine change and possibly get over the road in less time. To that end it borrowed an Erie S-3 Berkshire with 70-inch drivers (not a difficult transaction in 1929, when both roads were under the thumbs of the Van Sweringen brothers).

C&O shops boosted the S-3's boiler pressure and added a little weight to its drivers. Then the locomotive was put through her paces. The Erie engine, which was a Baldwin, incidentally, turned in a good day's work though she was not an equal of the articulated in sheer pulling power. After examining her dynamometer car readings the C&O decided that the engine it wanted should have the 70-inch drivers of the S-3 but considerably more power and a bigger tender. And since it felt that it would be "impossible to provide sufficient boiler capacity with driving wheels of increased diameter on an articulated locomotive" (a conclusion Lima later disproved with Allegheny type 2-6-6-6's), it ordered 40 Texas types from Lima in 1930. Among other considerations, the shorter length of a 2-10-4 would permit it to have a longer tank and still fit the turntables that accommodated the articulateds.

The Chesapeake & Ohio T 1, when delivered, was the most powerful two-cylinder locomotive in the world. Her debut on the road, running through without change from Russell to Toledo, indicated as much. She more than met the tonnage requirements and she managed that feat on 14 per cent less coal. The H-7a articulated that the 2-10-4 replaced was only four years old at the time and was considered an excellent design. Licking such a sixteen-drivered engine on its home ground with a ten-coupled unit was the final vindication of Will Woodard's Super-Power. More than ten years later the T-1 still bulked big in the motive power world. During World War II the Pennsylvania selected it from among many good designs when War Production Board restrictions prohibited an original PRR blueprint. Lima draftsmen redrew its plans for construction as the Pennsy J-1, though the 125 Texas types the road acquired were built by Altoona and

Baldwin. To this day certain responsible parties assert that the Pennsylvania never owned a better steam locomotive.

The C&O engines were among the last big steam orders that Lima filled before the depression closed up its plant. The only work that kept it open into 1932 was a Pennsylvania order for the Works' first and only electric contract: the construction of cabs and running gear for 30 box-cab 2-8-2's. For many months after their construction these motors, which General Electric was to have fitted with electrical equipment, sat behind the Works in sheds. Eventually all were shipped to the PRR and scrapped shortly thereafter. Presumably by that time the GG-1 had been adopted instead.

Once the electrics were completed, Lima paid off its workers and locked up its buildings; only a handful of designers and office personnel were left on the payroll. The next new locomotive did not leave the plant until May 3, 1934. There was a year-to-year net deficit during those times but the company was in sound financial shape to take the stress. It had no bonded debt, no bank loans, and only one class of stock. Joel Coffin, the man whose salesmanship and organizational ability had done so much for Lima, died in 1935.

At last the railroads picked themselves off the floor of the stock exchange and a few orders trickled into Lima. Furloughed employees were recalled from the farms surrounding the city, and fire again burned beneath the forges. A batch of beautiful Boston & Maine Pacifics were shipped east, while the Detroit, Toledo & Ironton (which operates through Lima) took four 2-8-4's. Something of a record was established in the construction of C&O's first 4-8-4's: an order for five such engines was received on July 10, 1935, and the first of them — the *Thomas Jefferson* — was sent out of the Works on December 11.

The locomotives that created the most excitement around the shops in those prewar years were the GS-2 class 4-8-4's for the Southern Pacific. The biggest railroad in the West (a region where not a single Super-Power engine had been sold) wanted six streamlined Northerns for a swank new coach train to be called the *Daylight*. Lima itself styled the handsome dress of the red-orange-black locomotives with a broad skirt and a "skyline casing" over the domes from the stack to the cab. The top casing also made an admirable smoke lifter and the Espee eventually rebuilt most of its heavy Pacifics and Mountains with it.

The GS-2 acquitted herself nobly over the California Coast Range between San Francisco and Los Angeles and the road immediately placed a repeat order for an 80-inch drivered version. In the years that followed, Espee acquired a fleet of 60 Lima-built *Daylights* and they became its standard heavy-duty passenger power. The miles they rolled and the trains they pulled during the war are legend across the Far West. One of them, GS-4 No. 4459, managed to squeeze over a million miles into her first eight years of service, a fact which earned considerable publicity for the makers of her SKF roller bearings.

In 1939 Lima added to its Espee laurels by building the road's heaviest steam power, a dozen 2-8-8-4's. These engines, called the only "semistreamlined articulateds" because of their skyline casings, slightly outweighed the system's more famous cab-in-fronters.

Eleven years after Lima Locomotive built the Chesapeake & Ohio T-1, the plant constructed the articulated that the road had deemed impossible in 1930. The new Allegheny type, being a Lima design, naturally carried a big firebox. It was so large (135.2 square feet of grate area) that it required a six-wheel trailer truck, rendering the H-8 a 2-6-6-6. For an articulated, the new engine was remarkably trim and compact. She was also the largest locomotive ever built by Lima. Once she hit the road there was reason to recall Ephraim Shay's remark about her builder — "they put more brains in their work . . ."

The H-8's performed yeoman service over the mountains as both road engines and helpers and they were also used to supplement T-1's between Russell and Toledo. One of them ran dynamometer tests on the latter line — tests that Lima hurriedly made public. The graphs indicated a maximum drawbar horsepower of 7498 with frequent readings between 6700 and 6900 in the 42-to-46-mile-an-hour bracket. The 2-6-6-6 was purposely stopped with a 160-car, 14,083-ton coal drag on a level, tangent line for an acceleration test. The Allegheny was moving 19 miles an hour within a space of one mile and within 6 minutes; five minutes later she had the bituminous coal rolling along at 29 miles an hour.

Lima built 60 of the Super-Power articulateds for the C&O and there is talk that the road wishes it had ordered more of them before Lima closed up its order books in 1951.

Lima's last great stand was the Second World War. It built a factory for the production of tanks, and employment was doubled to reach a peak of over 4000 men and women. Its normal business was swelled by the railroads' critical need of more and more new locomotives — smoke-deflectored Mohawks for the Central, additional Espee GS's, C&O articulateds. But orders from the War Department dwarfed these large common carrier contracts. Somehow the Works contrived to outshop 661 2-8-0's (more than all the Berkshires ever built), 70 Mikes and 37 six-coupled switchers for overseas shipment. In one month 40 locomotives were turned out. In those days Lima had more locomotives than Carter had little liver pills.

As the war relaxed its grip upon the Continent and the Far East, Lima shifted to the production of power for peace. Some 280 smoke-deflectored Mikados were built for the French National Railways. Two lots of locomotives were shipped that later fell prey to the Communists: 20 Republic of Poland 2-10-0's and 45 Consolidations under the U.N.R.R.A. program for China. And there was one contract for a nonbelligerent, a set of 14 Belpaire-boilered 4-6-2's for Argentina.

The company came out of that peak production period as confident as ever of steam and what it could do for the railroads. Albert J. Townsend, its able vice-president of engineering, waded into an enormous research program while the shops filled orders for new 2-8-4's, the old sales stand-by. It was announced in 1946 that Lima had patented a double-Belpaire boiler. Townsend combined it with Franklin rotary-cam poppet valves (Lima had rebuilt a Pennsylvania K-4 with poppets back in 1939) to create the company's postwar design, and went knocking on the railroads' doors for a buyer. There was a healthy chance that the diesel boom could be checked, and Lima's advertising indicated that the Works would not give up without a fight.

Then the news broke: the stockholders of Lima Locomotive and General Machinery of Hamilton, O., were considering a merger of their properties. The Hamilton firm's interest in such a combination was obvious. It produced diesel engines, and in 1947 the railroads were a bonanza market for diesel engines — mounted in locomotives. The company also had a free-piston gas turbine under wraps that looked like a natural for locomotive use. Corporation lawyers ironed out the details and the Lima-Hamilton Corporation was formed. Two years later, in 1949, Lima-Hamilton completed its first diesel and its last steam locomotive. The diesel was a 1000-horsepower yard engine for the Nickel Plate; the final steam power to carry a diamond data plate was also NKP: S-3 2-8-4 No. 779.

The Lima-Hamilton line of diesels was subject to normal development pains, but the locomotives were good enough to send back one repeat order after another to the home plant. Built into each one of them was a measure of Lima's traditionally fine craftsmanship. Upstairs in the drafting rooms the old staff worked overtime to acquaint itself with the innards of the newcomer it had fought so diligently. Plans for locomotives with double-Belpaire boilers were filed away while the diesel line was expanded to include a 1200-horsepower road-switcher and a 2500-horsepower transfer unit. And a wash drawing of the new gas turbine was prepared. The diesels — 172 of them — were foreign to the world of the late Will Woodard, but at least Lima was building locomotives.

One noon a Lima man dropped into his broker's office during the lunch hour. The tape inching out of the ticker told the unbelievable story: Lima-Hamilton was merging with the Baldwin Locomotive Works. Henceforth both would be the Baldwin-Lima-Hamilton Corporation ("hardly an inspired title," as the *Investor's Reader* commented). He rushed back to the plant that summer day of 1950 to break the news. Nothing much seemed to get accomplished that afternoon. As TRAINS saw it, the marriage was "hardly a happy wedding." Both companies had switched horses in midstream after the war and neither had made a genuine success of steam or diesel. There was, moreover, widespread duplication of product in the BLW and L-H locomotive lines.

The result was inevitable, and it took place on September 11, 1951. Pennsylvania Railroad No. 5683, a 2500-horsepower transfer engine, was pulled out of the erecting hall into the sun. It was Lima's last locomotive, the final decimal point after over 7700 locomotives. Quite a force from the office and shops was on hand to look it over. In other, happier years there had been confident talk and proud smiles when a new engine left the "Loco." But there was no talk and there were no smiles when the Works' tiny Plymouth diesel took Pennsylvania No. 5683 out through the plant gates. Twenty years before, locomotive production had ceased, too, but then the cause was hard times and sooner or later everyone knew the Works would reopen. But hard times had nothing to do with what took place this day.

It seems incredible that the crane and shovel trade, organized as a sideline in 1928, is now the full-time occupation of Lima. The machines that made it famous are too close at hand in 1952. The office building looks down on a Nickel Plate engine terminal where Lima-built Berkshires are being coaled and greased for the road. And the windows of the entire plant vibrate when a pair of the Baltimore & Ohio's Lima-built 2-10-2's go rampaging south to Cincinnati with a hundred hoppers behind their Vanderbilt tanks.

Today in Lima, O., the cab driver reports in to the fleet dispatcher:

"Going out to the 'Loco.'"

Only somehow it isn't the "Loco" any more. ∎

Editor's note: "Super-Power" was the first half of a two-part article entitled "The Lima Story." The second half, which appeared in the March 1952 issue, dealt with locomotives Lima proposed but never built: a 2-12-6 intended to replace 2-8-8-2s, a streamlined 4-4-4 for fast, light passenger trains, and a dual-service 4-8-6 with double Belpaire boiler and poppet valves.

All heat and sound and sweat

HANGING in our apartment is a Ghost of Industrial Past, a reproduction of the number plate from a Lake Superior & Ishpeming 2-8-0, given to me by the engine's owner, Hocking Valley Scenic Railway. The numerals 33 are encircled above by THE BALDWIN LOCOMOTIVE WORKS and below by PHILADELPHIA, U.S.A. The words are successively proud, personal, limited, and specific to a degree that would make contemporary public relations counselors blanch.

To wit, the function word THE acts as a fanfare to herald the founder's name BALDWIN which in 1916, year of the Consol's birth, still identified America's most famous, if no longer largest, engine builder. Then LOCOMOTIVE — no pluralism here, simply a be-all and end-all of a word. Finally, WORKS. The word is the smokestack Webster's definition of "a place where industrial labor is carried on," i.e., forges, lathes, presses — all heat and sound and sweat. It is not a word suggesting a division, a conglomerate, an umbrella over hosiery to soft drinks. The anchor: PHILADELPHIA, U.S.A. When Mr. Baldwin began building his locomotives there, Philadelphia was the largest, most important city in America, and it remained for more than a century lineside to the track of his biggest, most faithful customer, and port to a world that would host his engines on every continent with rails. Baldwin and Philadelphia were complementary, synonymous, inseparable, singular.

In 1984 there seems no place in the U.S.A. for a personalized, one-product, single-plant, hammer-and-tongs industrial giant. To draw from an inaugural address, the torch has been passed to a new generation of Americans. Whether it shines as brightly or as long is problematic. ⊥

33

The diesel that did it

The story of the 83,674-mile test that doomed steam

SUPPOSE you were asked this question: What single locomotive constructed since 1900 has had the greatest impact upon U. S. railroading? Surely your answer would have to be Electro-Motive No. 103, the 193-foot, 900,000-pound, 5400-horsepower machine on page 35. When the 103 eased through the gates of her La Grange (Ill.) birthplace in November 1939, diesel-electric road freight motive power was only a theory, and by her builder's own admission this dark green, yellow-striped locomotive was an experiment. Eleven months and 83,764 miles later steam's century-old grip on the freight train had been permanently broken and No. 103 was the prototype for the world's first standardized, mass-produced line of diesel freight locomotives. There is no equal in the annals of railroading for such a swift closing of the gap between fancy and fact.

The 103 (its shop serial number, incidentally) was what transpired when a man met an engine. The man was Richard M. Dilworth, Electro-Motive's Chief Engineer. The engine was GM's 567-series 16-cylinder diesel. Dilworth, an infinitely practical man, began mixing oil and railroading in the unlikely year of 1910. Fresh from a hitch in the Navy, he hired out with GE, was soon deep in the business of building and nursing gas-electric cars. He switched to fledgling Electro-Motive in 1926, formed its first engineering department, laid out the design of the articulated power cars of the first *City* and *Zephyr* streamliners, and built the original nonarticulated road passenger diesel which could be termed a commercial success. Dilworth, more than any other single man, knew that the diesel would be doomed if the industry forced upon it existing steam formulas. So he junked such sacred cows as carbody-mounted brake cylinders and solid cast-steel frames,

evolved a brand-new rulebook for a brand-new motive power. And gradually railroading learned to listen to the blunt-spoken onetime Navy electrician who carried a slide rule in his pocket and liked to sketch out his beloved locomotives on 36-inch-wide grocery-store wrapping paper.

The 567-series diesel engine was just as practical, just as tough. The 567, in essence, was a sturdier, more powerful, more accessible, and mass-produced version of Charles F. Kettering's extraordinary lightweight, two-cycle diesel, the frankly experimental 201 model which first spun a locomotive generator aboard the original *Zephyr*. Production of the 567's began at Electro-Motive's two-year-old La Grange (Ill.) plant in 1938, and on August 12 the first 16-cylinder model came off the line.

Sixteen cylinders could deliver 1350 horsepower to a main generator, sufficient for a single-engine diesel freight unit if all axles were powered. Dilworth began to sketch with his soft black pencil. Instead of the A1A-A1A wheel arrangement (i.e., a pair of 6-wheel trucks, each with 2 powered axles and a center idler) used under high-speed passenger units, he adopted two 4-wheel trucks, all axles powered — a B-B unit. A pair of such units, a cab and a booster semipermanently coupled with a drawbar, would create a 2700-horsepower locomotive — the equal, Dilworth figured, of the typical 2-8-2 or even 2-10-2 then hauling U. S. freight trains. Add another diesel of identical description and a 5400-horsepower diesel would result — powerful enough to take on the heaviest articulated steam locomotives.

Electro-Motive issued no press releases on the project, solicited no advance orders, made so little noise about Dilworth's

Electro-Motive photo.

103, in fact, that erection floor photos of the event are nonexistent today. The trade press carried not a line on the experiment.

The two cab units and two boosters that took shape on the erection floor were noticeably shorter than EMC's E6 passenger units — less than 50 feet over couplers instead of 71. The E unit's long, slanted nose was cut back into a jaunty "bulldog" front end. The 103 units were geared for a maximum speed of 75 miles per hour. A steam generator was shrewdly mounted in the rear of each booster unit so that the newcomer could be turned to passenger work if the occasion developed. Finally, the four units were painted dark green, emboldened with a broad yellow stripe; fat GM capital letters were placed upon the snout of each cab; and the assembled locomotive was numbered 103, with the individual units sublettered A, B, C, and D from front to rear. Early in November 1939 the experimental slipped through plant gates for a brief shakedown on the Baltimore & Ohio. She came back to La Grange for final adjustments, then on November 25 set forth to do battle with tradition.

Virtually all of the railroads which Electro-Motive had contacted in advance about the possibility of tonnage tests agreed to having the 103 on the property, but quite a few had reservations about its capacity. In 1939 any number of modern 4-8-4's and

articulateds were rated in excess of 5000 horsepower. A diesel of equivalent output, particularly an expensive and complex creature nearly 200 feet long, was not apt to upset established railroad economics. Why, the new *City of San Francisco* was pulled by a 5400-horsepower diesel in 1939, and didn't Espee have to call out a dependable cab-forward 4-8-8-2 to help the streamliner across the Sierra? Again, as a subsequent textbook put it, imagine the maintenance costs of a locomotive with 64 cylinders!

Two days after Thanksgiving (that was the year F.D.R. switched the holiday to one week earlier) No. 103 moved out of La Grange on an 11-month, 83,764-mile test that was to lead the freighter through 35 states on 20 Class 1 railroads. Dilworth's 912,000-pound cradle for four 567-series V-16's would operate at altitudes ranging from sea level to 10,240 feet, encounter temperatures from 40 below zero to 115 degrees above, pit herself against steam power ranging from 10-year-old 2-8-2's and Berkshires to brand-new 2-10-4's and Challengers. Few if any locomotives have ever been subjected to a fairer analysis of their potential.

The West End of Baltimore & Ohio's Cumberland Division, with its several summits, tunnels, and 2.2 per cent grades, was a natural research center. The toughest grade against the eastbound movement of coal was 11.4 miles of 2.2 per cent extending from M&K Junction to Terra Alta, W. Va. B&O rated a 2-8-8-0 with two 2-8-8-0 helpers at 4590 adjusted tons, and these three articulated required 1 hour 20½ minutes to make the climb at an average speed of 8.4 miles per hour. No. 103 left M&K alone with 1952 adjusted tons and topped Terra Alta in 41.3 minutes by averaging 16.6 miles per hour.

The 103's characteristic of a constant power curve with reduced vulnerability to curvature and varying track surfaces indicated itself on the opposite side of the continent between Pasco and Spokane, Wash., on the Spokane, Portland & Seattle. Out of Pasco east the diesel and a 4-6-6-4 each took a train of 6000 tons over 98 miles of continuous 0.4 per cent grade. No. 103 ran steadily at 26 miles per hour; the articulated's speed varied but averaged out to 10 miles per hour.

A similar reaction was experienced on a real mountain railroad, the 127-mile Moffat Tunnel line from Denver to Bond, Colo. The first 50 miles of the run ascends almost a mile on a relentless

2 per cent grade; there are 30 tunnels, including the 6.21-mile Moffat, and the curves get as tight as 10 degrees. An L-131 2-8-8-2 could move 1800 adjusted tons west in 6½ hours. No. 103 took 1 per cent less tonnage — 1780 adjusted tons — but made the run in 5 hours 20 minutes. The diesel didn't slip on wet rails, curves, or in the tunnels, didn't lose power at an elevation of 9200 feet, and didn't create a smoke problem inside Moffat. The 3600-series articulateds could asphyxiate sheep in stock cars.

The fabled "Rathole Division" of Southern's subsidiary CNO&TP between Cincinnati and Chattanooga afforded the 5400-horsepower diesel a chance to demonstrate how it could reduce train miles. The standard steam engine, a heavy U.S.R.A. 2-8-2, could handle a respectable 3100 tons south from Cincinnati to Danville, Ky., and 3000 tons from Oakdale, Tenn., into Chattanooga. But the grades encountered on the backbone of the run from Danville to Oakdale cut the Mike's rating to 1750 tons, thereby almost doubling train miles in this 138-mile stretch. The touring diesel took 4000 tons over the entire Cincinnati-Chattanooga run and sliced 1 hour off the normal 6 hours allowed from Danville to Oakdale.

Erie had a similar bottleneck between Marion, Ohio, and Meadville, Pa., a roller-coaster run of 212 miles with scores of 1 per cent grades that throttled the road's big Berkshires to 2800 tons from Marion to Kent and 3100 tons beyond to Meadville. Making the same running time, No. 103 hauled 5000 and 5700 tons, respectively, on the same route.

The toughest grades and most modern steam power which the 103 encountered lay in California's Tehachapi Pass. Santa Fe played host, the rival was the system's huge, 74-inch-drivered 5001-class 2-10-4, and the run was the 152 miles between Bakersfield and Barstow. Out of Barstow the Texas type, with helpers on Tehachapi, could take 2200 tons through in 5 hours 55 minutes. No. 103, without helpers, took 2180 tons in 5 hours 4 minutes. In the opposite direction the 2-10-4, with helpers, took 1630 tons through from Bakersfield in 7 hours 50 minutes; No. 103, minus helpers, took 1800 tons in 6 hours 6 minutes.

The 25 miles of 2.55 per cent from Caliente up to Tehachapi Loop is the critical segment of the operation. A Santa Fe 2-10-4 alone could lift 1100 tons up those 25 miles in 2 hours 15 minutes;

a Southern Pacific cab-forward 4-8-8-2 could move 1350 tons in the same time. No. 103 took 1800 tons upgrade in just 1 hour 31 minutes. During such comparative tests it became clear to startled operating men that Dick Dilworth's unheralded, untried experiment was far more than a match, engine for engine, in time and tonnage, with the culmination of more than a century of steam locomotive design.

Some of the subtleties of diesel design became apparent to astonished dynamometer car crews. For example, all 16 axles under the diesel were driving axles; it had no pony or trailing trucks which, on a steam locomotive, guided or supported weight but also subtracted from tractive effort. Not to mention the tender, which, on most modern engines, weighed two-thirds as much as the locomotive it trailed. Again, the rigid wheel base of a diesel truck was only 9 feet, and the distance between truck centers on a cab unit just 27 feet 3 inches. No wonder that a locomotive 193 feet long could be as flexible as a Pennsy 0-4-0 shifter, or that a 456-ton locomotive could possess an individual axle loading of just 57,000 pounds. Thus in that one shining 11-month moment were railroading's formulas and indexes and traditions thrown into a cocked hat. No. 103 was the biggest change in railroading since the air brake.

Although it was not a freight-train operation, perhaps a Northern Pacific experience best sums up the impact No. 103 had upon standard railroading. The date was March 18, 1940, and the diesel had just completed a series of tonnage tests. Now NP wanted the locomotive to handle Nos. 1 and 2, the *North Coast Limited,* between Livingston and Missoula, Mont., 240 miles of mountain railroad with a change of more than 2000 feet in altitude. Included were two helper districts, grades of 2.2 per cent. The schedule was 6 hours 30 minutes westbound, 6 hours 38 minutes eastbound. A 4-6-6-4 could handle up to 10 cars alone, 12 cars with a helper. Two helpers were called if the train exceeded 12 cars. So much for the *status quo.* No. 103 took a 17-car, 1316-ton No. 1 west without helpers in 6 hours 19 minutes; brought a 17-car, 1344-ton No. 2 east without helpers in 6 hours 24 minutes.

Numerous other by-products showed up in the demonstration. Flexibility, for instance. On the Monon No. 103 put on a

Sun glints off the polished nose of 103 standing with a solid train of Pacific Fruit Express refrigerator cars on the Western Pacific at Garfield, Utah, milepost 913. Electro-Motive photo.

time, ran off 12,871 miles. On a Chicago-Denver round trip for the Burlington, the 103 spent 79 hours on the road and 2 hours refueling without shutting down its engines. In a 10-day stint on Missouri Pacific the diesel had a 90 per cent utilization factor, ran off 4350 miles. In all of its operation the diesel was handled by regularly assigned enginemen — with no time lost for special instruction. The drawback there lay in the instinct of most engineers to take slack or to notch out too rapidly when starting. These were excellent steam tactics but the 103 snapped knuckles and pulled drawbars as a result because of its starting tractive effort of 220,000 pounds. Or as Dilworth had it, "It pulled a lot of trains in two and others uphill."

The test could only hint at the potential economies of total dieselization. Indeed, the May 9, 1940, *Oakland Tribune* quoted Western Pacific brass as noting that the 103 did not portend the death of all steam power since it would be "economical for certain runs only." Dilworth's freighter was sprung on the industry too quickly to expect many observers to total up savings from the abolishment of roundhouses, water tanks, ash pits, coaling towers, and other steam appurtenances. Just the comparative fuel costs were revealing enough in 1940. On Kansas City Southern the 103's fuel bill per 1000 gross ton-miles was .0978 cent vs. .1798 cent and .1642 cent for coal- and oil-burning 2-10-4's, respectively. On Mopac the diesel cost .0384 cent/ M.G.T.M. vs. .0539 cent for a coal-burning 2-8-4. And nationwide the 103's fuel costs averaged .067 cent/M.G.T.M. vs. .137 cent for the steam power with which it competed.

3-in-1 act; as well as operating in its usual four-unit makeup, it performed as a two-unit, 2700-horsepower locomotive, and a three-unit, 4050-horsepower engine. On Great Northern's 160-mile St. Paul–Duluth run two units of No. 103 regularly handled passengers by day and freight trains at night without changing the gear ratio. On the Rock Island the four-unit diesel hauled 3174 tons from Chicago to Silvis, Ill., and was split there into a pair of two-unit locomotives. One took 1550 tons beyond to Council Bluffs; the other moved 2200 tons on to Kansas City.

Availability on the entire 83,764-mile test was 100 per cent; not a single delay was charged against the 103. Which says much for not only the locomotive but also its EMC test crew who kept on top of the bugs that inhabit any new piece of machinery. In 32 days spent on the Santa Fe the 103 was utilized 74 per cent of the

By the time Electro-Motive's barnstorming baby returned to La Grange, she not only had proved her point but had become the prototype of the builder's original line of freight units — the 1350-horsepower FT, available as a cab or booster, in multiples of one to four units. Santa Fe was the first customer to sign up, and placed its No. 100 in revenue freight service February 4, 1941. Baltimore & Ohio, Great Northern, Milwaukee Road, Rio Grande, Seaboard Air Line, Southern, and Western Pacific followed suit. Ironically, FT production was cut back, then stopped altogether just when the 5400-horsepower diesels could have done the most good. A shortage of certain alloy steels in World War II obliged La Grange to curtail locomotive output for several months in

1942–1943. Alarmed at the critical motive power shortage (and duly impressed by railroad claims for the diesel), the W.P.B. relented and the big diesels went to war again.

Eventually the FT owner list included Atlantic Coast Line, Boston & Maine, Burlington, Erie, Minneapolis & St. Louis, Missouri Pacific, New York Central, Northern Pacific, and Rock Island. (Many of these units ran off a million miles and more and were then returned to La Grange for upgrading into 1750-horsepower GP9 hood units.)

As for the 103: it was reconditioned, repainted green and white, and sold to the Southern as Nos. 6100, 6150, 6151, and 6104 of that system's subsidiary CNO&TP. All units of the pioneer are still in service more than 20 years later, although at least one has been souped up to 1500 horsepower.

And for all its enormous impact upon the railroad scene of 1939–1940, the 103 was just a beginning. Northern Pacific dispatcher R. V. Nixon recalls that because of a wreck on a low-grade freight line the railroad decided to send the demonstrator over the passenger line from Missoula to Paradise, Mont., keeping the 93-car, 3947-ton train intact. Assisted by Mikes 1781 and 1835 and 4-8-4 2611, the diesel managed to pull the longest, heaviest train in history up the 2.2 per cent of Evaro hill. "It is interesting to note," says Nixon, "that EM 103 used 4 hours 25 minutes on the test train from Missoula to Paradise. The run is now made with F9's in about 2 hours 30 minutes." ⅒

Editor's note: Elsewhere Morgan wrote: "Perhaps the most influential piece of motive power since Stephenson's Rocket," TRAINS once labeled Electro-Motive 103, and the editor found not a whisper of complaint in his mail.

The startling statistics in this story were produced by a "four-section" diesel (the word "unit" didn't appear in EMC's vocabulary until later), essentially a pair of semipermanently coupled cab and booster B-B's operated back to back and arranged for multiple control from either end. In each unit was a V-type, two-stroke 16-cylinder diesel (8½-inch bore, 10-inch stroke) direct connected to a D.C. generator which, in turn, fed four truck-mounted traction motors. Each engine was rated at 1350 horsepower at 800 rpm. No. 103, born at La Grange, Ill., in 1939, weighed 912,000 pounds, stretched 193 feet over couplers, carried 4800 gallons of fuel oil (good for approximately 500 miles), was geared for 75 miles per hour, and was rated at 228,000 pounds maximum tractive effort.

Yet for all of their modernity in the 1940's, the FT series diesels which No. 103 sired are dated indeed today. For example, transition (changing of the motor circuits to obtain desired tractive effort and speed) was a manual operation on the 103 with its own lever on the control stand; today it's fully automatic. The 103 had no dynamic brake; that innovation was introduced on Santa Fe FT's. And the engineers aboard the 103 had to observe short-term overload ratings on the traction motors lest they become overheated. As for power output, an FT unit had a continuous tractive effort (indefinite-term power output without overloading motors) of approximately 32,500 pounds;

today's 1750-horsepower GP9 has a continuous rating of 50,000 pounds.

Several hundred FT units were produced to the blueprints of the 103. Santa Fe, with more than 320 on its roster, bought the most; Great Northern with 96 was runner-up. GN was the only buyer to specify steam generators installed in some of its FT's so that they could be operated in dual service, but after World War II Santa Fe regeared a few FT's and added boilers when its *Super Chief* and *El Cap* were placed on daily schedules. Most of the FT's saw wartime traffic at its peak. Western Pacific employed its three 5400-horsepower FT's as a "flying squadron" which were ordered out to wherever bottlenecks threatened. Milwaukee Road used its FT's to bridge the 212-mile Avery (Ida.)-Othello (Wash.) "gap" between its electrified zones without reducing train tonnage — as had been necessary with the 2-6-6-2's previously used. Santa Fe virtually dieselized its Winslow (Ariz.)-Barstow (Calif.) district when excessive helper mileage and the necessity to import boiler water threatened to tie up the railroad.

Many FT fleets have been reincarnated as GP9 hoods today via EMD's upgrading program; the familiar quadruple-portholed carbodies have vanished from B&M, C&NW, and Milwaukee. But the sizable studs of Santa Fe, Burlington, and GN FT's roll on . . . as does 103 herself on the Southern.

Most famous of faces

THE diesel entered railroading inside a carbody that looked for all the world like a box-cab interurban motor minus its trolley poles. A decade later the engine destined to become the *enfant terrible* of the steam foundries was born again within shovel-nosed and articulated "streamline" trains that sped past what the writers called "the century mark" on the speedometer so many times that people quit talking about Charlie Hogan and the 999. And then, in 1937, the diesel put on long pants and became a genuine road locomotive. General Motors' stylists thereupon created a "step-down" nose which, at one stroke, was functional and esthetic. And so obvious and sound in principle that it would endure (and be imitated, here and abroad) for 20 years — until sidetracked by the hood mania. The GM classic appeared first in more subtle, even feminine cast on B&O and Santa Fe 3600 h.p. *Capitol* and *Super Chief* power; was blunted into its present "bulldog" outline as early as 1939 on the first diesel freighter; and acquired its complementary 45-degree-angle number boards after the war with the advent of the F3. Behold it here on a Burlington (Colorado & Southern) F7 . . . the sturdy, slanting snout to ward off the unwary at a grade crossing, the crew riding high for visibility as well as protection, all the appurtenances: jutting headlight, roof-top horns, angled side windows. Seldom in industrial design has styling been so patently "right" — right from the start.

Photo by Ed Wojtas.

If you knew Katy . . .

I WONDER if I might put in a word here for Matthew Scott Sloan who ran the Missouri-Kansas-Texas for a long spell (1934–1945) which will remain forever memorable . . . for sensitive souls . . . for me. Now Mr. Sloan was a railroad neophyte; an electric utilities exec with a home address in Brooklyn, N. Y.; a strong-willed, bulldog-tempered man; the man who barehandedly hauled Katy out of the depression and through the war. But he wasn't content to fiddle with finances; he wanted to run the trains, too. He went roaming on his railroad in a Chrysler on flanged wheels to see if the ballast had a fine, straight edge, to see the Denison Shop turning out box cars in bright yellow per his memo, to see the *Texas Special* thunder past on the advertised as he had insisted that it should. I never met the man. But I did see his Katy. Glory, but it was a fine experience: the green passenger equipment with gilt lettering and red-and-white embossed Katy heralds hung between the baggage car doors; the rock-ballasted iron with not a stone out of place from one semaphore to the next; the dining car meals so rare that a Dallas businessman used to ride out to Greenville just to have a Katy dinner. Mr. Sloan didn't have any diesels then; he didn't even have a modern or a sizable steam locomotive. But he did have maintenance. His engines shone. They had in common graphite smokeboxes, glossy black jackets, white tires and running board edges, and the inevitable raised Katy heralds. See here as the window of the *Bluebonnet*'s diner in San Antonio reflects the nose of Pacific 380 — that was Sloan's Katy. Seems now in retrospect that Katy survived so de luxe for so brief a season. But how fine to remember when a railroad could look an institution as well as be one. I

Photo by Philip R. Hastings.

Can Mr. B. save Miss Katy?

WHAT recommends itself as the incongruity of the season is this: The man who coined, defined, and broadcast the term "super-railroads" (and who presided over a reasonable facsimile of one — Pittsburgh & Lake Erie — until his retirement at the end of 1964) now finds himself wrestling with the likes of the Missouri-Kansas-Texas. When John Walker Barriger was summoned to the Katy's bedside a year and a half ago, the 2869-mile carrier's only superlative was the rapidity of its descent from grace. Not only did Katy have scarcely more than gauge in common with the Barriger dream (electrified mains of 0.5 per cent grades and 1-degree curves carrying 70 mph 150-car freights), but the line was dying. Katy faced not bankruptcy but liquidation.

In fact, the railroad was so close to extinction that Barriger spent his first 24 months on the property simply assessing the dilemma. He found one out of every five freight cars out of service, awaiting repairs, yet the ancient, "out-of-Noah's-ark" car shops had been closed for four years. Track had deteriorated to the point where even a 25 mph speed limit could not prevent wrecks, and the Dallas terminal area was reporting almost a derailment a day. Mainline service was down to a freight each way a day, and triweekly or even weekly frequency was the rule on branches. Large shippers had taken to blackballing Katy, notably for its failure to pay damage claims dating back more than two years. Employee morale hardly existed. Abandonment for some 18 per cent of the road's route-mileage had been petitioned. The company required a gross of 60 million dollars a year just to break even, but it hadn't taken in that much since 1958 and seemed destined for its worst year since before the war. Katy owed 8 million dollars, yet had a bank balance of only $925,000.

Lest their investment follow Fort Smith & Western and New York, Ontario & Western into that Valhalla of railroading, Katy's 3886 stockholders required in the spring of 1965 a missionary, realist, salesman, and magician; and they hired him in John Barriger. For it requires a human quotient compounded of more than knowledge, experience, and drive to restore a detectable heartbeat to any corporation in such straits. It requires a certain moxie, a touch, an indefinable quality that you can't put through a computer or print in an annual report. John Barriger has it . . . and Katy was to demand every iota of it.

Typical of the man, his first move was to reinstall Katy's phone exchange in its St. Louis headquarters and rehire the girl who had manned it. Then he began calling for cash, customers, and confidence.

The railroad's shops and right of way were littered with scrap iron in the shape of everything from surplus passenger diesels shoved out to pasture to wrecked box cars that had never been picked up. The cleanup drive produced no windfall; derailments are expensive to clear away, and scrap dealers had already advanced money on much of the debris. Still, Katy found approximately $750,000 of pocket money in the weeds. Add a 1-million-dollar bank loan, which one assumes was secured by the sheer weight of Barriger's personality. Another 2.3 million was pumped into the blood bank by liquidating company bonds held in the treasury of a wholly owned subsidiary, Southwestern States Management (which owns real estate and mineral rights in four on-line states). The largest single source of financial energy lay in the unused balance of 4.7 million dollars remaining from an

41

I.C.C.-guaranteed loan of 12 million obtained in 1963 to improve the line and participate with other roads in the purchase of the Muskogee lines. The purchase deal had fallen through before Barriger arrived on the scene; he was able to persuade the Commission to allow Katy to spend the money to put its house in order.

Cash — $3000 of it per day — was retained in Katy's treasury effective July 1, 1965, the day the railroad became freight only. Its two passenger trains a day each way between Kansas City and Dallas had lost that much money on an out-of-pocket basis and had been carrying only 10 revenue riders each per train-mile.* Proceeds of the sale of equipment (the cars went as far as the Spokane, Portland & Seattle and an excursion line in Arizona; Atlantic Coast Line leased the diesels from an equipment dealer) were scant — $23,000, for example, for six coaches valued on the books at $100,000. What mattered was that a million-dollar-a-year cash drain had been stopped.

As fast as he could raise money, John Barriger spent it — on plant, on service . . . and simultaneously. He virtually doubled schedule frequency, running two or more trains each way a day on main lines, restoring daily-except-Sunday service on branches, and stepping up the number of yard tricks. The road had spent so much for overtime in the old hold-for-tonnage days that the payroll remained relatively stable as train-miles climbed. In essence, a few extra gallons of diesel oil put a lot of entries on the train sheet.

Trains require track, though, and by 1965 a decade of deferred maintenance had left Katy a railroad in name only. In that period it had never installed more than 10 miles of new rail a year and sometimes as little as 2. Of every 10 ties in main tracks, 3 were bad. It costs more, much more, to rebuild from scratch than to maintain as you go. What perplexed Barriger was the 23½ to 24 million dollars' worth of deferred maintenance confronting him because of the prior management's failure to spend 15½ million dollars on maintenance of way. By June 1965 he had

John W. Barriger.

a mechanized track gang in the field and by fall had leased enough equipment to add three more; a fifth crew was outfitted this year. Concentrating on Katy's heaviest-density main — Kansas City–Dallas/Ft. Worth — they had repealed enough slow orders by the end of 1965 to raise the speed limit from 25 mph to 55. They patched up the St. Louis–Parsons (Kans.) main sufficiently to allow freights to run 25/35 mph instead of only 15/25; plugged the worst holes in the branches out to Rotan, Tex., and up into the Oklahoma Panhandle; then turned south. Barriger couldn't afford new rail last year, but he had the satisfaction of seeing his gangs hit a pace of replacing more than 2000 ties and lining and surfacing 4 miles of track a day.

The frustration was more than occasionally overwhelming. Between Ft. Worth and Houston, 287 miles, an inspection team reported poor line and surface, curve-worn rails, and 1000 bad

---

* On May 20, 1965, Katy had asked the I.C.C. for permission to discontinue the trains on June 30, and in an order dated June 18 the commission had said that it would not investigate the proposal or hold a public hearing. On June 30 the I.C.C. changed its mind — too late, MKT replied, to give the carrier 10 days notice in advance of discontinuance. Result: the trains came off on June 30. The Commission held hearings in August and found in an order dated November 22 that the discontinuance had been justified.

ties a mile. Moreover, removal of block signals on a subdistrict had automatically reduced the maximum legal speed to 49 mph and eliminated broken-rail and open-switch protection from 176 miles of line. Despite 22 5-to-20 mph slow orders, 25 train derailments involving 12 locomotive units and 70 cars took place in the first two months of 1966 alone, including a couple that isolated an inspection special carrying Barriger and his long-term friend and former boss, Al Perlman (who lent NYC consultants to itemize the road's requirements for M/W mechanization, shop overhaul, and equipment purchases).

But the tide is turning. This year, for example, Barriger aims to replace 500,000 ties; lay 35 miles' worth of new 115-pound rail; surface, line, and reballast more than 300 miles of main track . . . yes, and reinstall those block signals into Houston.

Trains require cars, too; and one of the basic causes for Katy's decline was its inability to supply equipment to its shippers. Although 21 per cent of its 9966 freight cars were in bad order, Katy had not only closed its car shops but almost quit buying new cars. Barriger found cars which could be returned to service for a mere $150; others required only a half day's work or only wheels and stenciling. More than 1500, though, were beyond recall, and the daily output of 9 to 10 cars from the reactivated shops could not cope with the problem.

Barriger couldn't come up with the 20 per cent cash down payment required of installment-plan equipment trusts, so what he couldn't buy he leased. He signed 15-year leases for close on 4000 cars, combined trade-ins and wreck insurance on other units to finance a dozen 3000 h.p. GP-40's, and ultimately placed 61½ million dollars' worth of new equipment on the property. In so doing he established a record. His thousands of new red cars (everything from cushion-underframe box cars to mill gons to covered hoppers to pool-service cabooses) and low-nose Geeps totaled approximately 125 per cent of 1965's gross. "It is believed," said Barriger, "that this is the first instance in all railroad history in which equipment orders have exceeded a single year's gross receipts."

Trains, tracks, cars, and diesels constitute a railroad. But Katy has something more going for it in 1966: that intangible imprint of the Barriger personality. At age 66, the man disburses himself as deftly and freely as ever, and his spirit manifests itself in innumerable unorthodox, engaging, productive ways.

What does Barriger do that's so different? He hits the pavement and rings doorbells for business, terming himself "Traveling Freight Agent . . . and President" in that order. He talks endlessly — to shippers and railfans and train crews and editors and fellow railroad presidents; to anyone who'll listen. They do listen, and they find themselves caught up in Katy's fight for survival. He mixes, he requests, he passes around the credit; his 1965 annual report message pointedly thanked Brotherhood officials for their aid in revitalizing the railroad. He knows that it's not enough to be plucky; one must look it, too. So he engages artist Howard Fogg to dress up the annual report cover with a painting, he restores the old Katy herald, he spreads the word with an advertising budget that shames railroads thrice Katy's size, he coins phrases such as "Katy Did." He drives his people hard, but himself harder. Recently he had breakfast in Pittsburgh, lunch in St. Louis, dinner in Dallas, and went to bed in Houston.

It is precisely because John W. Barriger so unabashedly enjoys being a railroad president that he is quietly angry over what he regards as the unnecessary misfortune that overtook the Missouri-Kansas-Texas and is singlemindedly intent upon proving the point by restoring the road's solvency. He argues that prior management hacked instead of pruned, that it was goaded or panicked by the road's top-heavy financial structure into undoing the very plant and service which alone could rescue the line. He notes that Katy is the only railroad in its region that did not share in the post–Korean War economic boom in the Southwest; that as a consequence it began contending with Lehigh Valley and New Haven for the bottom rung on railroading's ladder.

Question: Does it really matter, in territory as crisscrossed with rails as Katy's, what happens to the road? It does to the owners, of course; and naturally to the employees — and to a Katy town such as Parsons, Kans. And it matters to Barriger on at least two counts: a solvent Katy would possess attractions as a merger mate (it owns the shortest rail route between Kansas City and north Texas); and historically as well as in terms of 1966 economic pace, the territory can support a solvent Katy.

Next question: Can even Barriger save a railroad that has been picking up speed downhill in the midst of a boom; that has been deep in the red since 1963; that needs 1100 carloads a day just to break even, but counted only 856 last year? The trends to date say Yes. When Barriger arrived on the scene in mid-March of 1965, Katy was toting about 825 cars a day vs. 875 in 1964, 950 in 1960, and 1250 in 1956. By summer he had slowed the decline in carloadings and in August reversed it. At year's end, 1965 was a scant 0.06 per cent behind 1964 in carloadings and would have been ahead but for the fact that 1964 was a Leap Year with 366 days. By March 1966 the railroad was moving approximately 940 cars a day — almost the same pace as in 1960. This year Barriger expects to gross 56½ million dollars (up from 49.6 million in 1965) and cut the loss to 4 million from 7.7 million last year. Then, assuming the boom keeps on booming, he sees a gross of 60 million or more in 1967 — a figure Katy hasn't posted since 1958. Even if the boom softens a bit, that goal seems attainable. From 1948 through 1956, when the nation's economy was considerably smaller, Katy never took in less than 72 million dollars a year and exceeded 85 million twice. So the business is there; and judging by past performance, a traveling freight agent with the persuasion of John Barriger ought to be able to load it inside the railroad's new red cars.

Meanwhile, it's exhilarating to watch Barriger elongate a career that already runs 4½ column inches in *Who's Who in Railroading*. To his prior credits as merger prophet, Government adviser, author, and elder statesman of the industry, he now appends his third railroad presidency and first board chairmanship. And as much as Katy was the very antithesis of the railroading he championed when he took his latest job, the marriage of Mr. B and Miss Katy was and is in another sense as fitting as a pantograph on a GG1. For John Barriger was born (Dallas) and reared (St. Louis) in Katyland, and if he wandered far afield in useful pursuits after he left home in 1917 to work as a shophand for the Pennsy in Altoona, he was ultimately available in the railroad's darkest hour.

Because of him the Katy is suddenly larger than life, a railroad more pertinent than its route-miles or gross or daily car count would imply. As Al Perlman remarked to a newspaper reporter during the inspection trip over the line, all of railroading is watching the Katy . . . watching John Barriger, that is; and wishing him well. ⊥

Editor's note: Morgan's favorite railroad was the Louisville & Nashville. Everyone knew that. The Southern Railway was certainly a close second, and most TRAINS readers knew Morgan had warm spots in his heart for the Central of Georgia, Florida East Coast, Southern Pacific, and Milwaukee Road. Fewer would guess his affection for the Missouri-Kansas-Texas, but it appeared in the pages of TRAINS far more often than its size and importance would warrant. In the late 1950s the Katy got into financial trouble, and in the August 1960 issue Morgan reported on the efforts of William N. Deramus III to turn it around. Katy's decline halted only briefly. In 1965 stockholders brought in John W. Barriger to do what he had done 20 years previously for the Monon. And that he did. By 1985 the Katy was healthy enough that Union Pacific made a bid to acquire it (purchase and absorption took place in 1988).

We'll adjust but it won't be easy

I REPLACE the high-backed wooden benches with pews, add an altar or a pulpit, and you could have turned the waiting room of Missouri-Kansas-Texas' San Antonio passenger station into a church. That's how well its architects and builder managed to blend functionalism with mission-style construction native to the region when the facility was completed in September 1917. It was a beautiful, serene place, a civilized transition from one's taxi to the observation-lounge of the *Texas Special,* a building Katy itself once extolled as "one of the most distinctive stations in the Southwest." When the photographer, Dr. Hastings, came upon the depot more than a decade ago he found therein Mrs. S. A. Agnew, "a lovable, kindly Southern lady" who had been station matron in San Antonio since the waiting-room doors were first unlocked. So here is Mrs. Agnew, presiding beneath the arches and chandeliers of a classic, a gem, a monument. Those are John W. Barriger's words of definition. It fell to him to demolish the building in 1967 when a fallen-from-grace, freight-only Katy required the real estate for other occupancy. But gentleman John could not bring himself to dismiss the place without a suitable epitaph in the company's annual report. He wrote, "the [passenger station] at San Antonio, built in 1917, was renowned throughout the United States as a gem in the finest tradition of classical mission-type architecture. Much of the material and nearly all of the fixtures used in the construction of this beautiful building had been imported from Spain and Italy. As in the case of other railroad monuments, most notably the Pennsylvania Station in New York, the San Antonio depot had to give way to the necessities of contemporary progress with its demands to transfer increasingly precious space within the heart of growing cities from lesser to

Photo by Philip R. Hastings.

more important assignments." So we'll take Mr. B's word for it, we'll remember his kind farewell, we'll adjust, but it won't be easy. It never is when friends part for good. **I**

45

A conversation with A. E. Perlman

He's still painting his own picture

I IN MY EXPERIENCE, the typical railroad president is less than candid with young journalists. I think he suspects their knowledge; he lapses into AAR-handout answers and he looks relieved when his p.r. aide summons him back aboard the company jet.

Alfred Edward Perlman is not your typical railroad president. He is a man of strong likes and dislikes; and when he dislikes something, somebody hears about it. Thus it was that I first met the man in 1956. I was riding an *Xplorer* press trip to Erie, Pa., there to inspect a CTC machine which he had had installed to reduce New York Central's main line from four tracks to two. I was minding my own business, thumbing through the press kit, taking in a 2-8-4 we were overtaking on the parallel Nickel Plate Road, when suddenly Perlman was easing into the seat beside me, shaking hands, and in that deceptively mild voice of his, taking me to task for a critical editorial TRAINS had published about his passenger policy. I was taken aback. Railroad presidents don't seek me out, yet here he was citing chapter and verse and statistic to prove he was right and my editorial was wrong. Stung, I argued back; and as the debate warmed it occurred to me that this man was proud, positive, critical, yes — but pompous, no. Had not a company flack pulled him away, he would have ridden clear to Erie defending his mission of saving Central from all and sundry, including errant editorialists.

Western Pacific photo.

I liked him, as I do anyone whose passion is a better way to run a railroad; so I remember without malice those subsequent occasions in his office and in the board room at 230 Park Avenue, New York City, when he charged me with touting the wrong railroad executives and writing off his 183.8 mph jet RDC as good theater. For one doesn't have to agree with Perlman in conversation to recognize industry insights few possess, as well as an enthusiasm geared to logic.

46

Today Al Perlman — Chairman of the Western Pacific Railroad, and erstwhile President of Penn Central; President of New York Central; Executive Vice-President of Denver & Rio Grande Western; Government consultant on Israeli and Korean railways; rail examiner for the Reconstruction Finance Corporation; assistant engineer M/W for Chicago, Burlington & Quincy; and roadmaster, icing facilities inspector, track laborer, and field construction draftsman for Northern Pacific — is 71. At an age when most of his contemporaries are out on the golf links, Perlman is completing what he terms his third railroad turn-around, attending board meetings of the AAR, and otherwise adding notches to a 50-plus-year career of uncommon industry rank and merit.

For 4½ hours in his office and over lunch on a mild March 1974 day in San Francisco, Al Perlman reflects on that career. Did he always want to be a railroader? He seems surprised by the question. Yes, yes — of course. He was born in St. Paul, but he was raised in Southern California; and there were transcontinental train trips to visit relatives in the East. He would camp on the open observation platform and absorb the clickety-clack and the receding rails. Trains, structures, track — the entire scene preoccupied him; and immediately following his graduation from Massachusetts Institute of Technology in 1923 he joined the maintenance of way forces of the Northern Pacific.

He moved rapidly up through NP's engineering ranks, and he was ready and he was known when the Republican River entered his life at approximately 4 a.m. on May 31, 1935. The river, swollen by cloudbursts in southern Nebraska, suddenly went berserk, rising an estimated 10 feet and killing nearly 100 people and wiping out crops and livestock. The wall of water struck the Chicago-Denver main line of the Burlington with unprecedented fury, knocking out reinforced concrete trestles, removing 41 miles of track from the roadbed, and isolating 216 miles of main. Perlman's crews reopened the main line in 23 days, 48 hours sooner than the predicted schedule. He made maximum use of a technique for which he would become famous: using off-track equipment instead of work trains. Draglines pulled track back into position, laid shooflies around smashed bridges, and restored embankments.

In the aftermath of that flood, which rates a special mention in Perlman's entry in *Who's Who in Railroading*, Perlman's weight fell from 160 to 128 pounds. For the floods had attacked the Q in three states, and full restoration took a year and cost one-third more than the road netted in 1935.

The Denver & Rio Grande Western was the bonus. In the summer of 1936 co-trustee Judge Wilson McCarthy urgently needed a bright young man to pull his bankrupt mountain railroad out of the mud, so Ralph Budd lent Al Perlman to McCarthy for two years. The two years became four — and well, Perlman never went home to the Hill Lines.

What was wrong with the D&RGW? Perlman smiles wryly at the recollection. (I have asked him the same question before, and his list of answers keeps getting longer.) The narrow gauge, he replies, accounted for a third of the system and had a 200 per cent operating ratio. And the main line had mud for ballast, 15 mph slow orders, and rocks so close to the track that "we were regularly knocking petcocks off the cylinders of our engines." Also, he says, the Grande was suffering from its legacy as a link in George Gould's stillborn transcon; therefore, the connections to which it catered were the old Gould lines — *i.e.*, Mopac in Pueblo and WP in Salt Lake City.

I tried to pin down Perlman by suggesting that his D&RGW years (1936–1954) were his happiest railroad term and he came close to concession. After all, there was the David-and-Goliath contest of living in the shadow of Union Pacific, the chance to exploit his off-track equipment concepts by virtually eliminating the work train, the drive to supplant expensive narrow gauge with a truck-and-bus subsidiary. In effect, the D&RGW was a test tube with which to prove his once-quoted belief that "given the traffic potential and good management, other obstacles become insignificant."

Perlman is essentially an outdoors man, and there's a lot of outdoors in the Rockies and the Wasatch. And the Grande was small enough so that everyone was on a first-name basis.

I know this: It is almost impossible to hold a conversation of any duration with the man without Rio Grande's being mentioned. The railroad's turnaround is the credential that put him on Park Avenue. Just ask any NYC man of the 1950's how often the new boss from Colorado ended arguments by saying, "Out on the Rio Grande we do it this way . . ."

Perlman is chary of giving adulation. In our long talk I could bring him to nominate but three men who were major influences upon his railroad career. Ralph Budd of the Burlington, of course, the consummate railroad man. (In my first conversation with Perlman, aboard the Xplorer, Al railed against a corporate image built out of press releases; rather he wanted to create an image out of service for the Central — the way Budd did on the Q.) Then Judge McCarthy, the kindly solon who held the creditors and regulators at bay while his team of young turks made a railroad out of mud ballast and 3 per cent. Finally, Robert R. Young.

The partnership of Young and Perlman was illogical. Young was the financial gadfly, the populist of Wall Street, the Establishment baiter — the stormy petrel who berated Pullman for rolling tenements; banker-directors for lack of competitive bidding on equipment-trust sales; and the industry for nonmechanical reefers, friction roller bearings, and hogs that crossed America without changing trains while passengers used Parmelee.

Now, why on earth did the renowned market player seek out a V.P. of a 2200-mile Western bridge line to run the 10,000-mile Eastern trunk he had just won in a bitter proxy fight? Perlman accepts the validity of the question, and he remembers that after the fact, a dozen or more people told him that he'd received Young's nod on their recommendation. But what did Young say? He didn't.

However illogical, the relationship might have derailed in the negotiation stage if Young had been as capricious as his clippings oft-times indicated. Perlman resisted those who advised him to have nothing to do with such an anti-AAR force as Young, but Perlman also told his prospective employer that he had no truck with unfounded accusations against the industry. More important, he laid down specific demands relative to salary, stock options, a seat on the board, and an open door between the offices of the chairman and the president. Young wanted to compromise; Perlman would not. At one juncture the Rio Grande outlander had left the financier's office and was waiting for the elevator when Young rushed out and declared that their differences could be resolved.

So began the climactic years of Perlman's career, the experience to which he warms and is ready to recall. In the summer of 1954 the name Perlman was, outside of the industry, unknown, not in the ranks of the Budds, the Gurleys, the Russells, the Whites. Suddenly, under the impetus of a maverick, he was astride the right-hand seatbox of the nation's No. 2 railroad. But that railroad, to Young's chagrin, was on the brink of bankruptcy. For all its Vanderbilt heritage, Water Level Route, *20th Century Limited, et al.,* New York Central was running out of payroll dollars, to say nothing of economic meaning in the real world of 1954. A lesser man wouldn't have touched the job, or at best would have fled back to Denver upon realizing its awful dimension.

I do not think it ever occurred to Al Perlman that he might fail. Rather, I think he knew he couldn't step on a tie, enter a shop, examine a train sheet, or glance at a balance sheet without seeing a way to boost net or cut costs — or both. He had no friends on Central; hence he could hire and fire without those qualms which beset a man who has risen through the ranks. In the microcosm of the Rio Grande he had honed the edge on those techniques from CTC to the M/W mechanization with which he would rationalize Central's physical plant. And just as important, he had the gut instinct to accomplish the rest: to confront city and state officials with his — and hence their — commuter and tax problems; to assemble a marketing department worthy of the name; to hire a real-estate pro to hypo NYC's Manhattan landholdings; and to field a management team of bright young men.

Now, that story has been told and retold and ought to be a book. But in 1974 what does Al Perlman want to comment about it? First, his men. The proof of the new New York Central, he declares, is where its creators are today. He ticks off the names: Walter Grant, his treasurer, now high in the ranks of Con Ed; Wayne Hoffman, his No. 2 man, now chairman of Flying Tiger; John Kenefick, his operating man, now president of Union Pacific; Robert Flannery, an up-through-the-ranks NYC man, now president of Western Pacific. The names, the titles, flow too rapidly for me to jot them all down; but the point is made: *his* boys made it good on the outside.

And why? "They were all permitted to paint their own picture." One gains the impression that if you want to survive under Perlman, you'd best find an understudy (insecure men "don't want any stars in their department"), leave a weekend phone number ("We might have a wreck on Saturday"), get out on the property (a Navy peajacket and boots are standard gear in Perlman's wardrobe), ask and answer your own questions, and be sure — to use a 1940 quote of his — you can say at the finish, "I've done my share."

As for what he made of New York Central, Perlman reiterates a favorite compound adjective; the railroad was "depression-proof."

Al Perlman does not dodge the hard, obvious issue of Penn Central. For a man who strove mightily for an East gathered under the two tents of NYC and PRR as opposed to a union of Nos. 1 and 2, who feels that the promises made to him as president and chief administrative officer of PC were broken, who was aghast at the shape in which he found Pennsy, and who argues that he was denied the authority he needed to bring order out of chaos, Perlman is remarkably dispassionate about PC's collapse. No, he insists, a successful merger was not impossible. He was out on line, wrestling with the mechanics of unifying the biggest, trying unsuccessfully to keep a liaison open with headquarters . . . and time ran out. He was sealed off, and ultimately was shunted aside in what future historians must chronicle as one of the great ironies of big-time railroading in the 1970's. Granted, one must be an unblinking disciple of Perlman to accept the premise that, unfettered, he could have kept Penn Central out of Judge John P. Fullam's court. And yet, would the odds have been any worse in 1968 than they were in 1954?

The man doesn't deal in ifs. What might have happened to Penn Central is academic; what is happening to Western Pacific is reality.

In a sense, Al Perlman's railroad career went into reruns effective December 1, 1970, when he assumed the presidency of the WP. Little 1496-mile WP operates in the deepest shadow of big 11,387-mile Southern Pacific — once again the David vs. Goliath confrontation. Control of WP had been purchased by financier Howard A. Newman who, being no neophyte to Wall Street or to the ways of railroads, sought out a man to protect his investment — shades of Bob Young. Finally, in common with both D&RGW in 1936 and NYC in 1954, WP in 1970 was sick. That year WP posted an operating ratio of 94.1 per cent and lost 8.1 million dollars on a gross of 68.5 million.

How long did it take Al Perlman to figure out what was wrong? He looks surprised at the question. Why, why — well, an inspection of the line by hy-rail car told him, of course. That and what he found in headquarters at 626 Mission Street, San Francisco.

For instance . . .

• WP had completed a new diesel shop in the wrong location — Stockton. "Should have been at the foot of the mountain [Oroville] where we have to add units to go uphill."

• WP had no staff meetings, no organization chart, no job descriptions, no cost controls.

• On a spur of subsidiary Sacramento Northern he found 100 bad-order box cars which had been stored so long that their journal brasses had been stolen. WP's computer didn't know the cars existed. But the computer did say that WP had 16,600 freight cars on line. Perlman ordered a field hand-count. The actual number on line: 8000 cars.

• WP's San Francisco switchboard did not open until eight o'clock in the morning — Pacific Time. Which meant that a traffic manager in New York couldn't ring the railroad about a missing car until eleven o'clock — Eastern Time.

Perlman had Western Pacific in the black in three months flat. He netted almost a million dollars in 1971, knocked more than 12 points off the operating ratio, won back some unhappy shippers and earned some new ones, added a trucking subsidiary, and made Marketing more than a name on the door.

A long conversation with Al Perlman moves rapidly and candidly over a lot of route-miles. His mind is too incisive, too quick, to be confined by a reporter's prepared set of questions.

Always there is Robert R. Young ("We were like brothers"), the man who entrusted him with New York Central, The Big Chance. The sense of gratitude is deep and surfaces frequently.

(A long-distance call takes Perlman out of his office in Suite 700 at WP's headquarters, and there's an opportunity to take in the room that has a view of the Bay Bridge. It's simple: a clean desk [when he arrived it was covered by thick reports and an adding machine rested in one corner]; on a shelf behind, a collection of seven pipes, an HO-scale NYC S-class motor, an HO box car, and a caricature of a handcar labeled D&RG and two trackmen; on one wall, a photo of a family group posed in front of a PC coach, plus an informal shot of Perlman and Newman; and on another wall, a seascape.)

Perlman reflects that there are three professions of compelling power — the stage, railroading, and journalism. He feels these are callings for which the monetary reward is secondary.

Mention is made of wrecks on another carrier, and he frowns. On WP, he says, a hy-rail car precedes every freight moving through the Feather River Canyon as a safety precaution against slides. Also, WP has a stretch of 100-pound rail remaining in the main line and over it the speed limit is 40 mph. Knock on wood, he says, tapping his desk, because metal failure in an axle could cause a derailment; but so far in his administration, WP has been keeping 'em on high iron.

The subject of containerization comes up. He fails to understand why the railroad industry didn't buy his Flexi-Van system. He ticks off the virtues of boxes aboard skeleton flats: no license plates needed, less tare weight, less wind drag, a lower center of gravity. Why, Central and Santa Fe proved the worth of Flexi when they rolled a container special coast to coast on passenger-train time. But the railroads ignored the lesson . . .

Back to Bob Young's bid to lead NYC — what if Perlman hadn't taken it? He thinks of the company he met at the top: the Duke and Duchess of Windsor; Thomas E. Dewey; Nelson Rockefeller, Presidents Kennedy, Johnson, and Nixon; Premier Nikita Khrushchev and his son — not simply famous people but for the most part uncommonly interesting people, people whose paths he would not have crossed back in Colorado.

On that mild March day in San Francisco we lunched in the Bankers Club atop the new Bank of America Building, and when we left, Al Perlman stopped on the way to the elevators and did something that took me back to his New York Central days. He paused and chatted a moment with a table of restaurant employees who were taking a coffee break after the meal hour. Years ago I had ridden an NYC security-analysts special — a sizable consist of bedroom sleepers, diners, and lounges led by well-scrubbed E8's — whose select clientele was made up of Wall Streeters, whose opinion weighs heavily in the world of equipment trusts, stocks, debentures, refinancings, and such. By day we inspected Flexi-Van, trilevel automobile racks, computers, and push-button humps; by night we rode.

President Perlman captained our team of railroad hosts, and along about 9 in the evening he would slip into the observation-club-lounge to talk railroading with analysts and reporters. Tapping the inevitable pipe, nursing a Scotch, he would explain and debate and argue the cause of his beloved Central (and anybody else's railroad you cared to mention). But by 10 or so he headed back to his bedroom (the office car had been left in New York), and the crowd would turn to cards and market talk.

Now — and this is the point — Al Perlman didn't just stride up the train as would be the wont and the right of a man who had brought the nation's No. 2 railroad back from the brink. I know. I watched him. He unfailingly would pause at the galley and engage the waiters and the chef in conversation. I could discern no difference in the attention he accorded their talk than that he gave to Merrill Lynch or to *Business Week*.

In my knowledge, he was that kind of a guy.

He still is. ⅂

Alfred E. Perlman, 1902–1983

HOW will we remember Al Perlman, who died in San Francisco on April 30, 1983, at age 80? His own credo comes first to mind: "All it takes is common sense and modern equipment." Thus armed, he rose in railroading from a Northern Pacific track gang to the presidency of the New York Central, leaving behind an indelible imprint of how to run a railroad. En route to Central's 230 Park Avenue, New York City HQ, he recaptured Burlington's main through southern Nebraska from a rampaging Republican River in 1935 in 23 days flat and received signal credit for lowering Rio Grande's operating ratio from 90 to 64.8 per cent during his 16-year term with that once-bankrupt mountain road. Of his 1954 jump into the big time, he said, "I had one more chance"—accepting Robert R. Young's offer, against the advice of the Establishment, to trade a comfortable slot on solvent 2200-mile D&RGW for the top job of a 10,000-mile "bankrupt but didn't know it" NYC.

Those were the glory years (1954–1968) of this deceptively mild, immensely self-confident man who turned Vanderbilt's paradise lost into a lean, aggressive plant. He heretically substituted reverse-signaled CTC double track for Central's cherished four-track mains, introduced 70mph Flexi-Vans to fight off truckers, sublimated the road's passenger orientation, replaced across-the-board rate hikes with marketing strategy, and defied politicos who mistreated his railroad. But before Central could become "depression-proof," Young committed suicide, and thereafter Perlman was thwarted in his effort to bring off a Chesapeake & Ohio-Central-Baltimore & Ohio merger. Frustrated by what turned out to be a powerless presidency of Penn Central (long after its collapse, he insisted PC could have made it), he returned to the West in 1970 at the behest of Howard Newman to rescue that financier's ailing Western Pacific, putting the road back into the black in 90 days.

What manner of man was Al Perlman? An abrasive, impatient egotist? Yes, you could form that opinion if you questioned his course. Chary of praise? Yes, only three men — Q's Ralph Budd, D&RGW's Judge McCarthy, NYC's Young — occurred to him in an interview once as major influences on his life. Contemptuous of his peers? Yes, if he deemed them unequal to what he thought of as the essential labor of bringing railroading into the last half of the 20th century. A railroader's railroader? Unquestionably. He was at home trackside, he delighted in bringing up Young Turks and giving them free rein, he numbered souls as disparate as Lucius Beebe and John Barriger and lounge-car waiters and John Kneiling as confidants, he thought trains were work so engrossing that monetary reward came second.

He perhaps shone brightest in adversity. A Central employee said Perlman was the calmest individual at 230 Park Avenue when a recession threatened to inundate his rebuilding of the system, saying in effect we've done our job, we can't worry about what is beyond our control. Again, a lesser man might have become an embittered recluse after Penn Central. Instead, Perlman accepted the Western Pacific overhaul with gusto, addressing his new 1400-mile charge with all the drive he accorded his 1935 war on the Republican River, speaking of "Great White Father" Espee in the same context as he had addressed competitor Union Pacific in his Rio Grande days.

Al Perlman once observed in 1940 that the mark of a man was to be able to say at the end, "I've done my share."

He clearly did his.

Editor's note: Morgan reported on his first interview with Al Perlman in the June 1957 issue. Morgan obviously felt his readers should become reacquainted with him in 1974. Few railroad officials rated a full obituary in the pages of TRAINS, but Perlman (like Barriger) was one who did.

The railfan

What makes the train-watcher tick?

WHO on earth would give a fig that, say, locomotive No. 3530 of the Atchison, Topeka & Santa Fe Railway was constructed in 1914 by the Baldwin Locomotive Works under serial 41247 as a four-cylinder balanced compound 4-6-2, or that she was rebuilt into a simple engine with Walschaerts valve gear at San Bernardino in February 1922 and finally was scrapped there on August 30, 1940? Certainly not the Santa Fe, which dieselized years ago. Nor Baldwin, which doesn't build locomotives of any type any more.

But chances are you care, if for no other reason than the fact that you paid 50 cents to read a magazine that would have access to and print such seemingly pedestrian data. And because you care, you've automatically classified yourself as a railfan (alias railroad enthusiast, train-watcher, ferroequinologist). Certainly you cannot be segregated by occupation or residence or age or nationality or by almost any other index except sex. For instance, using this journal's readership as a guide, approximately 85 per cent of hard-core fans are not employed by railroads or railroad suppliers. Or if we sample the occupations of several prominent free-lance railroad photographers, we find an Iowa psychiatrist, an Eastern Air Lines captain, a California newspaperman, a Western Electric photo-technician, a U. S. Navy officer, a North Carolina college instructor, and a Nickel Plate claim agent. A fan might be described as anyone who enjoys the railroad without or beyond the considerations of employment or ownership.

Train-watching is not a particularly popular pastime, assuming we count as serious those fans who invest in books or cameras or tickets to advance the avocation. The largest nonprofit national fan organization numbers about 2000 members; a hard-cover railroad book under any byline but Lucius Beebe's which sells more than 5000 copies must be counted a good success; the net paid circulation of this magazine slightly exceeds 37,000. Even if we added a few other-than-long-suffering wives plus prototype-oriented scale model railroaders, it would be difficult to peg the total number of inner-circle enthusiasts at more than 100,000. Which is to say, .05 per cent of the U. S.

The impact of fans is in inverse ratio to their numbers, though. Last year 75 groups sponsored 160 railroad excursions on more than 85 lines, held a three-day national convention in Chicago, made the pages of *Life,* created a bonanza book and recording season, and — for the first time — were directly appealed to by the Association of American Railroads for aid in overcoming the industry's political handicaps. Personal ownership of locomotives is becoming all but commonplace; the list now includes a Consolidation in Iowa, a 4-6-2 in Chicago, and a 4-6-0 in the East. Fans own and operate such tourist pikes as Tweetsie and Black Hills Central as well as the common carrier Strasburg. The redoubtable Mr. Beebe no longer cruises the land in lonely splendor aboard the Virginia City. At least three fan clubs bring up the markers' end of excursions with an old 12-wheel open observation, and among the solariums being acquired by individuals is a streamlined Pennsy car of Broadway Limited ancestry.

As he thus emerges from total obscurity, the train-watcher is apt to find himself described in the secular press as someone who never quite outgrew his tinplate toys. And be it granted that the movement, because of its strong emotional appeal, will

Illustration by Gil Reid.

always have its minority of wild-eyed bell-ringers. Still, the second-childhood image does not fit the majority of participants in a rapidly maturing avocation. The fan is proving himself an indefatigable historian, doing a first-rate job of preserving the mechanical detail if not yet the over-all economic sweep of the past. The best of his camera work is no longer put to shame by the occasional forays into railroading of the mass-circulation national periodicals; and he has replaced the Pennsylvania wall calendar as a source of railroad artwork. Finally, his public relations value to the industry is quite real, if unmeasured; if the fan did nothing else than call attention to the fact that there still are railroads in an auto-oriented America of the 1960's, he would be worth the railroads' indulgence of his excursion requests, but there is evidence that he represents an informed opinion force on the railroad dilemma that will be heard increasingly in our time. All of which is quite remarkable. No other industry in the land possesses such an audience. It is unpaid, inquisitive, full of good will, enthusiastic. There is simply no counterpart for it in America, for whoever takes a fan trip to a steel mill, or charters DC-7B's (not to get anywhere, but just to fly in a DC-7B, that is), or publishes $15 rosters of Greyhound's equipment? Moreover, the railfan is a comparatively recent phenomenon, at least as an organization man. The patriarch club, the Railway & Locomotive Historical Society, dates back to 1920, but the first bond of national unity came about in December 1929 with the revival of *Railroad Man's Magazine*. Throughout the 1930's — when fan trips were few and far between, and railroad police were the greatest hazard to the man focusing his Brownie on an 0-6-0, and Van Metre's *Trains, Tracks and Travel* was virtually the only text on the subject — the untrimmed pulp pages of *Railroad* were precious beyond price; they not only informed the faithful but lent enthusiasts an incalculable morale boost in the knowledge that they were not alone. Slowly, painstakingly, the railroad enthusiasm gained strength: the Railroad Enthusiasts operated the first recorded fan trip over the 10.9-mile Hoosac Tunnel & Wilmington on August 26, 1934 . . . the first chapter of the National Railway Historical Society was formed m 1935 . . . Beebe's epochal book, *High Iron,* came off the press in 1938 . . . and a slender but slick-paper monthly called TRAINS appeared in November 1940.

At that juncture the fan stood quite innocently on the threshold of (1) a glory age he could not fully enjoy; and (2) a revolution and a retrenchment in ferroequinology he did not anticipate. For the railfan movement took hold when the industry had everything but traffic. Steam ruled the main, but there was the novelty of the *Zephyr;* D&RGW operated named narrow-gauge limiteds on year-round daily schedules; there were enough Mogul-powered short lines around that later L. Beebe would be prompted to fill a 368-page book with their antics; and if the C&LE and Indiana were faltering, why the Insull tractions would endure forever. Indeed, the very depression-caused lethargy of the rails made of them a never-never land of sentimental delights that could not last.

Then abruptly war broke out and the trains were full and new locomotives were arriving. And because of military conscription, travel restrictions, and censorship, the fan was sealed off from his avocation just as the industry made its all-time maximum effort. Just as abruptly, the emergency was over and the great disenchantment slowly set in — even as it did for the railroads themselves. Grimness amongst the fans turned to horror as it dawned upon the fraternity that dieselization meant torching 10-year-old 4-8-4's, that seniority could not save such names as the *Black Diamond,* that even Class 1 standard-gauge properties such as O&W could go under with the facility of Rio Grande Southern. In retrospect, the sudden loss of steam and the reduction in passenger train-miles hurt most. Unlike steamboat or antique automobile buffs, railfans had been used to having their cake and eating it, too. Such strategic lines as Pittsburgh & Lake Erie were scandalously neglected by photographers in the prime of four-track main and 2-8-4 power until suddenly C.T.C. and olive-drab Geeps had erased what had been taken for granted. Similarly, one never quite got around to riding the *Olympian* or the *Black Gold* until it had quietly slipped from the thinning pages of the *Guide.*

Once the disillusion was total (dating from the news item that Norfolk & Western intended to dieselize as soon as possible), the fan went off in three directions — sometimes all at once. He became a historian. He also journeyed to Canada, then into Mexico or overseas, to ride and photograph the trains that had vanished from the American scene. And/or he began to accept the new and spartan posture of railroading, riding behind the Q's 5632 whenever he could, of course, but also learning a wheel arrangement code expressed in hyphenated letters instead of numerals, taking a new look at humps and junctions and other fixed facilities that had escaped his thought in steam days, and rejoicing in the coming of piggyback. There were several indices of his change of heart. The number of fan clubs increased. It became possible to break even on a nonsteam excursion. Book production soared.

Future biographers of the fan will do well in this regard to reflect upon what took place when a Lincoln (Nebr.) reader of this magazine made so bold as to suggest an all-diesel issue to balance the all-steam number which has been an annual habit of TRAINS for six seasons. As the staff had expected from past experience with the same delicate steam vs. diesel question, reader response was prompt and intense. Except that in 1961–1962 the mail has been running more than 3 to 1 in favor of a diesel issue. A sampling of this correspondence leads to several conclusions. A sizable segment of those who wrote in did not necessarily relish the prospect of steamless editorial fare — they simply thought it would be fair in view of the all-steam number, or only logical in view of the absence of steam power today (one man observed that he was "wholly" concerned with steam and traction, then went on to spell out in detail what he expected to be included in any diesel reporting). It is also apparent that a second generation of fans exist, a group of enthusiasts who because of age never became acquainted intimately with the steam locomotive and therefore mourn her not. They grew up around F3's, wait impatiently for new U25B orders, and want to hear the latest on the diesel-hydraulics. Save your explanation of exhaust-steam injectors; they'd rather know what all those jumper cables are for on the nose of a GP20. Even the older train-watchers who regard the diesel not only as the dreariest of man's inventions but also as the agent of destruction of all that was once beautiful on the high iron — even these seem to accept at least the possibility of an issue devoted to diesels, and they simply ask that the editors note that fact upon the cover so they'll not squander 50 cents.

It all proves not so much an affection for the new as a continuing interest in the railroad, whatever locomotives are employed.

Not inexplicably, the enthusiast and the railroad still regard each other with reservation. Obviously, if almost any activity is one man's job and another man's hobby, these men will not always agree. The fan thought the Pennsy I1 2-10-0 an extraordinary hippo of a locomotive, a fine thing to focus upon as she came thundering, waddling upgrade to Shamokin with three sisters helping her lug 90 cars of ore. But to a fireman, the Decapod was a hard-riding, filthy cab behind a firebox of such modest grate area that keeping the pressure anywhere near 250 pounds taxed the brain as well as the back. Again, the observation car is the bane of management because it has to be turned at terminals, it has to be switched again if cars are added or cut out during a train's run, and space in it is hard to sell because most passengers don't like the ride at the rear end; yet the enthusiast delights in the observation because of its visibility and because, externally, it belongs at the tail of any named train as much as a period at the end of a sentence.

At best, the industry gracefully tolerates its fans, running their excursions, perhaps providing a meeting room in union station, and occasionally issuing for them a booklet about engines. At their best, the fans refrain from asking the railroads for 8 x 10 photos of all the engines the lines own or making off with data plates from stored-serviceable locomotives or breaking safety rules on fan trips.

The pity is that in its hour of greatest need for friends, the industry will take its case to practically anyone who'll listen — employees, shippers, editors, financial analysts, mayors — except fans. In those quarters of management that have contemplated the fan at all, he is too often written off as an eccentric or sentimentalist — likable enough, perchance, but hardly a useful political ally. And for his part, the fan senses and objects to condescension. He is by nature inclined toward the railroad cause but objects to having his vote taken for granted. He resists the speaker who shows up at the club with a dry mimeographed party-line text when, before an audience of sympathetic and knowledgeable listeners, the representative might be expected to talk informally and as if among friends.

The unspoken conflict is at least closer to resolution than ever before. Of inestimable help is the fact that a number of enthusiasts have become so intrigued by the industry that they have wound up employed therein — and at management level, too. A rate researchist devoted weekends on end to committing triple-headed B&O Mikes to film. The president's aide entrusted with some of the largest secrets of an affluent major road knows more about a long-abandoned narrow gauge than any other living soul. A public relations director can tell you as much about traction, from Birneys on up, as anyone in the land, save George Krambles or Ira Swett. And a traffic exec so admires the steam engine profile, that he paints them in suitable winter surroundings for his personal Christmas cards. Such men bring more to railroading than management skill. And sooner or later, their enthusiasm for the game may be reflected in the industry's attitude toward its admirers.

The fan is not an easy man to understand. Railroading for him is simply too big, too private, and too obvious an emotion to be able to explain. He sees five F7's climbing the hill to Brookfield in the last notch, with the high cars rolling and grumbling in their wake, their wheels rimmed in the snow of the last grade crossing — and like Mallory's mountain, "it's there," and what more can be said? It either reaches out to one or it doesn't. It's a natural rather than an acquired urge, more a passion than an interest. The coin collector, the bridge player, the hi-fi addict can usually tell you when and why he took up the pursuit. But not the train-watcher. It seldom occurs to him to be introspective about it, but even if he were, he could do little more than acknowledge the influence of a boyhood spent at the depot or a father who once worked in the shops at Sedalia or an Ives train set of tender memory.

This enthusiasm, this passion, breeds the specialist and the isolationist to the degree that its slaves can often barely countenance each other, much less the Outside World. There is the man who, appalled at the immensity of total railroading, makes the Colorado & Southern, say, his Holy Grail and becomes to it what Sandburg is to Lincoln; he may not be quite sure (or care) which side of Pittsburgh the Horse Shoe Curve is on, but he can tell you that C&S 615 (formerly 475) had a new firebox applied in 1908 and that the siding capacity at McClellands (M.P. 69.85) is 12 cars. There is the rider who finds an irresistible challenge in the statistic of 217,100 miles of railroad line in the U. S. and sets forth to see what percentage of it can be ridden in a lifetime (no one but the legendary Rogers E. M. Whitaker would dare believe that all of it can be ridden, nor is anyone else apt to achieve such a goal); he will jet across the continent to take in an excursion that will add 40 miles to his "total" and he will condone the gloomiest of red-plush coaches on 11 p.m.-to-6 a.m. milk trains if it means "new mileage."

The merest scrap of conversation is all that the initiate needs to identify an enthusiast:

"It's a Harriman standard, probably ACF Jeffersonville, rebuilt with ice-activated air conditioning in 1935." Passenger-car specialist.

"The NOGN had the line out of Jackson to New Orleans. GM&N bought control in '29, but then in 1932 it went into receivership but came out in 1933. Which was when GM&N again took possession under a 99-year lease." Historian.

"The only J-4 with a Worthington feedwater heater was the 1824. All the rest got Elescos as they were rebuilt. Except the J-4A'S, of course — numbered 1891 to 1914. They had 'em when they came from Baldwin. And a Delta trailing truck — but no booster. That came later." Locomotive man.

"At 8:30 the local, 101, showed and then, behind him, running as Second 101, came the Bullet. In other words, out of Cincinnati they ran the hotshot as a first-class train. About 30 minutes ahead of No. 1." Schedule authority.

Fans seldom specialize out of all contact with the rest of the avocation. Instead they prove the infinite expanse of railroading. The majority of enthusiasts are reasonably cosmopolitan in outlook today, not without their individual likes and dislikes, but more willing to go afield than was the case before the war. For example, there was a time when one could afford the luxury of disdaining the spartan standardization of an N&W or an IC in favor of dwelling upon the lines or roster complexities of a Southern or a Mopac, but as the diesel swept the land it became a case of making do with a Y-6 or a 2500 or doing without. And then when even this compromise was nullified, the fan went to Canada in search of steam. And today, he finds the East African Garratt not so abhorrent as he thought and/or makes his peace with the ubiquitous Geep.

And so, on balance and in both retrospect and outlook, train-watching remains an immensely satisfying pursuit and, however unremarked, a visible candle in the darkness that has fallen over railroading in our time. It becomes more painfully apparent with each percentage point loss in carloadings that the industry, of itself, cannot reverse the misfortunes which beset it.

Railroading is a notoriously involved business to explain and consequently to argue for. The man in the street cannot comprehend why five o'clock commuter trains with standee loads do not make money. He subscribes to the myth of pin-striped robber-baron management waxing wealthy on land grants. He hears that the rails want rates which would destroy their competition, that they are forever trying to derail such progress as the St. Lawrence Seaway, and that they're insensitive to the welfare of their employees. The fan, conversely, recognizes such nonsense and knows who sponsors it and why. At the same time he is not so naive as to believe that angelic forces command all railroad HQ's or that all of the industry's ills can be blamed upon external circumstances. He is informed, then — and the railroad cause recommends itself to the informed.

Railroading requires friends — friends who understand its complexities and can explain its virtues, friends who without thought of reward are curious and concerned about this business of flanged wheels on steel rails. Friends who, for lack of a better word, might be called railfans. ⊥

Why boys leave home

I EACH revolution of her ten-coupled 57-inch drivers shakes the seatbox and jars the cocks and gauges. The heat from over three score square feet of inflamed coal crust seeps through the Butterfly firedoors until sweat dampens your socks and trickles down the small of your back. In the tunnel blackness, her stack hammers hard against raw rock, and the thick, pungent, gassy smoke swirls back into the cab to slow your breathing and film your face; always the cinders are creeping past the red bandanna around your neck. The noise is rhythmic, constant, deafening: the pound of a harness of main and side rods, crossheads and valve motion; the monotone of the stocker screw; the asthmatic whine of the injector; the exhalation of brass valves; the rattle of deck plates.

Yet for this a man would leave the security of a shoe store, the smell of fresh-plowed earth, the regularity of factory hours. Or he'd suffer the conscious frustration of having passed up the great adventure for cash or comfort or acclaim. For the reward of the smoke and the sweat is to hold in the palm of your gloved hand the throttle of a 189-ton Baldwin, to know that each notch on the curved ratchet overhead feeds more superheated steam into a pair of 28-inch diameter cylinders with a 32-inch stroke, to realize that this rocking, pounding boiler stuffed with tubes and charged with 200-pound-per-square-inch energy is yours to urge and restrain. **I**

Southern Railway engineer Frank Pinkston pilots a 2-10-2 into the Blue Ridges. Photo by Frank Clodfelter.

Biggest travel news since the 747?

"Rame a turbine a gaz" sounds French — and is

IT SEEMS to me I've spent my life reporting crusades to reconstitute the American passenger train. In the pulp pages of Frank A. Munsey's 15-cent *Railroad Stories* I learned of UP's M-10000 and of the Q's *Zephyr*. On the brick platforms of Englewood (Ill.) Union Station I witnessed the formalization of streamlining in Henry Dreyfuss's gray ghost of a *20th Century Limited*. And thereafter, through the good offices of A. C. Kalmbach, I was aboard with press credentials as the carbuilders and their clients tried again and again — and again . . . with the dome and the RDC, with the Slumbercoach and the Pioneer III, with the Aerotrain and the Talgo, with the bilevel and the hi-level. I watched President Lyndon B. Johnson sign the legislation that installed the Metroliners. I saw the old ovals and diamonds and shields and wings of private ownership come down and the pointless arrow of a quasi-public corporation go up.

So in Chicago Union Station on the rainy morning of September 28, 1973, I thought to myself, "Here we go again." For a band was playing and flashbulbs were popping, and Chicago Mayor Richard J. Daley was saying something about Chicago's being the transportation center of the country. All this activity was in progress between a pair of strange-looking low-slung red-white-and-blue passenger trains which would be hailed in subsequent Amtrak radio commercials as "the biggest travel news since the 747."

I was reminded of the parting of the Red Sea as an aisle was opened through the crowd for the departure of His Honor the Mayor. Then it was time to climb aboard and ride one of the trains to St. Louis on a preinaugural run down the Illinois Central Gulf (formerly Gulf, Mobile & Ohio, nee Alton Route). *Keep an open mind,* I told myself; the men who insisted that a train called

Running as train 301 to St. Louis, a Turboliner picks its way through the slip switches of the south approach to Chicago Union Station on October 1, 1973 — its first revenue run. Photo by Robert P. Schmidt.

X was the answer and that *Zephyrs* made money are confounded, dead, and buried — give the guys and gals who picked up the torch a chance. If they say that this little train is a peer of Boeing's best — why, let's get aboard.

"The biggest travel news since the 747" is a pair of RTG's (for *rame a turbine a gaz*) — 423-foot, five-car, bidirectional gas-turbine/hydraulic trains built in France and leased by Amtrak at a monthly rental of $107,000 for 18 months with an option to buy. The implication of the imports is that Amtrak wants an alternative to its United Aircraft Turbos for nonelectrified intercity corridors. Development of Canada's diesel-locomotive-hauled LRC (for lightweight, rapid, comfortable) train is stalled, and Britain's turbine-powered APT (for advanced passenger train) remains in prototype form only.

To understand the RTG's, you must bear in mind that they are off-the-shelf French trains, members of a 36-train order placed by the French National Railways (SNCF) with the firm of ANF-Frangeco and modified only in detail for U. S. service. Indeed, according to the French magazine *La Vie du Rail,* two of the extras added in France which most intrigued French observers were "the traditional American train bell" and "fountains with fresh drinking water."

My ride on September 28, 1973, proved that Lyons-Nantes on SNCF is similar to Chicago-St. Louis on the old Alton in 4-foot 8½-inch gauge and in precious little else.

In France, where RTG's serve a rail-oriented society at speeds up to 125 mph over high-ballasted multiple track, such trains reportedly have boosted ridership 25 per cent where they were substituted for conventional equipment. But here . . . well, a single stroll through Amtrak's leased RTG convinced me that for the U. S. more than a bell and ice water is in order.

Jottings from my little black notebook:
• A stepbox is required to board a low-slung RTG from ground-level platforms because (if memory serves) in France the railroad operates from semi-high-level platforms.
• RTG's seats — half of which face forward and half backward — are airline-Y-class narrow, are covered in warm-to-sit on vinyl, and have only two positions — neither particularly comfortable.
• The aisles are too narrow to allow for the food-and-beverage trolley service called for by the limited sit-down dining facilities in the center bar-grill car.
• The windows are a generous size by U. S. standards — the opposite of Metroliner's rifle-slot-size lookouts — and accordingly will

The bell was mounted just ahead of the front truck of each power car. Visible behind it is the gearbox on the axle. Photo by Randall M. Keils.

attract the rock-throwers who, alas, now must be counted as a fixture of the American railroad scene (and not just in the ghettos).
• Car-to-car passageways are a nightmare and require an understanding of French train design deeper than my own. To exit a car, first you pull a glass sliding door — and the exercise is the opposite of that required to open domestic push-on-a-panel air-actuated slide doors. Now you're in the vestibule, and the steps on either side are not covered by trap plates — women with children, elderly persons, and middle-aged editors beware. Next you encounter a double set of non-automatic sliding doors (try opening them with a suitcase in one hand), which gains access to the buffer plates across the buffers and screw-type coupler, and to the double slide-type doors on the other side . . . then on to the single slide door into the interior of the next car.
• As you cross the vestibule you can look down to ballast, rails, coupler, and buffers — which means, I suppose, that an Illinois blizzard can push its ice and snow upward into the vestibule. Doesn't it ever snow in France?
• The center bar-grill car seats 24 at tables while the train as a unit has 296 revenue coach seats. Considering the habits of the cocktail crowd traveling this corridor — to say nothing of the three meal hours encompassed in the RTG's schedules — somebody's going to go thirsty or hungry or both.
• The low, round glassy front ends of the power cars at either end of RTG provoked the question of grade-crossing protection for the enginemen. An Amtrak mechanical official replied,

Between the cars of the Turboliners were standard European screw couplers and buffers and tubular rubber diaphragms. Photo by John H. Kuehl.

"Do you think a Metroliner engineer is better off?" Maybe not, but at least the glass area is less, and the New York-Washington corridor has fewer highway grade crossings than the Chicago-St. Louis route.

• Protruding from the end of each power car is a big American automatic coupler, wedged tight by skips of wood. In a grade-crossing accident, this coupler predictably will punch a hole in the side of the vehicle the train hits and most likely will lock onto it. Less important is what this coupler arrangement does for the RTG's esthetics.

Otherwise, the RTG's are pleasant enough to ride. Their twin 1140 h.p. turbines produce an acceleration rate of 1.05 mph per second; their combination dynamic-disc-tread brakes can slow the 496,000-pound trains (empty weight, ready to run) from 100 mph to a stop in less than a mile — in 4400 feet to be exact. The RTG's are reasonably quiet, save for a jiggle which comes from beneath the floor over the trucks; and they ride reasonably well over our staggered-joint rail and over most turnouts and crossings. The point is, p.r. releases imply that *rame a turbine a gaz* translates into something superior to our E9's and domes and

diners and coaches; and from the viewpoint of the passenger, this simply isn't the case.

Never mind — I may have missed the point of the festivity on September 28. On the historic platform at Springfield, Ill. — which has witnessed everything on rails from Abraham Lincoln's funeral train, to George M. Pullman's No. 9, to the delivery passage of the *Electroliners,* to the 1935 dedication of the streamlined *Abraham Lincoln* (*Lord Baltimore* 4-6-4 and all) — an Amtrak executive, ex-railroad and knowledgeable in mechanical affairs, admitted the shortcomings of his new imports. He then remarked that what really mattered was that with the RTG's Amtrak was doing something on its own, something other than painting pointless arrows on old depots and laying wall-to-wall (and halfway up the wall) carpeting in 25-year-old cars beset with undiagnosed air-conditioning troubles. After all, Amtrak inherited the Metroliners and the United Aircraft Turbos; and Amtrak's new diesels, however much they are an improvement over the elderly F units they displaced, are not hardware to which the customer can relate. Trains with all the magic words — gas turbine, low center of gravity, French-built, bright and cheerful — are machinery to bring out TV cameras.

The distance for Amtrak between Chicago and St. Louis is 284 miles. The RTG's are scheduled to make that in 4 hours 59 minutes, including four intermediate stops (three fewer than conventional trains make); and Amtrak charges no premium for riding RTG — just $14.50 for a one-way coach ticket. The jets make the trip in just under an hour, and airlines charge $28 for coach; this does not include 34 miles' and 1½ hours' worth of driving time to and from the airports involved. Greyhound's nonstop expresses take 5 hours; the one-way ticket costs $12. Or you can drive in the American Automobile Association-rated time of 5 hours 49 minutes (291 miles at 50 mph average) and at varying expense, depending on how many miles per gallon your automobile gets, the number of passengers you take along, and whether you throw in depreciation and insurance.

The variables are almost infinite. What happens when Chicago-Springfield-St. Louis Interstate Highway 55 is completed all the way? Amtrak at present holds to a 79 mph speed limit, which could be erased by Federal dollars expended on track and signaling. One planemaker has talked up a downtown-to-downtown seaplane service from Lake Michigan to the Mississippi River. And Greyhound has just unleashed a vehicle dubbed the MC-8 which offers the passengers coffee-and-snack service, a hostess, and restroom facilities. Item: Hovering over all modes of passenger transport (but least of all over the train) are the issues of air pollution and fuel shortages.

In terms of what has ailed the passenger train since World War I, and would have buried it but for Amtrak, equipment has been less a factor than have, say, labor, terminals, and track. And the French turbine trains, for all their 2.7-million-dollars-apiece pricetags ("assuming a fairly stable monetary situation," to quote Amtrak) can have but faint impact upon these gut issues.

But economics have become blurred since Amtrak was created. An incontrovertible avoidable cost or above-the-rail expense is about as difficult to isolate as a straight line on Sophia Loren. Amtrak advocates — some of them in Congress where support counts — argue that, what the heck, with all the billions invested in the Interstate Highway system and in airports, a few million more bucks in a national rail passenger system don't matter. But I have the feeling that I want more for my share of the tax burden involved than just another low-center-of-gravity lightweight train.

Again, I may not be the one to say. Amtrak's RTG's aren't aimed at the over-the-hill set who grew up with illuminated drumheads, swivel parlor-car seats, white linen tablecloths, and all the other evidences of elegance preserved in the pages of the works of Beebe, Dubin, Kratville, and Wayner. Today's market equates travel with the six-abreast seating of Y-class jet service; with Greyhounds with tiny restrooms; and with VW's and LTD's, either self-owned or rented from Avis or Hertz. These customers are apt to feel right at home on an RTG, assuming that fare, frequency, and timetable jell; and that a U. S.-built production-model RTG (Rohr Corporation has been licensed to produce the trains here) has weatherproof vestibules, easy car-to-car access, protection for the engine crew, and otherwise overcomes the French equipment's most noticeable shortcomings.

In late afternoon the brightly painted *rame a turbine a gaz* provoked grins from the crews of diesel yard and transfer units sprinkled across that railroad patchwork on the east bank of the Mississippi. The RTG trundled across the river, rolled under the shadow of the Gateway Arch, and slowly nosed into the dark emptiness of the enormous arched trainshed of St. Louis Union Station, parallel with rows of platforms bereft of tracks and the trains they once held. At 5 p.m. on September 28, 1973, "the biggest travel news since the 747" pulled up to the bumper post, and its turbines died with a sigh.

With press kit in hand, I swung down and looked about in the gloom for the ghosts of the *Sunshine Special, Colorado Eagle, Banner Blue Panama Limited, Southwestern Limited, Diplomat,* and *Spirit of St. Louis.* I looked, but I did not tarry. For I and the group of reporters and Amtrak brass who squeezed into the only two taxicabs at the station entrance had planes to catch. ⌶

Editor's note: The ANF-Frangeco Turboliners were attention-getters in the Chicago-St. Louis, Chicago-Detroit, and Chicago-Milwaukee corridors, but they proved expensive to operate — an idling turbine doesn't use much less fuel than one that is operating at full throttle. Moreover, the European-style couplers between the cars made it difficult to alter train consists. Three of the second group of French Turboliners were rebuilt in 1988 for service between New York, Albany, and Niagara Falls, but the others were scrapped.

My finest train trip

"Unquestionable proof to me that the potential of American railroad passenger service is both unlimited and untapped."

⊥ Milwaukee, March 15, 1950

Mr. R. E. Barr
Vice-President, Traffic
Illinois Central System
135 E. Eleventh Place,
Chicago 5, Illinois

Great guns, Mr. Barr,

but I have failed to uncover any mileage in my file of railroad travel experience that can even equal my passage on the *Panama Limited* out of New Orleans on January 5, 1950. Illinois Central No. 6 was 921 miles of unquestionable proof to me that the potential of American railroad passenger service is both unlimited and untapped. The *Panama* was the concrete realization of a caliber of performance that I had begun to believe was an impossible illusion, a dream that could only hold sway in the minds of impractical idealists.

But first let me present my credentials lest you believe that I am a one-man advertising agency on the make for an IC account. I am one and the same guy who protested about Iowa Division passenger service on the IC in a letter to you last August. The dome lights were never darkened all night in my *Hawkeye* coach, and pillows cost 25 cents each; on my eastbound trip the station switching on No. 12 at Waterloo, Ia., past the midnight hour could only be defined as rough. I suggested that the lights be off, the pillows free, the switching smooth. In writing that letter, I tried to assume the attitude of an average passenger who, unlike myself, might ride Greyhound or drive his car to Waterloo unless the IC put its house in order.

Just for the record, let me say right here that you neither ignored nor dodged the issue. I was informed that the road was equipping both new and existing coaches with blue aisle-lights. My car was simply one of a minority yet to be so modernized. The quarter pillow rental was simply a service charge to cover costs: a fair if debatable reason. As for the nocturnal yard practices at Waterloo, you would check into that promptly. The letter regretted the cause for my complaint, promised a finer *Hawkeye,* and thanked me for writing.

My *Panama Limited* trip may be nothing more than a routine ride on the all-Pullman overnight streamliner; if so, this second letter will be of no great moment. For all I know your desk is stacked high with fan mail and your phone rings ceaselessly because IC No. 6 has been doing just what comes naturally. I don't know. I just think that the person who can find the paper and postage to fire even friendly criticism is also obliged to report such an example of quality passenger service.

One more point, Mr. Barr, by way of preface. The magazine assignment which took me into New Orleans on that sultry afternoon of January 5 had no connection with the IC. After a week on the road — haunting roundhouses and backshops, talking to traffic solicitors, running down rumors, jotting down fact and figure in my black notebook — I was, in fact, quite happy to look at railroading with no editorial strings attached. If the *Panama* had

E7s and cars of the Panama are scrubbed down at New Orleans. Photos by James G. La Vake (left) and Roy C. Meates (above).

been tagged for TRAINS, you would have heard from me about net earnings, train personnel, equipment names and like material long before this income tax deadline.

I was familiar with the *Panama Limited* tradition, however — aware that it was to the Mississippi Valley what the *Crescent* was to the Piedmont Plateau and the *Lark* to the coast of California. I liked to think of all these Pullman limiteds as handsome testimony that all of railroading's onetime fine gilt edge had not been swallowed up by coach streamliners and name-the-train contests. Luxury trains, that is, that merited the traffic of the discriminating year in and year out without recourse to bus fares or air line hostesses. I seldom rode these trains, but I liked to think they were

drumming along each night with their old "rights over everything."

I also recalled photographs of the *Panama* when it was powered by decorated 4-8-2's, held to a more leisurely schedule than today, and when IC charged an extra fare that included dinner — the train that Lucius Beebe (in his *Trains in Transition*) said "deserves to be preserved in service as an eloquent souvenir of heartier times and more spacious tastes in comfort." And if memory serves me faithfully, the streamlined *Panama* that followed upon the heels of Beebe's lines was under construction on December 7, 1941, frozen by W.P.B. directive, then released from the shops of Pullman-Standard into service as the last new passenger train until peace.

Interesting incidentals, I suppose, but hardly strong research for an inveterate train rider in for the wonder of his rail mileage. All I asked of Illinois Central, as a paying passenger aboard No. 6, was dinner and breakfast, a night's sleep, and a *Morning Hi* connection next a.m. in Chicago. A *Hawkeye* customer could expect the same.

I checked my topcoat and bag out of a concourse luggage locker the moment a switcher had parked the *Panama's* 14 cars of streamlined orange-yellow-brown in Union Station and the train gate was opened for loading. No. 6's observation-lounge-sleeper was my first tangible hint that the train it trailed was something special; its recessed IC-diamond drumhead, its *Panama Limited* in neon tubing script mounted in shallow boxes on either side of the car, its venetian blinds and simulated window panes, all blended into a design for which I could recall no postwar challenger. In common with its companion equipment ahead, the observation reflected full-fledged streamlining in its skirts and wide rubber diaphragms. Cleanliness of the cars indicated a thorough job earlier in the day at the train washer.

My spring suit, which is notably comfortable on a winter day in Corpus Christi, where I bought it, felt consciously warm in the humidity of a Louisiana January 5 — and car 616 was only three back from the front end. So on I trod past the red caps, car inspectors, diner and lounge to *Prairie State*. I had the last lower on the right to the rear. I gave bag and coat to the porter and stayed on the ground for a Camel. Up ahead they were loading mail and coupling up a 4000 horsepower cab-and-booster Electro-Motive E7. An EMD shifter shuffled arch roof Espee baggage cars two tracks over.

"'Board! All aboard!" The first of many calls echoed up the polished panels of the *Panama*. I flipped my smoke away and climbed the steps into the coolness of *Prairie State*. Over across the way the Texas & New Orleans had tied one of its memorable big Baldwin P-9 Pacifics, No. 622, onto a victorious Orange Bowl special being dispatched west to California as Second No. 1. Inside my car, complimentary copies of the New Orleans *States* had been placed on each seat, in each room and compartment.

Prairie State rocked a bit to the curve on which it was standing as two pairs of V-12 GM diesels accelerated from a lazy idle to a businesslike 325 revolutions per minute and kept climbing. Five o'clock on the nose; the *Panama* was on its 921-mile overnight journey from sun to snow. A running brake test punctuated by a couple of air horn blasts, then the IC roundhouse was passing on the left. An Alco-GE passenger diesel with the sunset herald of the Espee on its box nose caught me off guard — new power for the *Sunset* standing in the joint T&NO-Gulf Coast Lines-IC stable. The P-9's had at last been bumped.

A pause to pick up passengers at Carrollton Avenue, then a highball for Hammond. No. 6 held up avenue traffic crossing the boulevard and rails of a Tulane-route street railway line. Minutes later the long classification tracks of Mays Yard were sweeping by: the miracle yard rushed to completion in 1944 to blast the freight blockade that threatened the Port of New Orleans during World War II — the yard cited as the best investment the Illinois Central has made during the last 40 years.

Dinner seemed a good investment for me. Almost subconsciously I observed that the *Panama* was riding well (vestibules are a convenient lab) — far better, in fact, than the much-advertised streamliner on which I had left Chicago shortly before Christmas.

A wide window in *Vieux Carré,** the diner, lent a truer expression of the Panama's pace. I estimated offhand that we were hitting at least 85 miles an hour, maybe more. Aboard this Illinois Central train splitting the still of the swamps at 85 within 100 miles of New Orleans I discovered an almost perfect duplicate of a Milwaukee Road speedway schedule — little variation in gait, equal riding calm and quiet. It was good track being used to its full advantage by modern equipment and inspired dispatching.

Starting with the filet of walleyed pike at $2.60, the menu indexed a delightfully extravagant content of food and drink. It was a rather difficult selection for a traveler adjusting himself to the austere one- and two-entree service of other dining cars which labored under the blanket of economy (a dim way out, perhaps in view of the once-merited and still-blurbed joy of eating on a train). I settled on the select combination grill ($3.25), resisting the temptation of a shrimp cocktail (only 30 cents extra) for the orange juice test.

---

* Also the title of a standard-weight Pullman buffet parlor in the Chicago-Louisville afternoon service of the Pennsylvania years ago.

Orange juice it was — no canned overtones of taste nor obvious artifice — but real, honest, American, iced orange juice. The ham and chops and vegetables and coffee and dessert that followed were uniformly excellent served in an atmosphere of cordial hospitality by a waiter who did not mistake long delays between dishes for true sophistication. The car itself, with photomurals of an antebellum South and a tiny end-of-diner windowless nook embracing an embossed Creole mosaic, was a setting I had begun to believe existed only in the *Car Builders' Cyclopedia.*

I assume, Mr. Barr, that *Vieux Carré* is no stranger to the silver-plated rule that all railroad diners lose money. Yet I can conceive of no more profitable manner in which the IC's passenger traffic department can pen red ink on its accounts.

Next door in *General Beauregard,* a three double bedroom, one drawing room, one compartment lounge car, I found another *Panama* Pullman of original design. Panoramic prints of Latin American vistas topped a curving wall at the rear while through a mirror-flanked archway lay a perfect miniature of what I guessed to be French Quarter architecture. At any rate, I remember iron chairs with black leather upholstery, a bar worthy of Leadville, wooden shutters crowned by crescent glass, and a cast iron grilled door with flower design opening into the aisle down past the sleeping rooms.

My description may seem inaccurate on a point or two and possibly ornate to you but I want to record one traveler's impression of *Vieux Carré* and *General Beauregard* while it is still fresh — and also free of the embellishments and exaggeration that might become a measure of memory. The plans of the carbuilders for mass production of a few standardized blueprints find a robust argument in lower cost, but such a program could never produce a *Panama Limited.* And I like to think that No. 6 may create much of its repeat revenue simply because it is different from the run-of-the-mill, pastel-shaded, chrome-lined streamliners that rely almost solely on their names for individuality. Detroit automakers cut costs by mass production, but Detroit also displays a new model a year.

No. 6 braked to a creeping 10 miles an hour over the trestled Manchac Bridge, then traveled on through scattered rain to Hammond. Talk and laughter in the lounge was of good humor and small significance — mostly southern businessmen whose lack of planned pretense seemed to compensate for formal-fit black and navy blue attire. In particular I recall a large man with a voice that would carry over open safety valves who variously pointed out the best hotels of small towns the *Panama* passed, paid the bill on drinks for an assortment of friends and utter strangers, and related an earthy brand of Tennessee humor.

As No. 6 heeled to the curves entering Jackson, Miss., the fat man chided passengers who found it difficult to navigate down the lounge and was not in the least perturbed when a bottle of soda water finally gave up the fight with gravity and slid neatly into his lap.

As the *Panama* stood in Jackson, I awaited the jolt or thud or both that would signal the uncoupling of No. 6's New Orleans-Jackson parlor car and the addition of a Pullman that originated in Gulfport. But instead of a jolting thud, I detected a weak tremor, as if a car inspector had opened a journal box cover on our car (naturally not the case because the *Panama* rides on roller bearings). Either there was no pickup and set-out in Jackson on the night of January 5, or the IC switchmen were masters of their art.

Sleep was hard to come by, in spite of a lower berth, correct car temperature, good roadbed, and all the other details that make for rest. Maybe by that hour I was thinking of the *Panama* in terms of TRAINS, anxious to write even a personal, subjective account of the journey. Or I might have mused that I could endorse No. 6 for even so stern a critic of railroad manners and morals as a brother who is gainfully employed in the aviation industry.

Unless I was aboard a rare trip of the *Panama,* this Pullman streamliner was a precision-engineered operation drafted to hold its own in the de luxe passenger market by offering satisfaction — not simply a package of speed and orange-yellow-brown cars and diesels, but a careful handling of the details from the type face of the menu through to choice and training of personnel. One felt a guest aboard this train. That was it: a guest, not just a ticket number going along for the ride.

Moreover, this was a train that rode right through the factual barbed wire so often strung up in answer to passenger service criticism. Seniority didn't stifle train crew courtesy on No. 6.

Diner deficits didn't cut the quality of meals to meat loaf standards. I was pleased with but did not pay for the New Orleans newspaper. The Jackson station switcher had to lock into the identical couplers employed on other roads. Were all these extras the exclusive right of the *Panama*? Comment of friends on the dawn-to-dusk *City of New Orleans* made that answer doubtful. Was it the controlled-capacity, long-distance pattern of the *Panama* that made quality feasible? I had ridden similar mileages on other streamliners and never been unusually impressed by the service.

The answer was almost too clear. On *my* adding machine, at least, the *Panama Limited* performance could be commonplace provided other carriers invested the time and cash and effort of the Illinois Central. This was not to say that IC had a corner on the market. My own travel experience, on which this letter is based, is too limited to underwrite an opinion like that. But on the basis of my own traveling, coupled with printed and vocal notes of repute on the subject, I venture to say that not more than 15 per cent of the nation's feature trains are providing the full scope of service expressed in the *Panama*.

Morning came to me at Mattoon, Ill. Snow and ice lay over the land. Three quarters of an hour later, in Champaign's high-level station, I could look down from the diner to a man throwing salt over the slippery ground about the express office. Meantime, breakfast was just as fine as dinner the night before.

Up forward, the distinctive lounge of *General Beauregard* maintained a reversed look. The drinks and jokes and talk of the previous evening had faded; a couple of passengers smoked and rendered the expected comment on Illinois weather, another studied the sports section.

Frequently the lull was lost when a modernized Mountain or 2-8-2 slammed by in the opposite direction, its rapid exhaust buried in a banging roar of tonnage. It was good to be riding a road on which the steam locomotive still held down both the hot shots and the drags in the old tradition. How long would it last?

No. 6 was running late, the conductor said, and the train had grown during the night. He sat on one of the iron-leather chairs and identified the three diesel-powered passenger hauls that hurried by on the southbound main as (1) the *City of New Orleans,* (2)

the coach section of the every-third-day *City of Miami,* and (3) the Florida streamliner's Pullman section.

The captain figured that we should be in Chicago by 10 a.m., allowing for the fact that "when you've got 17 cars and two units, you're not going to set the world on fire."

Maybe not, but 4000 Electro-Motive horsepower at least had the globe smoking as they gunned through Matteson, riding over the fill that hurdles the tracks of the Elgin, Joliet & Eastern and the Michigan Central. At Homewood No. 6 flashed into the electrified zone and skirted huge Markham Yard on the west side.

And then came the names of Chicagoland: Cook County Lumber, Electro-Motive, Buda, Van Cleef Brothers, IC's Burnside car shops. We rolled over Grand Crossing (beside the Nickel Plate and over Pennsylvania and Central) with the porter calling out 63rd Street.

A two-car Chicago South Shore & South Bend electric train slipped past toward Michigan City, then a four-car South Shore schedule paralleled us out of 63rd Street. South Shore gained speed, passed No. 6, tunneled under our main line to reach high-level suburban platforms. A couple of New York Central trains (more correctly, Michigan Central and Big Four) rolled by toward 63rd Street.

The *Panama Limited* entered its station track, drifted by the red caps and passenger agents, spent its motion at approximately 9:55 — just 25 minutes late but in comfortable time to make the *Morning Hiawatha* departure at 10:30.

I call that my finest train trip, Mr. Barr, but permit me to define the compliment as meaning over-all excellence of service. I have tried to keep the average traveler's needs and wants in mind, yet pull no punches from a critical railroad point of view. The *Panama* was not the most exciting nor the most enjoyable rail journey I have known. To say that would be dishonest to a pair of Louisville & Nashville K-5 Pacifics that staged a dazzling run of the *Flamingo* one wet evening in 1945 from Louisville to Junction City, Ky. Nor could I ever forget a Burlington 5600-series Northern racing 17 cars through Nebraska one early morning at a steady mile-after-mile gait of 80. Not only these two selected memories occupy my mind, but also mixed trains and troop trains that brought the rider nearer to the pulse of railroading than is permitted by the soundproofing and diesels of IC No. 6.

But such journeys do not encourage the trade of the disinterested, so to the *Panama* must go the orchids. You have real reason to be inordinately proud that it carries the Illinois Central's diamond insignia. ⊥

Editor's note: The "Kalmbach salutation" on a letter, long since abandoned, looked contrived and artificial unless it was done well — and Morgan was the only person in the office who could do it . . . and "Great guns, Mr. Barr" has it all over "Dear Sir" as an attention-getter.

Travel West, 1964

There isn't a train we wouldn't take, either, Edna, including the streamliners

I MY favorite lady poet, Miss Edna St. Vincent Millay, committed to verse many, many moving, compassionate, sensible thoughts but none finer in my estimation than her willingness to ride any train regardless of its destination. My sentiments exactly. A corridor window on a local on the Riviera is the ticket for mixing sun and surf and sand with steam. A cupola seat on the Reader is genuinely bucolic. And the sensation if not the fact of 90 mph is present when Long Island's M.U.'s gather speed out of Penn Station and plunge beneath the East River.

Less esoteric but no less deserving of our consideration is the streamliner, that soundproof mix of roller bearings and double bedrooms and tinted dome glass and leg-rest seats and stainless steel that remains the civil way of getting from here to there. I'm intrigued by them. I have been ever since I first saw the *Zephyr* in print and the *South Wind* in person. I admire the long aristocratic E units that lead them west from Harmon and Harrisburg to Seattle and Oakland and L.A.U.P.T. I like the smooth, silent tug of their disc brakes, the vantage point of their Dutch doors, and the welded, fluted contours of their silvery cars.

And so last March the urge arose anew to sample the streamliners. Milwaukee was overcast and cold, there was business to transact on the coast, the *Guide* lay open on the desk. I jotted down layovers in Denver, Salt Lake City, Las Vegas, San Bernardino, L.A., San Francisco, and Dallas; sewed them together with 6010 route-miles of six railroads on a 16-day schedule involving 11 trains; and phoned in the space requests. The tab was reasonableness itself. Under the family fare plan (*i.e.,* depart Monday-Thursday, return any day; 1½ round-trip tickets cover two), first-class transportation plus bedrooms or parlor-car seats

for my wife and me totaled $365.05 — or 3 cents a mile per person. And they threw in Moffat Tunnel, domes, 113 miles of surfside running, and the Great American Desert for nothing extra. Yes, the time had come to explore again that established folklore that the best trains run west of Chicago.

Zip is the word for what North Western's 400's do between Milwaukee and Chicago. The green-and-yellow trains aren't as fast as they once were, but 85 miles in 95 minutes with four intermediate stops (which is what No. 206 is called upon for on the 8 a.m. departure out of our town) leaves the throttle in the No. 8 notch quite a bit. Two random thoughts: C&NW has never succumbed to the horrors of Continental breakfasts (*i.e.,* no bacon or eggs) which afflict its neighbor road; and at Great Lakes Naval Training Station a GP7 was switching beneath the catenary of the defunct North Shore, supporting an idle notion of mine that sooner or later a Geep will roll over the last foot of 4-foot 8½-inch gauge.

A taxi, a business luncheon, another cab, and we were at the check-in desk for Milwaukee Road-Union Pacific No. 111. The *City of Denver* will always mean to me that grille-nosed articulated that bared its teeth at the Q's *Zephyr* from 1936 onward, but of course the old streamliner is long gone. Indeed, since 1959 its namesake has simply been the *City of Portland* routed west via Denver instead of Cheyenne, with perhaps a setout coach or two for Denver in season. Which, memories aside, remains a good way of bridging 1048 miles and climbing a mile, for 111 averages about a mile a minute and consists of glossy yellow cars including very de luxe domes.

A pair of UP E9's slipped our 11 cars out of Chicago Union Station and into a wintry afternoon . . . and just as quickly, just as quietly, deadlines and phone calls and urgent memos dissolved behind the marker lamps. What is an evening aboard such a train? It's the good things: good drinks, good food, good conversation. And above and behind all, the good secure feeling of putting away the miles without so much as a tug on a seatbelt or a glance at a stoplight. I was asleep before Omaha. Next morning there was sunshine, bacon and eggs under dome glass with a backdrop of Rockies, and a punctual arrival in Denver Union Station.

There are few incentives for anyone to depart Denver, but Rio Grande 17, the westbound *California Zephyr,* qualifies. The *CZ* pioneered the cruiseliner or non-train concept of Western rail travel. Actually getting anywhere is a secondary excuse for the stainless-steel, dome-studded schedule; its purpose is, quite simply, fun. You're invited to don a sports jacket or shirt, stretch out, wind a film into your camera, say hello to strangers, exclaim over the biggest mountains on anybody's railroad in the U. S., and ignore a diet. The only intrusion of traditional railroad orthodoxy which I noted on the run was in the buffet-lounge. Margaret asked for a Coke which, being a "beverage," could be jotted down on a slip by the waiter whereas my coffee was "food" and required a check written by the customer — no verbal orders accepted.

Incidentally, after boarding in Denver we elected to have breakfast in the diner which meant that we didn't have a prayer of nailing down dome seats or even observation-lounge chairs by the time our four F7's rounded the great curve at Fireclay and started up the 2 per cent to the Divide. But we found windows and we stared . . . and I wondered how much one misses at 30,000 feet in a 707. The plane overlooks, ignores, but the train must needs come to grips with elevation and canyons and streams. So the car floor cants noticeably and the exertions of V-16's penetrate sealed double-plate glass and you know you've been somewhere and seen something.

The *CZ* is a train you can unwind on, too — a kick-off-the-shoes-and-take-a-nap train , a stretch-the-legs-at-Grand-Junction train, a how-do-they-manage-five-entrees-for-dinner train. I rode it last March for rest rather than research, so my recollection is fragmentary: the GP30's that kept parading past on hotshots; the moon-crater terrain west of Grand Junction; the heeling to the curves on the climb through the dark up and out of Helper, Utah; and the chat with the Filipino attendant in the observation lounge.

Oh, yes — our Pullman car name: *Silver Chasm*. That's what Webster's means by the word "appropriate."

I wouldn't insult your intelligence by arguing that today's 1136-page *Official Guide* contains half the wonders of its 1536-page counterpart of 1940, but there are exceptions to the rule. Union Pacific 5 out of Salt Lake City, for example. It has no name in the timetable (though I noted later that it's labeled the *Mail* on the San Bernardino station bulletin board) and it traverses an especially unpopulated region of the West by daylight which the City streamliners shun unless their headlights are burning. Yet I noted in its consist a cafe-lounge as well as a Pullman (out of Omaha and destined for L.A.) which implied that 700-plus desert miles to Vegas could be covered with a modicum of comfort.

UP 5 is scheduled out of Salt Lake at 10 a.m. but it actually departed at 11:42. With 3 E9 units, 10 head-end cars, 3 coaches, a heavyweight cafe-lounge, and the sleeper *American Progress.* We crept across city streets, past warehouses, beyond to the yard

limits, behaving as if mail and express trains delighted in their tardiness and proving just how inaccurate first impressions can be. For suddenly we were off to the races, running like the M10000, building up the pace through 45 to 50 to 60 and continuing to accelerate. Margaret and I have a line we exchange on occasions such as this, the Victorian quote from Beebe's first book that goes, "Bless me, this is pleasant, riding on the rail." UP 5 was that sort of train, no pretensions, plenty of clickety-clack, a work horse with Santa Anita instincts.

The Pullman porter was an amusing soul, full of anecdotes and jokes and lineside notes. He'd made his first trip the night after Carole Lombard died in a plane crash (how's *that* for dating your career start?) and been on the Omaha-L.A. run ever since. He could remember Vegas when it had a population of less than 10,000. We had a good cafe crew, too, serving up fare expected of a dome diner.

And the scenery was big, wide, and often engrossing, including one genuine and, so far as I know, quite unremarked horseshoe curve. It was SD24 country; we overtook a brace of the low-nose C-C's at the division point of Milford, Nev., and met another in a canyon.

We were steadily recovering our 1-hour 42-minute schedule loss, too, as 7200 h.p. hurled back the miles. The porter said that the engineer on the last lap into Las Vegas was the oldest man on the district and the fastest. Clearly he was a pro, for as we broke out of the mountains and began our curving descent to the rainbow lights of Vegas on the valley floor below it was apparent that we might just go in on time. I mean precisely that, too: on time. Not a couple of minutes off, either way, or even a shading of seconds. We drifted down the platform, the speed dwindled, the air exhaled, and at seven o'clock straight up we stopped — dead on time. We had run off 450 miles in 498 minutes.

Our one-night layover in Las Vegas gave us a chance to sample what might be termed America's Most Unusual Streamliner: Union Pacific's *Las Vegas Holiday Special.* The train (Nos. 115 and 116) began life as the *City of Las Vegas,* a name which survives on its stepboxes and plastic eating utensils. Initially it ran with a leased GM *Aerotrain,* assisted over Cajon by a GP9. Today's conventional equipment — an E9, a full-length lounge, a "Chuck

Wagon" buffet diner, and however many coaches are needed — operates week ends in the winter and daily June 15 through September 13. A Los Angeles–Las Vegas round-trip ticket, meals included, costs you a flat $20 (or $16 each if you and your wife travel under family fare tariffs); all drinks are 75 cents each. Now compare that with the one-way turboprop airline fare of $13 and you (1) understand why people could skip the time advantage of flying, and (2) wonder how UP breaks even on the service unless Vegas underwrites any losses.

Economics aside, the *Special* is a novel experience. Its passengers board fresh from the gaming tables, roulette wheels, and slot machines, either gleeful over their winnings or strangely philosophical over their losses, much in the manner of trout fishermen. The food laid out on the buffet counter is varied and good and abundant; all one needs is the knack of balancing to compensate for the sway of the train. UP cooperates. Although the *Special* is the fastest schedule into L.A., the first miles out of Vegas are flat and straight, and the E9 deliberately dawdles — or so it seemed to me. The patrons compare their luck in Vegas, drink, play cards, eat, then retire to their coach seats for a long nap. I wonder if there is any stranger way in which a railroad grosses $3600 or more for a round trip of 670 miles than transporting a trainload of Californians into the Nevada desert for a week end of uninhibited fun, thanks to a contrast in state laws.

Would Art Dubin call the *Special* a "classic train"? Hardly. Would Beebe call it anything? So far there's been not a mention in any of his books. What about Kratville's *Steam Steel & Limiteds*? No, not there either. Perhaps a train requires a more fundamental, useful purpose in life to warrant such permanence in print. I do not know. I do know, though, that you'll search far and to no avail in the *Guide* for the train's equivalent.

We disembarked in San Bernardino, spent the next day quite rewardingly atop Cajon Pass with Santa Fe operator Chard Walker, then encountered reader Gordon Glattenberg, a man with a recommendation. Why not, he said, ride on into Los Angeles on Santa Fe No. 7, the Fast Mail? Uncle Sam's transcon is no longer listed in the public timetable, but its consist includes two heavyweight passenger cars — a midtrain combine and a coach at the rear — and it will accept those riders curious enough to be aware of its existence. So we did, and the 140-mile run via Fullerton over the Third District of the Los Angeles Division was fine: 23 cars . . . 50 to 65 mph . . . and a splendid locomotive. Imagine four big long-nosed 2000 h.p. Alco PA-1 passenger units in A-B-B-A formation, all silvery and red, fresh from the Barstow washer.

And now may we address ourselves to a familiar question: does Southern Pacific really give a darn about passengers? Its current color scheme, automat cars, train consolidations, and public pronouncements would appear to argue "No" whereas its passenger deficits and the similarity of behavior of other roads would suggest that Espee has less of a choice in the matter than some would give it credit for. By way of personal answer I offer you No. 99, the *Coast Daylight,* on March 18, 1964. First, its size was a shock — two E units, a combine, two coaches, the automatic buffet car, a dome, and a parlor-observation. Second, it was scrupulously clean and the crew was as cordial as any encountered in our 6000 miles. Third, the ageless scenery was as swank as ever — Santa Susana Pass, 113 miles of Pacific Ocean coast line, a horseshoe curve and Santa Margarita Pass, orange groves, almond trees, and a view of the Bay Bridge entering San Francisco. Fourth, the baggage elevators in the coaches and parlor — a fine Espee exclusive — were no longer operative, the automat car ran out of its main entree — Salisbury steak — at noon and the coffee was only fair, but both sight-seeing and service in the dome were excellent.

Considering the competition, we might want to place our memories of *Daylight*s, morning and noon, with 4-8-4's and 16 cars each in proper perspective and be thankful there's a 99 at all. Between 5:45 a.m. and 11 there are, by rough count, a minimum of 18 Los Angeles–San Francisco (excluding Oakland) flights.

I wonder if a six-car 99 isn't a reflection upon mankind as much as anything else. Considering the content of the other pleasures which occupy us in 1964, the *Daylight* should be so popular that Espee would be begging Budd to expedite deliveries of more new cars, including diners.

After San Francisco we were in the hands of Santa Fe — on the *San Francisco Chief* to Clovis, N. Mex., on an unnamed connection beyond to Dallas, and aboard the *Texas Chief* back to Chicago.

Quickly now, what does AT&SF connote to you? How's this: a minimum of 6000 h.p. up front with you seated in deep plush, carpet beneath your feet, surrounded by stainless steel, a windowful of American desert outside your window, and Fred Harvey announcing another meal?

The train to which the buses from San Francisco drew up alongside in Richmond, Calif., was first class — in and out of the employee timecard. No. 2 comprised 3 big Alcos and 13 cars, including a diner, full-length dome lounge, and a sleeper with a lounge; and we had aboard approximately 100 coach passengers and 30 in the Pullmans. I have it on good authority that Lucius Beebe patronizes the *San Francisco Chief* frequently, and I can comprehend his reasons, for they must be a faster-than-*CZ* schedule, de luxe equipment, and Harvey menus. A pleasant spring rain began to fall as we cut through the Franklin hills and away from the Bay Area toward the San Joaquin Valley, and it seemed — and was — a time for loosening tie and shoes. Behind was the last business appointment, ahead lay two nights aboard train in the custody of Mr. Pullman and Melvin, the dining car waiter.

The most interesting car on the train was the dome, No. 551 — upstairs just like the *Chief*'s but quite different below decks. The Budd 12-wheeler contained a dormitory for the crew downstairs, which reduced its cocktail lounge to a tiny bar facing just seven seats. Yet, upon the word of the waiter, it was the busiest bar on the railway, serving the upper deck, dining car, and Pullman lounge in addition to the lonely seven immediately adjacent.

It was raining buckets over Tehachapi, so Margaret took my word for the Loop and we went to dinner.

Next day was sunny, dusty, windy, and fast. Between Holbrook, Ariz., and Gallup, N. Mex., No. 2 gets into Donald Steffee's speed survey by running off 94.9 miles in 76 minutes at an average start-to-stop speed of 74.9 mph, and Santa Fe allocates five F7 units (on at Barstow) to see that the engineer has the horses to do the job.

At Clovis we changed sleepers and trains, diverting from the main line there on unnamed No. 76 toward central Texas and the Gulf. Another find in the *Guide,* too, with three Alcos, three head-end cars, three coaches, the lounge Zuni, a lunch-counter diner, and two sleepers — all lightweight save the R.P.O. It was a friendly train that batted along at 50 mph or so between such towns as Hereford, White Deer, and Pampa; a train with stops long enough to allow one to look over the express wagons full of lingerie, chewing tobacco, shoes, and fluorescent tubes from the station platforms; a train that eventually acquires a name *(California Special)* — but only between Temple and Houston. Our section diverged at Brownwood and went into Dallas 5 minutes ahead of time behind four F7's.

The *Texas Chief* rolled us back to the Middle West comfortably, overnight, and on time — more of the same Santa Fe service that one becomes used to with no difficulty at all. And from Chicago home — what else but Milwaukee Road 5, the *Morning Hiawatha?* That's an advantage we enjoy in this town. No matter where one travels, the last lap home is at 90 mph on double track that still offers a frequency of seven trains each way a day. I've ridden those 85 miles uncountable times across the past 20 years, and my reaction is the same. Milwaukee Road knows how to conclude one journey and set the stage for the next. ⌷

Editor's note: It is difficult to slip anything past the readers of TRAINS. The December 1964 issue carried letters from several readers noting that Morgan's train overtook the brace of SD24s at Milford, Utah, not Nevada, and, unless the dispatcher had made a serious error, train 76 must have carried Morgan through Lubbock, Slaton, and Sweetwater, not Hereford, White Deer, and Pampa. That aside, this article is one of my favorites, in part because the October 1964 issue landed in my mailbox a week or two after I returned from a trip that included the CZ, UP 5, and the Coast Daylight.

This is it

I THIS, for my money, is the most arresting single scenic site in all of American railroading: Hanging Bridge in the Royal Gorge of the Arkansas River on the Denver & Rio Grande Western. The boiling waters crash through a canyon just 30 feet wide at the base and more than a thousand feet deep. Each day at 10:17 a.m. and 1:36 p.m. trains 2 and 1, the *Royal Gorge,* pause 10 minutes so that the passengers can absorb it all. "Nowhere else does man come closer to realization of the Infinite," says the guidebook. For a few moments one is suspended apart from the trappings of civilization, insulated against the works of man. Here is the culmination of uncounted centuries of the knifelike action of river on rock. Here the distractions of asphalt and neon and print are nonexistent.

Down here there is simply God . . . and the Rio Grande. I

Photo by Jim Scribbins.

73

The perfect passenger train

A civilized approach to passenger-train deficits

I PERHAPS there once were perfect passenger trains in point of fact as well as in mellow memory. Lucius Beebe, seconded by Arthur D. Dubin, have acclaimed several editions of the *20th Century Limited* as such, with a degree of verification that renders further comment superfluous. No one who saw the Dreyfus-styled Nos. 25 and 26 would disagree, nor would anyone who caught the implications of magnificence in Walter L. Greene's NYC calendar paintings of a generation and more ago.

S. Kip Farrington Jr. once made quite a case for the *Chief* on grounds of its all-Pullman makeup, $10 extra fare, shower, three lounges, and 100 mph 4-8-4's. I am without firsthand knowledge; but in the absence of evidence to the contrary, I would like to believe that Seaboard's winter-season all-Pullman East Coast section of the *Orange Blossom Special* qualified, if only because its happy name sounded like some concoction blended of gin and clickety-clack, or because one of its Vanderbilt-tanked M-2 Mountains once piled up more than 20,000 miles in a month working from Hermitage, Va., to Baldwin, Fla., without change. Although we may once have had a dozen perfect trains (or thrice that number if we let nostalgia temper our recall), I doubt that one is left in 1966. Good trains, yes; but flawless, no. The candidates have lost their extra fares or their observation cars, or their trainmen no longer doff hats in the diner, or their cars have been entrusted to hood units, or their consists have been diluted

". . . my ballot would be cast in favor of long flat-nosed Alco PA's, ideally in A-B-A formation . . ." Photo by D. W. Johnson.

by coaches.* It is intriguing, though, to speculate on whether the mechanical components of a perfect passenger train are not still around and to muse over the concept that could weld them into the travel purity of old.

Of course we would need the proper power on the point. All else being equal, a pair of Burlington's slant-nosed stainless-steel-

---

* I am not anticoach. Indeed, I would argue that many a prewar all-coach streamliner put its Pullman-only brethren to shame — and it was high time that those who had to count their pennies received their just deserts. Still, perfection implies an ultimate of comfort, and a bed is more comfortable than a seat.

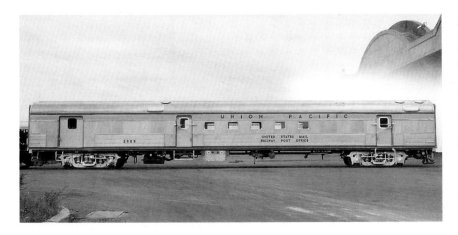

". . . a Railway Post Office . . . the Budd beauty whose image now adorns this journal's letters column." Budd photo.

sheathed E5's would be appropriate, assuming their nameplates were intact. But to the ear, the twin V-12 engines of any E have never quite been synchronized, so my ballot would be cast in favor of long flat-nosed Alco PA's, ideally in A-B-A formation and with their original 244-series V-16 power plants.

Tucked behind the Alco's grilled headlight casing on the trailing cab unit would be a Railway Post Office, either that arch-roofed delight that accompanies the *Broadway* or the Budd beauty whose image now adorns this journal's letters column. It would be the archetypal R.P.O. with a letter slot in its sides, a pickup arm, and a battery of clerks — one of them armed — sorting first-class letters through the night while the passengers behind slumbered.

Something borrowed, something blue — that would be next: the baggage-lounge that the *Capitol* carried up front until B&O's best lost its all-Pullman status. If memory serves, this vehicle was equipped with a big metal-studded leather bar, many mirrors, an exceptionally attentive crew, and — thanks to its location in the train — a total absence of people passing through on their way to the diner or the observation or wherever people passing through lounges are en route to. Seated therein, one could hear the air horns and the diesels' rpm's and feel the drawbar pull. It was one of those havens that named trains once had which only the regulars knew about. As for the baggage end, it is assumed that any

perfect train would attract at least a few passengers unable to get about without a steamer trunk or two to accommodate their accessories.

I would not be pernickety about the Pullmans in a perfect train save to insist that they afford a broad choice of accommodation and not simply the roomette/double-bedroom alternative provided today on once-plush limiteds from the *Southwestern* to the *Sunset.* The perfect Pullman de luxe must needs offer duplex rooms and compartments, drawing rooms and duplex roomettes, and — why not? — uppers and lowers. It goes without saying that these sleepers would incorporate disk brakes, faraway-sounding names, plenty of coat hangers and hot water, and a knock on the door within 30 seconds of the call button's being pushed.

As to precisely which cars to choose or whose builder plates they would bear — ACF or Budd or Pullman-Standard — I would abide by Arthur D. *(Some Classic Trains)* Dubin's selection, my sole stipulation being that he reclaim from the Illinois Central a 4-bedroom, 4-compartment, 2-drawing-room hand-me-down from the 1938 *Century* and restore its grand, unequaled name: *Imperial Chariot.* That I would ask. Wouldn't you?

Dining Equipment is something else again. I propose to be biased, dogmatic, insistent. The perfect passenger train must have Espee's *Lark Club.* Because *Lark Club* cost $247,000 in 1941 dollars. Because it's a triple-unit kitchen-dining-room-lounge. Because it affords more than 131 linear feet of recreation and dining space without intermediate vestibule, partition, or other obstruction. And because Pullman-Standard somehow managed this feat of articulation without impairing riding qualities or increasing noise level over that of conventional equipment. The *Club* was just that, not in name only — and possibly the most spectacular single piece of passenger equipment to emerge from the whole *Zephyr*-to-*Xplorer* streamlined era.

Perfection requires more than simply equipment, particularly in matters of the palate; and no reflection is meant upon Southern Pacific's culinary staff when I suggest that menu and crew be drawn from an interroad pool. We'd need a Northern Pacific steward, if only to write up meal checks; NP is, to my knowledge, the only carrier left which frowns upon the barbarism of "verbal orders not accepted." Surely the menu should offer

"The perfect passenger train must have Espee's *Lark Club*." SP photo.

". . . one of the 3-double-bedroom, 1-drawing-room dome-observation-lounges of the *California Zephyr . . .*" Photo by George H. Drury.

Illinois Central's umpteen-course Martini-to-creme de menthe, $9.85-and-worth-it King's Dinner; and every entree should be accompanied by a stab at Baltimore & Ohio's vast Roquefort-rich salad bowl. What's more, late risers and late diners should be able to order up bacon and eggs at 11 a.m. or a filet mignon at 11 p.m.

Next door I'd couple in one of those 5-double-bedroom buffet-lounges that used to grace the rear of the *Capitol* and are now operated adjacent to its diner . . . simply because they're comfortably laid out in blue plush and wood-finish paneling and employ waiters who never forget to alert their patrons when a dry state is impending. These onetime observations are admittedly a bit soft in the springs; and yet trains, even perfect trains, were intended to rock and roll a bit, canting to curves and grooving crossings and crossovers.

The marker's end of the perfect passenger train necessitates careful thought. Of course, the tail car must be a legitimate observation bearing an electrically lighted drumhead of one fashion or another; and of course, it should not be butt-ended.

So it could be one of the deep-windowed cars that trail today's *Century* or were specially designed for the Mid-Century edition of the *Empire Builder*.

We could do worse than to select one of the Sky-Top observation-sleepers that were fashioned for the *Olympian Hiawatha*.

I submit for your consideration, though, one of the 3-double-bedroom, 1-drawing-room dome-observation-lounges of the *California Zephyr . . .* with qualifications. Esthetics make it imperative that those illuminated lunchboxes of marker lamps on the *CZ* vehicle be replaced with suitable teardrop-shaped lights — agreed? And rear-facing seats in the aft lounge, as well as a speedometer and altimeter, would be necessary.

Still, the *CZ* car has two recommendations: a full-height see-ahead dome; and a shower bath in its drawing room.

(A shower on a train, even a transcontinental schedule, is scarcely a need, and — ask anyone who's tried one — it's problematical fun. But it is an experience. The natural sway of the train will cause one to grab for a water pipe for support, and the one you grasp is invariably the hot pipe. What's more alarming, the temperature of the water can fluctuate wildly if the engineer is recovering time, so that one can be alternately parboiled and quick-frozen in less time than it takes to scream. Nonetheless, an on-train shower is an indispensable prestige note. Long may they pour on the *Broadway, CZ,* and *Crescent,* the only U. S. trains which yet possess the [?] luxury.)

To equipment and personnel, we must finally add schedule. Not destination, but simply schedule, for the perfect train's creed must echo Robert Louis Stevenson's declaration that "the great affair is to move."

Should we not depart from Seaboard's pleasant little stub-end Spanish-style Miami terminal at eight o'clock on a balmy Florida winter evening? At eight sharp, too, leaving behind those who would fail to dignify a timetable . . . leaving them to the pointless freedom of their automobiles, which doomed perfection in passenger railroading to begin with; leaving them to ponder with fresh appreciation the wonder of a mechanism whereon the brakes are in release at 7:59:30 and forward movement begins on the second of 8 with the lift of our conductor's service-starred arm.

Other stations would warrant call: Cincinnati Union Terminal on a rainy spring night. And Dearborn, Chicago, where we would pause between throbbing ranks of Santa Fe F's on one side and Erie Lackawanna E's on the other. And Union Station, Louisville, because it's a grand old stone structure, which is reason enough (and conversely, why the perfect train must detour around Penn Station, New York).

The perfect train would surely cross Great Salt Lake at dawn, descend to the lights of Las Vegas at dusk, attain Tennessee Pass at noon, and expend long, sleepy afternoons batting across the Santa Fe desert east from Needles. It would travel up the Hudson River (quite possibly on the West Shore) at dinnertime, and be spinning down Pennsy's rock-steady tangent into Chicago when it's time to shave. Its lounge lights would be extinguished at midnight for those within to view Horse Shoe Curve, and seats in the dome would be at a premium topping Saluda as the brace of GP9 helper units behind settled into the No. 8 throttle notch.

Accountants in our audience, no matter how susceptible to the charm of rail-borne luxury, by now have computed the perfect passenger train as proposed herein to be hopelessly, magnificently uneconomic.

I concur. It would be surprising if the extra fare (what train worth its name lacked an extra fare?) would even cover the out-of-pocket dining-car deficit. For the perfect train, without apology and on a grand scale, would have extraordinarily high built-in labor costs. Its equipment, being the antithesis of those low-slung, tinted-window, contoured-seat speedsters now being readied for corridor-type runs in the East [TurboTrains and Metroliners], would naturally be expensive to operate and maintain.

Yet the perfect train is proposed, not wholly in jest or nostalgia, with the thought that even though American passenger trains still produce a deficit far exceeding 300 million dollars a year, for once the railroads which sustain this real and sizable loss might get their money's worth. They might, too, redress the grievances of those who did not flee the passenger train in its failing hour, who suffered without complaint the pains of higher-than-air-fares, late arrivals, automat meals, nonelectropneumatic brakes, 79 mph maximum speed, *et al.,* while resisting the temptations of the freeway and the jet.

Would the jet set be lured back downstairs by the perfect passenger train? Definitely not. They would scorn our sub-sub-sonic gait, $1.25 drinks, and absence of movies or Muzak.

Would the freeways offer a potential market? Negative. The occupants of the station wagon and the *Lark Club* have naught in common; each does not even know the other exists.

Who would the flawless streamliner impress, then?

Those whose appetites are sharpened by jointed rails . . . who wave at the flagmen on passing freights . . . who are unconsciously aware, without looking up, that the train is slowing for Connellsville or descending into Butte . . . who savor all of railroading's idiosyncrasies from QUIET IS REQUESTED FOR THE BENEFIT OF THOSE WHO HAVE RETIRED to, "What call would you care to leave for the morning?" — who, in short, know that travel, true travel, is an end in itself. **I**

It's dying where it all began

Omit Britain from a train-watcher's itinerary? Unthinkable!

I THIS . . . this is all the excuse one needs for an overseas rail safari. As the sun sets you're caught up in the turmoil of John F. Kennedy International Airport, New York, a bewildering complex of glass walls scented with kerosene and orchestrated with whining turbines. But just 8 hours later by your wrist watch, which is breakfast time beyond the Atlantic, you're standing on the high-level platform of a sooty brick railway station in Scotland named Kilmarnock, watching a dirty, listenable 2-6-0 play cat-and-mouse with a guard's van as bowler-hatted, umbrella-carrying types assemble with you for a train called the *Thames-Clyde Express.* You feel strangely, impossibly reborn, as if you should reach out and touch the smokebox of the Mogul with the expansive number 77019 to determine if it is indeed steel and fire and not illusion.

So it was with me on Platform 4 at Kilmarnock on a foggy morning in May 1965. I was happy with the absolute contrast between British Railways and what I was familiar with at home; glad of the fresh passport in my pocket that would be the key to this and other railway treasures on an itinerary reaching to the Indian Ocean; and most of all, pleased that I had not further postponed a reunion with international trains and the engines that propel them. For time is running out on the old guard overseas, just as irrevocably as it did here in the 1950's. Only a single major London terminus now sponsors steam . . . close on 5000 route-miles of catenary in France is condensing the ranks of domestic compounds and imported Mikes . . . English Electric and GE salesmen are doing to the Garratts of Africa what the ivory hunters did to the elephants of the same continent . . . Spain remains enchanting, but the RENFE units on the Alco assembly line in

Bulleid Pacific 34002, *Salisbury,* runs southpaw as she drifts downgrade between Mortehoe and Ilfracombe in Devon with the 5:20 a.m. train from Exeter. Photo by George F. Heiron.

Schenectady will soon turn the clock ahead. If such items intrigue, then you try to come up with the wherewithal and go; and if you've been before, you go back.

You may ask, "Why Kilmarnock?" Because it's in Britain, birthplace of the steam railway. And because its 401¾ lovely rail miles from London, one city which should be entered by train and not by airport bus. Glasgow's airport is Prestwick, and the 8:30 p.m. BOAC jet out of New York gets there at 7:45 a.m. Assuming it's on time, and there's no hang-up in immigration or customs, one can grab a taxi and get across to Kilmarnock (which is 24¼ miles southwest of Glasgow) for the 9:44 a.m. departure of the *Thames-Clyde*. It's a long red train of traditionally compartmented cars drawn by a 2500 h.p. 1C-C1 of Baldwin lineage on a route up and over mountainous moors attained by 1¼ per cent gradients, viaducts, and mile-long tunnels; thence through England's steelmaking and coal-mining industrial heartland.

The journey theme, then, is scenery punctuated by steam. Once you adjust to small cabs, six-wheel tanks, pipsqueak whistles, and an absence of bells, headlights, and pilots, the British locomotives spotted en route are charming creatures: a Pacific here named *John Milton,* a little 0-6-0T of the National Coal Board there done up in vivid green, War Department (theirs, not ours) 2-8-0's, even 60-inch-drivered Decapods which have been clocked at 90 mph plus. In their twilight years these engines are dirty, often indescribably so; but the good, clean British lines are there, make no mistake. Sheffield, England's Pittsburgh, is the place to see them.

For comfort, privacy, and visibility, a first-class smoking compartment puts the typical open-aisle American coach to shame. It's a deep-cushioned, cedar-paneled place in which to alternately look out, chat, read, and doze. The distractions are pleasant: a train banging past in the opposite direction with a screech of whistle and a thump of windowpane, and calls for morning coffee, luncheon, or afternoon tea in the midtrain restaurant car. You do have to beg for ice in your Scotch; but the noon meal, drink included, runs to only $3 for soup, roast beef with vegetables, cold cuts, salad, cheese and biscuits, and coffee. Season with the smoke of a 4-6-0 and you have a decent repast

At 6:15 p.m., St. Pancras Station, London, on time.

For the balance of my stay in England I concentrated on British Railways' Southern Region, which is at once BR's most distinctive if most compact operating unit, a sort of elongated Long Island Rail Road, a spider web of 630/750-volt D.C. third-rail electrification, and the proprietor of the last sizable stud of steam passenger power in the U.K. The most misleading statistic about the Southern is its 1696 route-miles, which would seem to place it between Cotton Belt and Central of Georgia in scope. Commuters magnify the region out of all proportion to its route size. Their weekday surge into London explains why Southern maintains six terminals in the city, experiences rush-hour traffic through suburban junctions at the rate of a train every 37½ seconds, and requires no fewer than 21 stub-end tracks in Waterloo Station. Southern is multiple track bearing more trains than the mind can cope with. An instance: One day I caught the 11:10 a.m. out of the seacoast resort city of Brighton for London, a distance of 51 miles, and en route our train of green M.U.'s overtook or passed 42 other trains. Equal that anywhere else in off-peak hours.

One would think that a suburban-oriented system such as the Southern, so necessarily committed to electric traction since World War I, would have cast a minor image in steam. Not so. Southern always provided its nonelectric mileage with handsome, interesting, capable locomotives, including four-cylinder 4-6-0's timed to exhaust eight instead of four times per driving wheel revolution and the island's largest 4-4-0's with a tractive effort of 25,135 pounds, a 79-inch wheel, and three cylinders. And in the Second World War an extraordinary engineer named O. V. S. Bulleid shocked the country with two series of 4-6-2's — a wheel arrangement previously unused by the company. For Britain, both the larger Merchant Navy class and the smaller West Country and Battle of Britain series were all but revolutionary, what with their hooded welded boilers, chain-driven valve gear, syphons, Boxpok drivers, and relatively high (280 pounds) pressure. They were scarcely handsome by ordinary standards, controversial from an engineering viewpoint, and subject to what the English tactfully term "teething problems."

By a quirk of history these Bulleid Pacifics, in original or rebuilt form, were destined to outlast all of Britain's orthodox mainline express power in passenger service. Diesels largely demoted the famous Castles and Gresley streamliners and Princesses of other regions; but Southern, engaged in the more time-consuming work of extending its third rail, thought it cheaper to stick with steam in the interim. And the interim will last until sometime in 1967; so until then Waterloo Station will resound to the exhaust and safety valves of engines named *Canadian Pacific* and *Westward Ho* and *601 Squadron.*

By all means discover them in Cecil J. Allen's admirable *British Pacific Locomotives* (Ian Allan Ltd., 1962). Then, if at all possible, transport yourself to Waterloo and inquire at the booking office for a first-class smoker to the West of England. The illustration on page 81 should resolve any doubts on the issue.

Oh, yes — it was a Bulleid 4-6-2, and an unrebuilt one at that, that conveyed Sir Winston Churchill to his final resting place. At first I thought the choice odd, for if *Winston Churchill,* alias 34051, was a steam locomotive and hence as traditional as the Empire itself, was not its unorthodox design out of keeping with its namesake's character? And yet . . . well, did not Sir Winston revel in a dash of the different, as in his pioneering advocacy of the tank and the plane? There is no record, I'm told, of any special interest in railways on the part of the prime minister; but had he been briefed on locomotive design in the U.K., I daresay he might have been in Bulleid's corner, voting for the fresh, and hang the problems. Yes, I rather think so.

What is train-watching like in England today? Let me give you a 1½-hour sample, selected at random on a warm, sunny Tuesday afternoon in the cathedral town of Salisbury, just 83 and a fraction miles out of London. I went to the station well ahead of train time, found a comfortable bench on Platform 4, and opened my notebook:

3:30: A diesel multiple-unit train set muttered into a stub track and discharged its passengers behind my back. Across the way, in a small freight or "goods" yard, a typically British diesel switcher shunted about. It weighed 25 tons or so, sat on six side-rodded drivers, and drove through a mechanical gearbox.

3:35: In from the West and destined for Waterloo came a train behind 73022, one of the standardized 4-6-0's introduced by British Railways after nationalization but before the abrupt switch to dieselization. She was of straightforward two-cylinder design, with all her running gear exposed in U. S. style — obviously an engine created to cope with Britain's postwar adversities of poor coal and minimum maintenance.

3:50: *601 Squadron,* one of the Bulleids arrived on a terminating train.

3:55: In from London arrived a blunt-nosed, compact 1700 h.p. diesel cab unit of strange breeding. Inside she packed a guttural Maybach-designed engine driving through a Mekydro hydraulic transmission, but the builder plate read Beyer, Peacock Ltd. This, then, was what the Garratt Foundry had been reduced to when the export market for its unique articulateds collapsed.

4:02: A sister unit arrived.

4:24: More diesel-hydraulics, these named for famous Royal Navy battle wagons: *Onslaught* east, *Formidable* west. Named diesels? Perhaps. But it will require a generation newer and more flexible than mine to be comfortable with the idea. *Formidable* — now, there's a nameplate I would have hung below the running board of a Big Boy.

4:45: Another BR standard 4-6-0, the 75066, rolled in.

By which time the American observer, busily writing and/or photographing, all the while feverishly thumbing his Ian Allan *ABC of British Railways Locomotives,* finds himself preoccupied and quite adjusted to the thump of opposed rail joints, the vantage of high-level platforms, and the offbeat exhaust of locomotives with three cylinders. I suppose the extraordinary traffic density does it. In England, especially on the Southern, there's always another train coming. Over there they produce train-miles as we do ton-miles. If there is scant they can tell us about how many tons can be hung behind a locomotive's drawbar, then there is naught we can relay to them on how to dispatch trains or people in the mass.

So what else was memorable about British Railways in 1965?

Museums, for one thing. I am frankly prejudiced in favor of the British approach to engine preservation. Judging by contemporary periodicals in England, it's threefold: restore the locomotive to her original physical condition or at least livery; send her on outings for the fans if possible; finally berth her under roof. Such museums are maintained by the Transport Commission in suburban Clapham outside London, Swindon, and York — to name three.

The repository in Clapham Common, just a brief ride on the Underground from Waterloo Station, is the most accessible one for overseas visitors and the best value for two shillings sixpence (say, 35 cents) in the U.K. The building is a converted carbarn, just around the corner from the subway station, and as you walk in you're confronted with the shovel nose of a blue streamlined

Pacific. Suspended overhead is the legend FASTEST STEAM LOCOMO-TIVE IN THE WORLD. She's *Mallard,* Sir Nigel Gresley's great three-cylinder, 80-inch-drivered speedster which, on July 3, 1938, touched a dynamometer-car-recorded 126 mph. That was, and is, the highest fully authenticated speed the reciprocating steam locomotive has ever achieved. In the quiet of the museum you stand beside those huge driving wheels (which seem so much larger than the identical drivers of, say, a Santa Fe 4-8-4 because of the tight British clearance diagram) and recall Cecil J. Allen's note that at the instant of 126 mph they were revolving more than 500 times a minute

That would be — let's see, something better than 8½ complete revolutions every second!

Clapham has much more . . . a Midland compound 4-4-0, a condensing tank engine once operated beneath the streets of London, carriages which conveyed Queen Victoria, double-deck trams, all manner of other railway memorabilia.

But *Mallard* is the star. It's an unmitigated shame we didn't do as much for our fastest, which in all probability was one of the Milwaukee's A's.

I would offer these vignettes from elsewhere in England that week in May:

• The excitement one morning in Chichester as a Bulleid 4-6-2 took over — No. 34086 of the Battle of Britain class, name of *219 Squadron* (and bearing that RAF unit's slogan: "From dusk 'till dawn"). I have in my notes: "Running up to 60, blowing off continuously en route, high-pitched whistle."

• Another instance of adventure — West Country-class 4-6-2 *Clovelly* speeding overhead as our electric suburban train out to Shepperton diverged from the main line not far out of Waterloo.

• Waterloo itself, with 4-6-2's *Spitfire* and *Clan Line* at the buffer posts.

• The sadness of time running out on steam, as at the country station in Horsham a few miles from the south coast where a 2-6-2T was departing on a local that would be, I was told, diesel drawn in six weeks.

• In the Britons' voices the identical note of dismay that was in our own a decade back as diesels blanked entire engine classes that we had somehow assumed would endure our lifetimes.

Bulleid Merchant Navy class 4-6-2 *Elder Dempster Lines* awaits departure time from London's Waterloo Station. Photo by George F. Heiron.

(British Railways owns approximately 6000 steam engines, about what we had in America in 1955 — though, of course, compressed into a fraction of our land area).

As the jet's turbines warmed at Heathrow Airport, London, at the initiation of Central African flight 893, I was moved to wonder whether my fourth visit to London since 1958 would prove to be sufficient. Or whether that ghastly, irresistible steam-off dead-line of 1967 might not be warrant for one more long look at the likes of *Spitfire* and 73022 and *Canadian Pacific.* ⊥

*Editor's note: Morgan knew that most of his readers had little interest in overseas railroading, but he was always eager to arouse their curiosity about railroading where GP7s, knuckle couplers, and standard gauge weren't the norm. He reported on three trips abroad: "*TRAINS Goes Overseas*" (June–September 1959; Britain, France, Italy, Switzerland, West Germany, and Belgium), "*TRAINS Goes Around the World*" (February–November 1961; Britain, Africa, India, Australia, New Zealand, and Japan), and "*Jet Search for Steam*" (January–August 1966; Britain, Africa, France, and Spain). This article and the one that follows are episodes 1 and 5 of "Jet Search for Steam."*

Where the trains catch the spray from the falling Zambesi

About a wonderful place to train-watch

IBREATHES there the man, with soul so dead, that he possesses not somewhere in his imagination a Shangri-la? For the likes of us, it is a place remote, rail-served, spectacularly beautiful, yet ultimately accessible. A place learned of in childhood from the pages of *Railway Wonders of the World,* and casting then an impression so intoxicant and indelible as to haunt us into manhood.

A year ago my Shangri-la became reality. For me that place was close on 10,000 air-miles from Milwaukee in southern Africa, and until the middle of the 19th century known only to natives, who spoke of it as *mosi-oa-tunya:* the smoke that thunders. Missionary-explorer David Livingstone came upon the spectacle on November 16, 1855, as he was paddled down the Zambesi, a sort of west-east Mississippi River of Africa. Livingstone saw "five columns of vapor rising 250 feet to mingle with the clouds" — spray produced by waterfalls that would in our time be termed "the world's mightiest curtain of falling water" and "the greatest sight in Africa." What he broke personal precedent to christen Victoria Falls (for Livingstone believed in native names for native places) was actually five falls in one, with a crest 4580 feet across, a height of 304 to 355 feet, and a widely disparate water flow of 3¾ million gallons (in October) to 75 million gallons (in April) per minute. A falls, that is, far broader than Niagara and of more than twice the height.

Shangri-la? Not yet. A half century would flow down the Zambesi before *mosi-oa-tunya* would concern those of the conviction that rails and geography complement rather than contend with each other. The shadow of empire-building Cecil John Rhodes fell upon the great fissure in the Zambesi as he was assembling his "phantom" railway — a Cape-to-Cairo line that would bind a continent from the Mediterranean to the Atlantic with 3-foot 6-inch gauge rails. If Rhodes is remembered today as an often ruthless colonialist, at least one of his contemporaries thought him "nearer the soul of things than the world knew." Rhodes never saw the falls, but his engineering mind grasped their dimension and "his gift of imagination" did the rest as rails neared the Zambesi at the turn of the century. Overruling his brother Frank — who wanted to bridge the river 6 miles above Victoria Falls lest the trains desecrate a natural wonder — Cecil declared, "Build a bridge . . . where the trains as they pass will catch the spray of the falling Zambesi."

Cecil prevailed. His engineers flung a cantilever arch across a gorge below the falls. The double-track main arch was 500 feet long, with approach spans of 62½ and 87½ feet, the whole affair consuming 1868 long tons of steel. Its builders — the Cleveland Bridge and Engineering Company Ltd., of Darlington, England — actually assembled the bridge in sections at the factory before dismantling the structure for shipment to Africa. Although the whole bridge program took over 14 months, the steelwork was riveted across the gorge in only 9 weeks. It is fitting, I think, that history records the first living creature to cross the bridge as "a fully grown leopard." Except for the single-tracking of the railway in 1929 to permit addition of a road and sidewalks, the Victoria Falls Bridge looks the same today as when it was opened September 12, 1905, by Professor Francis Darwin, son of Charles.

Until May 1965 I knew of these things only from print and

Safety valves lift on a 4-6-4+4-6-4 as she eases across Victoria Falls Bridge 360 feet above the waters of the Zambesi River. Photo by George A. Gloff.

photo, and from afar. Yet the supposition seemed valid that if one added Rhodesia Railways' largest Garratt locomotives to the scene and included a railway-owned, railway-adjacent Victoria Falls Hotel, the total could spell Shangri-la.

So we embarked upon the "all-classes" overnight from Bulawayo north, booked to cover the 280 miles to the falls in 12 hours 10 minutes behind steam. The journey was a pleasant prelude to Shangri-la, with a warm sizzle in the darkness at each meet announcing steam on opposing train movements and with daybreak bringing a repetition of what my namesake had seen 110 years before: "vapor rising . . . to mingle with the clouds." It was, it really was, and the columns of spray could be seen out the open corridor-aisle windows of our train from miles away.

Mosi-oa-tunya . . . what a sight, what a place to approach behind a great, black, shining 4-8-2+2-8-4.

We got off at Victoria Falls station, only steps from the lobby of the hotel, checked in, then joined a young Rhodesia Railways civil engineer for a closer inspection of the bridge and a view from the Zambian side of the Zambesi.

Trains descend to the bridge from either side on curving 1.1 per cent, then cross decorously at 5 mph, which makes for splendid train-watching from the shady terrace of the hotel. You can sip your gin and tonic *and* draw a direct bead on the bridge. You can watch to your heart's content while a train from Zambia appears and edges out over the gorge — 360 feet above water. Once the Garratt is across and leaning into the 1-in-90 gradient, you simply settle up the bill and stroll through the hotel gardens and lobby to trackside where, 5 minutes from the bridge, the 4-8-2+2-8-4 appears on a superelevated curve working upgrade into Rhodesia, Bulawayo bound. And there are trains, many trains — for as RR's press releases note, "every lump of Rhodesian coal destined for Zambia's copper mines and practically every ton of Zambian export copper [is] carried across the bridge," not to mention "merchandise and minerals, petrol and people." Smaller Garratts are seen, but the rule-of-thumb power at the Zambesi is a Class 20 "double Mountain" — one of the 60 700-series 4-8-2+2-8-4's built during 1954–1958, 95-foot fellows that exert 69,333 pounds tractive effort.

I reflected upon other railway hotels in other places, all of them of happy recall and some memorable. From the windows of Norfolk & Western's Hotel Roanoke one had the railway's passenger station and main line below, the shops to the left, and the general offices to the right; and the rumble of passing Mallets was ceaseless. And there was Chessie's Greenbrier at White Sulphur Springs, W. Va., with Dorothy Draper's white-and-green decor within and the owner's black-on-black on H-8's and hoppers without. Yes, and Canadian Pacific's Hotel Palliser in Calgary, Alta., where a breakfast bonus was a picture-window glimpse of the *Dominion*'s 2-10-4 coupling on. Once I even found a CP hostelry in New Brunswick — the Hotel McAdam in the junction of the same name — located on the second floor of a handsome old gabled stone structure whose first story was the depot itself.

Each was shy of Shangri-la, though. Shangri-la was Victoria Falls.

Shangri-la may not chance my way again.

I rather think it won't. ⌶

One afternoon in Austria

An encounter with a 4-8-0

AS a boy I had access to enough copies of *Railway Wonders of the World* to form the opinion that the European steam locomotive, seldom a handsome animal at best, declined steadily in esthetic appeal as one moved eastward from France. Or southward, for that matter. The engines whose pictures I pored over were in some instances so grotesque as to be stimulating — just as a sternwheel packet, the antithesis of a ship, nevertheless may possess a certain majesty.

My opportunity to ride behind and to inspect a genuine European locomotive arose July 5, 1961, in Austria. I took an afternoon off from witnessing the trials over Semmering Pass of German diesel-hydraulics destined for the U. S. and rode a couple of steam trains between Murzzuschlag and Bruck an der Mur, a 26-mile ride down the Murz River. The ride down the gently landscaped valley (in a brace of 4-wheel cars behind a 4-6-4T) was pleasant if unexciting, the weather was mild, the goal provocative. For in the junction town of Bruck I hoped to board No. 580, a Rome-Vienna express, for the ride back to Murzzuschlag. And "express" meant the high-mounted oddity of a 4-8-0 which you see in these photos. In she rolled, the 33.115, limping from an apparent hot axle bearing, towing 17 cars, steaming straight out of the pages of *Railway Wonders*.

How European can an engine be? The 33-class 4-8-0 (the word Twelve-Wheeler seemed too American to describe her) bore the thin stack that denotes a Giesl ejector; Germanic but split smoke deflectors; a cab with more size than protection; Walschaerts gear actuating O. C. Lentz valves; a bland smokebox door; and a grubby, overworked fireman. She rode on 66.9 inch drivers, dated back to the '20's, and had worked the Semmering

until electrification. I'm hopelessly partial to big power (aside from a few 2-8-4's, nothing bigger than the 33's was ever built by Austrian Federal for passenger service) and unusual wheel arrangements (the only other 4-8-0's I had seen belonged to the Espee), so the 33.115 enchanted me in spite of her gracelessness and grime.

The journey back to Murzzuschlag along the Murz was uneventful. Despite an assist from a 4-6-2T, the 33.115 only managed the 26 miles in 41½ minutes. Yet the sight of that lazy tandem leaning into it on the curves on a July afternoon in Austria is one that rests comfortably in the memory. I think it always will. ┴

Photo by David W. Beadle.

Amtraking west in search of the fast Flying Scotsman

It is written that all things are possible. They are, they are

BY MY WATCH our Western odyssey began at 12:20 p.m. in Milwaukee on September 12, 1971, and ended there at 5:50 p.m. on September 20, 8¼ days and 4793.7 rail route-miles later. En route we encountered a prairie fire that had engulfed a farming hamlet . . . a narrow river deep and swift enough to hide a 125-ton diesel . . . a world-famous locomotive steaming along more than 5800 miles from home . . . the only working passenger conductor on the railroad which coined the word "streamliner" . . . a schizophrenic train that couldn't make up its in between three names and a number . . . a route where to Amtrak was to backtrack . . . the most novel, albeit homemade, dome . . . steam on the Espee . . . and Milwaukee Road doing what comes naturally.

Any excuse for a train trip is a good excuse. All reasonable men grant that proposition. Yet the two reasons we had for going West were so sound and the rewards were so predictable that I felt I could have written this account in advance, simply leaving a few blanks in which subsequently to enter arrival times, car names, and the like. I was wrong. No one could have forecast that September 12–20 adventure across 14 states aboard trains 31/Extra LNER 4472 West/102/2/23 in the dimensions it developed — such as hanging on a 1.5 percent grade on a brake of unknown strength, revisiting a turntable under cover, and watching the dismantling of a storied rail passenger plant.

Two reasons for travel, did I say? Reason 1, of course, was Amtrak — not Amtrak *per se,* but Amtrak in the third quarter of 1971, a very special and quite perishable period in the youth of America's first national rail passenger system. For in the beginning, on May 1, 1971, Amtrak merely had hung out a banner or two, donned a red jacket here and there, changed a few routes, and otherwise simply picked up the tab for a business-as-usual operation. And toward Thanksgiving Amtrak was to assert its own personality — in scheduling, personnel, equipment, ticketing. But in September 1971, Amtrak was running off its train-miles in a twilight zone, in a betwixt-and-between season of old, new, borrowed, and blue. We, as taxpayers, wanted to examine any evidence of our new investment; as rail enthusiasts, we wanted to bid farewell to memorabilia familiar to Lucius Beebe.

Reason 2 was LNER 4472, Alan Pegler's elusive now-you-see-it, now-you-don't *Flying Scotsman,* and ensemble — the same train that had compensated the British for that tea party by slipping into Boston harbor in September 1969 and cruising south for an unlikely, climactic three-steam-engine-meet in Anniston, Ala., hosted by the Southern Railway ["Appointment in Anniston," February 1970 TRAINS]. The lightweight, vacuum-braked green consist had wintered in the wilds of Texas, had barnstormed across the Middle West the following summer, then had sought shelter from the snows again, this time in the custody of Canadian National in Toronto. Rumors that the 4472's 80-inch drivers would roll again, this time toward the Pacific, finally had been confirmed in a telephone call from Alan Pegler: *Flying Scotsman* was off and running, bound for display on Fisherman's Wharf in San Francisco via Spokane and Oroville; would we like to experience a division or two of the transcontinental adventure ?

Who could resist a betwixt-and-between Amtrak sampler and *Flying Scotsman*? Not I. Not my wife. Not that seasoned, gregarious Augusta (Ga.) radio executive George G. Weiss. To squeeze the odyssey between airtime and presstime deadlines, we decided to Amtrak west on the *Empire Builder,* overtaking

Amtrak 7, the *Empire Builder,* pulls out of a siding onto the main line in deepest Montana. Photo by George G. Weiss.

4472 somewhere beyond the Divide, and ultimately return on a combination Overland Route/*CZ* limited. For us, this just had to be *the* journey of 1971, in spite of prior associations the same year with Nos. 1 and 722 and 6218 and 759.

Ding, ding, ding. With bell ringing, into Milwaukee rolled the *Builder,* Amtrak 31, led by four old ex-NP F units and trailing 17 cars in 5 color schemes, the like of which will occupy fan slide shows a generation from now. From the diesels back, No. 31 consisted of a baggage-dormitory, flat-top coaches, a Ranch car (lounge-snack), dome coaches, a full-length Great Dome, diner, Slumbercoach, and three sleepers, variously dressed in old GN Omaha orange, new GN big sky blue, NP two-tone green, Q stainless steel, and BN merger green. Our spaces were in the last car,

Silver Ravine — a Budd 10-roomette/6-double-bedroom sleeper built for the second-generation *Denver Zephyr* of 1956. Altogether, it was one of Amtrak's most de luxe — nay, exotic — entrees.

If No. 31 was Burlington Northern in hardware, it was Milwaukee Road in hand on the throttle and in rail beneath the wheels; and at 12:20 p.m., on the advertised, the long train rolled from under the trainshed into a sunny 70-degree day, building momentum, making like a *Hiawatha.* The radio exec spread out his timetables, a Rand McNally rail atlas, Robert J. Wayner's *Car Names and Consists,* and black-and-white and color cameras and umpteen lenses (only a deserted Boeing 747 lounge could have coped with that library/studio); and Margaret and I went to the Great Dome for a preluncheon something on ice in tomato juice.

A recurring theme of the trip first struck us at this point:

What strange bedfellows Amtrak makes. Here we were ramming across the Soo diamond at Duplainville, Wis.; skimming around that splendid curve to the shore of Pewaukee Lake; doing 70-plus aboard that nemesis of the Milwaukee's late lamented *Olympian Hi*. Oh, the stylist who was hired, the money that was spent, the publicity that was printed, the fast miles that were run off by our hometown railroad to beat the *Builder* back in 1947; and here in 1971 only the train named for James J. Hill was left — and left on the *Hi*'s high iron. The gods of high iron are a sardonic lot, although they are not without humor.

The winner of the *Hi/Builder* contest rolled across a lush Wisconsin, bridged the Mississippi at La Crosse, followed the Minnesota shore of the river up to the Twin Cities, came within waving distance of, but wyed around, St. Paul Union Depot (I understand that city of 308,686 population was not amused by Amtrak's avoidance of it), and arrived in the old GN station on Hennepin Avenue in Minneapolis for a 45-minute layover — the time in which Continental Airlines says it can turn a 747.

Amtrak, I thought, is better for the soul on-train than off-train. The station was old (1914), almost empty (another train would not arrive for 12 hours), and depressing. A million dollars would be needed to dent its drabness, and for less than a quarter of that Amtrak could erect a new replacement shelter, complete with air conditioning and TV monitor. Anyway, who really cared? The passenger count on the condensed 11-car consist west from Minneapolis would show 99 in coach, 15 in Slumbercoach, 20 in first class — all hardy trainfarers long since adjusted to looking neither right nor left as we crossed waiting rooms, intent upon the leg-rest seats, white-linened tables, coffee, and/or made-down beds aboard the train on the track at the foot of the escalator.

No. 31 moved out, put metropolitan America behind its trailing *Silver Ravine,* and headed for a thousand and almost another thousand miles' worth of Jim Hill big sky blue country. Clickety-clack, clickety-clack, Amtrak-Amtrak-Amtrak . . . chanting 567-model two-cycle diesels up front were bringing us ever nearer the Rockies, the Divide, Canada (eventually to within less than 10 miles of British Columbia), and somewhere out there, the *Flying Scotsman.*

In Chester, Montana, the *Flying Scotsman* and train occupy the siding awaiting diesel aid required by bad coal. Photo by George G. Weiss.

Room D had a faulty floor heat valve which taxed the Pullman mechanical knowhow of the radio man; the upper-berth reading-light bulb was burned out in Room E. No matter. The sheets were crisp and the wheels were round.

Williston came at 6:55 a.m. [MST], on time — our last glimpse of North Dakota, and just across the state line from Montana, a state in which No. 31 stays for approximately 700 miles and 11 hours. Montana is big country, fine country — very productive for growing wheat and for turning out train-miles. Also, as we were to find at Milepost 239, it was incinerable country. Oswego,

Mont. (population 77) is, or rather was, at M239 (from Minot, N. Dak.) on BN's ex-GN main line — a tiny farming hamlet on an unmarked road, about halfway between U. S. Highway 2 and the Missouri River. Two days before our No. 31 showed up and took the passing track there, a fire had sprung up near the town even as most of its residents were off nearby dousing a grass fire touched off by lightning. The resultant conflagration burned homes, crops, livestock, and automobiles, and even attacked the BN (the intense heat hollowed out creosoted ties and left tie plates and spikes hanging in air). The dispatcher was obliged to route us under a slow order down the siding which, by virtue of being on a lower grade, apparently was protected from the worst of the blaze that obliterated Oswego. Nobody died, but it was a close call and the damage was nearly total.

The West, we decided, still can be wild.

On the *Empire Builder* rolled, past Glasgow and Havre, and on up the old GN's gradual ascent to the Rockies . . . and into the hole at Chester, Mont., at 1:45 p.m. We had company. Also in siding, on the other side of the main, stood ex-London & North Eastern 4-6-2 4472 and her train, dying for steam because of a diet of indigestible lignite coal, awaiting an assist from a Geep which the DS had ordered removed from the power of the eastbound freight holding the main. The *Scotsman* was 24 hours off its schedule and could get who knows how many days later — but we had zeroed in on her on our map and had arranged with the conductor to mark our tickets "Off at Whitefish" for an early-morning encounter with the 4472 west of the Rockies.

"Only 55 miles of the line above 4000 feet," boasted the old Great Northern maps of the line's lenient 5213-foot Marias Pass crossing of the Continental Divide. For that very reason, GN's bridging of the Rockies is not as spectacular as that of the NP or the Milwaukee; yet it was a major reason every Hill Lines executive from James J. on down to John Budd wanted to create a Burlington Northern in order to move all of the system's westbound tonnage over 1 instead of 2.2 per cent. John F. Stevens verified the existence of Marias Pass for Mr. Hill, and at the summit is a statue of the man who walked the pass in 1889 — in 40-below-zero weather.

The descent of the 1.8 per cent of the western slope through open-sided gallery-type snowsheds reminiscent of those of Austria's Semmering Line — that's the ride I enjoy. Freights climbing east up to Marias require wide-open four-unit helpers on the rear; the *Builder* dropping downgrade often shrouds its trucks in blue brakeshoe smoke. The sky is blue and the clouds are white. This is the aspect of train travel lost upon all but the few, the very few, who still take the time and pay the tab to ride west by rail — and hence is the index of the travel sophistication of the majority of passengers today.

Whitefish, railroad division point and lumber town, close by the Whitefish Range of the Rockies, on the southern end of Whitefish Lake — surely an incongruous spot for a rendezvous with the *Flying Scotsman.* Still, in the chilly predawn darkness of September 13, 1971, No. 4472 stood with steam up by the yard office just west of the depot, an ocean and almost a continent away from her birthplace in Yorkshire, England, in 1923.

She was there, though. The trainmaster's walkie-talkie radio said so. Over it crackled an order to "C&E, Extra LNER 4472 West," perchance the strangest-sounding order to travel over Montana railroad radio airwaves. And at 6:40 a.m. [MST] the green Pacific and her eight-car train slipped ghostily out of town. (Had anyone within the range of radio reception known what "LNER" denoted? Was the engine to which those letters referred just a foreigner, an alien without visa — or did someone out there know of her nonstop exploits and of her distinction as the first engine officially to exceed 100 mph? Perhaps, but not likely.)

Extra LNER 4472 West cruised around the shore of Whitefish Lake, then headed for the civil-engineering spectacular of contemporary American railroading: BN's brand-new 59½-mile line relocation in northwestern Montana necessitated by the Government's Libby Dam project, the bypass punctuated by the 36,970-foot Flathead Tunnel. When the 7-mile bore was opened to traffic on November 1, 1970, Flathead became (after BN's 7.79-mile Cascade Tunnel) the second-longest rail tunnel in North America, thereby bumping D&RGW's Moffat (6.2 miles) from No. 2 to No. 3 spot. At 8:45 *Flying Scotsman* dived into Flathead's 18-foot-wide, 23½-foot-tall portal and ran underground a long, long 720 seconds. Mile after mile after mile . . . we were *steaming* down through the No. 2 titleholder of North American tunnels . . . with an English train at that! It is written in Mark 10:27 that all things are possible. They are, they are.

We emerged from the west portal of Flathead at 8:57.

That day we rode through the canyon of the Kootenai, along the banks of the Kootenai River, diving in and out of shadow on its tree-walled shore. A bright sun glinted on the 4472's green jacket and lacy rods, an altogether enchanting sight as observed from a plush chair in the Pullman car *Lydia*. Now, the *Lydia* is an English version of our parlor car, a fine wood/steel vehicle painted brown and yellow (chocolate and cream, in English parlance), all varnished and carpeted and teaked and quite civilized. Seated in one of its chairs and chatting with Flying Scotsman Enterprises General Manager George Hinchcliffe, I found it possible to be in both the United Kingdom and the United States at once — a variation on the theme of, say, BOAC cabin service in a Boeing 707.

How was *Flying Scotsman* after 11,000 miles' worth of North America? I asked. Hinchcliffe rubbed his hands in satisfaction. He suggested that LNER 4472 had set a record that would not be broken easily, for a few days previous she had traveled from Chicago to Minneapolis on a single load of coal (her tender accommodates only 10 tons) and with no intermediate lubrication. Indeed 4472 had run too well, causing her sponsors to assure BN that she would burn anything. Subsequently she had been given lignite, and that strip-mined Montana fuel (Hinchcliffe searched his vocabulary in vain for a descriptive adjective) had reduced mileage per load from 400+ to 200–, had burned a hole in the grate, and had set a score of grass fires (but not the one at Oswego).

Aside from lignite, I asked? Hinchcliffe obviously thought the question was academic. The LNER A3-class three-cylinder machine scarcely was taxed with 8 English cars. She was built for higher things; in Britain she was "a passenger-moving machine" which had taken up to 16 cars (with 64 seats each) on prewar schedules calling for running into the 90's as well as operating nonstop over routes of up to 392.8 miles. Then when the war came in 1939 — well, the conflict wasn't all Spitfires and convoys. The war was also single-slotted LNER A3 Pacifics lifting as many as 26 cars, moving people by the thousands in trainloads, performing over their heads as steam and steel will granted design and personnel and motivation. Hinchcliffe remembered, and I had my own memories dating back to 1958 of these lovely green racers

What a lovely place is Wishram, Washington, tucked between mountain and trees and river, and populated by Alcos. RS-3 4064 gets acquainted with the visitor from Yorkshire. Photo by George G. Weiss.

thrusting forth from the high-level platforms of Kings Cross Station, London, intent upon diving into Gasworks Tunnel on the first lap of the race to Scotland.

A conversation along the Kootenai — a moment I will cherish, something worthwhile to share in TRAINS.

That day was a lazy, pleasant day for *Flying Scotsman* and her riders on the run from Whitefish out of Montana, across the panhandle of Idaho, and down into Spokane. And so was the following day from Spokane over the old NP main into Pasco, Wash. Those were days to absorb the vastness of the Pacific Northwest (more arid than green where we were) from the confines of cars built to the loading gauge of the world's first railways . . . days in which to talk steam with the BN crews (NP men always recall their favorite, 4-8-4 2626, the ex-Timken 1111 "Four Aces" of roller-bearing fame) . . . days in which to crawl through 4472's corridor tenders into a cab with dual throttles, vacuum brake, nonautomatic firedoor, and English engineers (drivers, over there) with high-bib overalls.

Lazy days, pleasant days. But *the* day was coming: September 16, 1971. It would begin pleasantly enough as well as terminate satisfactorily; oh, but in between would be a bit of Colorado Midland-like operation, storytelling stuff for sure.

It all began in Pasco, a few minutes after six o'clock on that unforgettable Thursday, September 16, 1971. Extra LNER 4472 West departed early in deference to a scheduled run to Bend, Ore., of 276.7 mostly-in-the-mountains miles — diesel assistance not requested, time allowed 10½ hours. Someone said something about 1.5 per cent grades and 10-degree curves in the offing in opposition to our 80-inch drivers, but our steed was possessed of 32,910 pounds tractive effort, we had a light train, and that lignite lay miles behind, so — so what ?

The day started innocently as we ran down the Columbia River on that SP&S water-level grade which, like most of BN's other strengths, is owed to the legacy of Jim Hill. Big steel spiked to good ties sunk in high ballast — 4472 ate it up, skimming along past miles of slide-detector fences, drinking in the scenery, reciprocating her Walschaerts in that imperious, imperturbable British manner of hers.

Then Wishram — railroad town, population 650, Alco haven; nestled between the wall of the Columbia River Gorge and the river, right across the river from Oregon. *Flying Scotsman* stood silently, accepting the curiosity of the townsfolk, ready to turn south now toward her appointment in San Francisco.

At high noon we were off, leaving the SP&S main to bear left across the bridge over the Columbia. Now the 4472 was on rails of the Oregon Trunk, the SP&S subsidiary that empire-building Jim Hill had thrust up the Deschutes River Canyon to the uplands of Oregon and beyond to the traffic treasures of California. This is the top end of the Bieber Line (or Inside Gateway), that chain of steel linked of SP&S, Oregon Trunk, GN, WP, and Santa Fe to create a second choice for shippers to Espee's Oregon-California backbone. The route was as fresh to me as it was to the green A3 Pacific — one of those remote, freight-only properties one knows only from the printed page and the published photo . . . and now we were riding it.

The Oregon Trunk's terrain is like what I imagine the San Diego & Arizona Eastern's Carriso Gorge to be, also like what India seems to be in that marvelous TV late-show movie *Flame over India*. In the Deschutes River Canyon, OT is a thin line of steel threading arid, inaccessible, rushing-river-sliced, raw, and dangerous country. Consider simply the river: It looked, well, if not suitable for bikini-clad swimmers, at least navigable by rubber boat (which it is). A few years ago, though, the Deschutes swallowed up a diesel victim of a rock slide — and it took several days simply to find the unit . . . downstream. Our British enginemen, in common with Columbus's crew, must have thought this climb was toward the edge of the world.

The grade looked worse than it was — something under 1 per cent — and 4472 walked right up, shuddering a bit on the sharper curves but making it.

The gutsy stuff began at Milepost 86, South Junction, where we left the Deschutes and began 27 miles of 1.5 per cent grade and 10-degree curves — track which limits a 1500 h.p. Alco to 900 tons, a 1750 h.p. EMD to 1000 tons. We wanted *Flying Scotsman* to take it in stride, to show these skeptical BN (i.e., SP&S) types that their bad mountain held no terrors for our high-born lady from England. And for a spell 4472 justified our faith — until Mile 91 at 3:30 p.m. There we were, wrapped around a 10-degree curve, out of steam, looking back down 1.5 per cent from an elevation of something like 2000 feet above sea level, hanging on a vacuum brake about which only a handful of those aboard knew the faintest thing. Seconds ticked off to 60, the 60's collected into minutes — then suddenly, at 3:43, *Flying Scotsman* moved — no slip, no audible exhaust, simply a great pull forward and upward.

But the suspense wasn't over. We stopped again, at Mile 95 at 3:56, then moved off at 4:08; stopped again at Mile 99 at 4:25, and moved off at 4:35. Then we were beyond the summit, at Mile 103.2, and leaving the 1.5 per cent behind, gathering speed south to Bend, Ore.

And that left the question: why? In a postmortem, Hinchcliffe put the record straight. Yes, the 4472 had run out of steam; the reason was bad coal that not only produced too few B.T.U.'s but also produced huge clinkers which had choked the fire. When pressure had fallen from 220 pounds to 160, the driver simply had shut off, stopped, and rebuilt his fire. Between pauses on the 1.5 per cent, Hinchcliffe noted, the 4472 had accelerated to 33 mph, so the power was there. But had the locomotive faced such a

Amtrak 102 is truly a rainbow as it curls across I-80 east of Colfax, California: SP's red on the diesel noses and the side of the dome car, Union Pacific yellow, Great Northern blue, and Northern Pacific green, all accented with Burlington (and Budd) stainless steel. Photo by George G. Weiss.

crisis before? Oh, yes — on several occasions. On one excursion in England the *Scotsman* had started a train of 12 coaches on 2 per cent without difficulty. In other words, then, 4472 had picked herself up by her own steam pressure, superheater units, and main rods, just doing what she was designed to do? Of course, Hinchcliffe affirmed smiling, of course.

Was the journey beyond to Bend and then to Klamath Falls the following day anticlimactic? It should have been, but Oregon kept piling on the scenery (would you believe a single-span bridge across the Crooked River almost as high — 320 feet — as it is long — 340 feet?); Extra LNER 4472 encountered the most alien rails of all south of Chemult, taking to Southern Pacific iron there by virtue of BN trackage rights (steam officially had vanished from Espee on October 19, 1958, with a 4-8-4 fan trip across the Sierra); and into Klamath Falls there was owner Alan Pegler himself at the throttle — or regulator, as he would correct me.

Our little party was reluctant to take leave of *Flying Scotsman* in Klamath Falls — *Flying Scotsman* and her rigid-framed, 56-inch-wheel tenders; her train of first- and second-class compartments,

parcels vans, *Lydia,* and observation car; her doughty crew of Britishers and volunteer American aides; her always obliging, sympathetic, alert escort of BN trainmasters, road foremen, enginemen, and trainmen. Once more, as in Georgia and Alabama and Mississippi two years earlier, we had fallen in love with the 4472, and with Romeo we were wont to declare "Parting is such sweet sorrow, That I shall say good night till it be morrow."

Except that on the morrow we had an important appointment in Sacramento with Amtrak. So we shook hands with the 4472's crew, turned around for one last look, then parted company.

It is possible to Amtrak from Klamath Falls to Milwaukee; but the Oakland *Cascade/City of San Francisco* connection between those two triweekly schedules requires a 24-hour layover, so instead we booked passage to Sacramento on a turboprop F-27 of Howard Hughes's Air West. In the process, I found that Klamath Falls (population 15,305) had a good airport and four flights each way daily, indicating that, contrary to popular legend, Espee had had assistance in pruning its Cascade Route passenger timetable.

Yet even if Southern Pacific did want out of the varnish trade (and I think its One Market Street HQ, NARP, the ICC, and you and I could agree on the answer to that one), the system obviously was cooperating with Amtrak at high noon on Saturday, September 18, 1971. The Amtrak No. 102, which Espee slipped into the Sacramento station that morning was the best of Amtrak I've seen — at once a rainbow train, a railfan's-delight train, a bright-red-ink train, a de luxe train, a shimmering train, and a schizophrenic train. From gray/red Espee A-B-A F units back, No. 102 unfurled like this: 1 UP baggage-dormitory — yellow, of course; coaches in three flavors, 1 each of UP yellow, Q silver, and GN blue; 1 NP green Lewis and Clark Travellers Rest buffet-lounge; 1 *CZ* diner, named *Silver Diner;* 1 SP silver dome, No. 3601; Q silver sleepers *Silver Swan* and *Silver Slope,* and our 10 & 6 UP yellow sleeper, *Pacific Plateau . . .* all scrubbed, all shining, all with freshly silvered trucks.

A paragraph about 102's star car, that Espee dome. It just could be the best dome ever built, albeit it was homemade. What the railroad did with its ¾-length dome was to allow the overhead glass to flow right across the floor-level lounge at one end of the car, thus creating a unique skylight room with a ceiling of almost

11 feet! Anyone — the Q or ACF or Budd or Pullman-Standard — could have done it; but only Espee *did* do it. In details, too, the car is a very comfortable vehicle, what with angled love seats upstairs as well as upper-level beverage service. It rides well too. There is one drawback: One must walk up and through the dome and down again to get beyond the car because it was rebuilt from an existing piece of *Daylight* equipment with a conventional center sill. Alas and alack, I can't spot these 3600's in Amtrak's purchase list [page 16, December 1971 TRAINS], so would you care to join me in a protest march on 955 L'Enfant Plaza, Washington ?

No. 102 was called over the p.a. system as the *City of San Francisco,* whose old number it bore; the BN timetable flyer we had picked up on the *Builder* referred to 102 as the *California Zephyr;* the regulation Amtrak timetable referred to it by number only; and we were to find that east of Denver where 102 combines with the *Denver Zephyr,* it would become just the DZ with Oakland connections.

Revenue passenger count: 97.

The engineer knew what he was about, even if the timetable authors did not. He eased No. 102 off at the scheduled 12:01 p.m. on the dot. He must have slipped his throttle into notch 1 to alert his V-16's and to warn the traction motors, then — very gently, very slowly — he latched back into notches 2, 3, and 4.

No. 102 rolled out of the station and around the end of Espee's Sacramento Shops complex (giving us a glimpse of restored cab-forward 4-8-8-2 No. 4294 behind Forge Shop No. 2), gathered headway toward Roseville and its immense hump and dozens upon dozens of high-horsepower hoods (does any other road amass so many at one site?), then explored the foothills of the Big Hill, up through Newcastle, Auburn, and Clipper Gate, up the easy 1.5 and 1.9 per cent to the 2.4 that had spawned the cab-forward articulated and made blessed the name of Dr. Diesel. (Inexplicably, the diner made its last luncheon call at 1:03 p.m. — *1:03!* — while all this scenery was abuilding. This left us the choice of deserting the dome in prime time or dining late at a counter in the Travellers Rest. Amtrak, please note.)

Well, Charlie Crocker, the railroad your Chinese workers drove from near sea level to Sierra summit at 6899.9 feet in less than 100 miles is as extraordinary as ever. The diesels get down on their knees and labor; the tourists exclaim over the view of the American River Canyon; the snowsheds tell of what winter always will mean at those elevations; and the turntable still rotates indoors under the shed at summit at Norden. Big-time railroading, this; wondrous railroading — and I'll wager that not more than 1 per cent, and maybe only 1 per cent of 1 per cent, of California's population (it must be 20 million people by now) has experienced it. The loss is theirs, and that is probably just as well by Espee.

Across the California/Nevada state line, down along the Truckee River, at the bottom of the eastern slope of the Sierra, there are two Renos — the neon and slot machine and casino Reno, and the railroad Reno. The first one (achieved this day on time at 4:50 p.m.) is Reno proper — where you can adjust your marital status, win or lose at the gaming tables, or play all night; and where 102 ties up Virginia Street traffic and is a momentary halt to the commerce of playtime. Three miles east is Sparks, the railroad Reno — where the crews change, and the scenery is shop and yard tower and rotaries; and where you can stretch your legs before dinner and the desert ahead.

That diner, *Silver Diner,* was as much multi-personality as its train. It was a *CZ* car, but the menu covers bore those unmistakable UP color scenes (you know, Bryce Canyon, the Mormon Temple, Sun Valley), the forks were stamped C.M.StP.& P., the syrup pitcher was Rio Grande's, and the napkins were variously CB&Q, CZ, GN, and WP. I wish the food had been as appetizing. Certainly no one went hungry — but vintage *CZ* that diner was not.

Breakfast time brought with it Green River, Wyo., and a new day on a new railroad — Union Pacific. No. 102 was a lonely passenger train in that place and at that moment. As the conductor removed his hat to walk through the diner, I thought, *My friend, quite a pass we've come to in 1971 At this moment you're the only working passenger conductor on the entire 9483-mile Union Pacific. Search the train sheets where you will, from Kaycee to Puget Sound, from Council Bluffs to L. A., there's no* City of Los Angeles *or* Portland Rose *or* Butte Special, *much less a* Forty-Niner *or an* Overland *or a* Challenger. *There's just we, unremarked Amtrak 102 behind three yellow E9's, riding a great multitracked main that but for the grace of D&RGW would be freight-only today.* But I said nothing aloud to the conductor. He already knew.

Not that a freight-only UP was inhibiting the Overland Route (or vice versa) that day. It was business as usual in Wyoming — hours of droning along all by ourselves, followed by interception of a fleet of freights. Rawlins was typical. As we arrived there on time, two of those Centennial 6900-series D-D's and a GP30 on a westbound hotshot leaned their collective 15,450 h.p. into their tonnage and moved out of town like a Metroliner . . . *and* there were two more westbounds behind him . . . and on the way out of Rawlins we overtook an eastbound getting under way behind two 6900's. Mr. Lincoln, Mr. Harriman: the Overland is very much in business, uniting the nation as you intended. Descending Sherman Hill into Cheyenne on the old line, running wrong main, we overtook yet another eastbound; and as our sleeper passed up the box cars I idly jotted down reporting marks — just to see if that "uniting the nation" idea was as valid as I thought. It was. The cars rocked along: CNW, PRR, IC, PC, EL, RI, UP, MKT, CNW, N&W, MP, Southern — from all over, traveling to all over, uniting, uniting, uniting on the road appropriately called Union Pacific. No. 102 arrived at Cheyenne at 12:29 p.m. beneath a clock in the station tower that had stopped at 7:07. Inside, the sparse newsstand apparently was in the final countdown, selling July and August magazines. And as the carman awaited the E9's moving around No. 102, he reflected on the work in progress ripping out four depot tracks and tearing down as many trainsheds. They could have all the business they could handle, he said, if they'd just advertise, make their connections, and give service. He had thought, or hoped, that Amtrak would turn back the clock; but Amtrak had failed him, and the clock was stopped . . . at 7:07.

(I despair of these scenes — these glimpses, these cameos if you will — of the majors dismantling their passenger plant, their once-great people-movers. I remembered Cheyenne from the winter of '45 — all streamliners and limiteds and main trains, supported by a whole roundhouseful of Pacifics, Mountains, and Northerns. And now, 27 years later, there was just the one 10-car nameless train about to back down to Denver, there to be surrendered to the Burlington. If I were that carman, I'd be bitter too, and there'd be no explaining to me what went wrong or why my pass was now just a piece of paper.)

Can Amtrak backtrack? Yes. Between Cheyenne and Denver — in both directions. Because Cheyenne lies east of Speer, where the line to Denver and the Borie cutoff diverge, the power on 102 was obliged to change ends to tow us back to the junction and thence southward; northbound the process is reversed, so that 101 will be heading in the proper direction when it departs Cheyenne for the west. Confusing, yes — but that's the way it works. Also confusing is a timetable that allows No. 102 2 hours 25 minutes for the 106 miles between Cheyenne and Denver — not that it hampers good timekeeping; our train left 11 minutes late and arrived 24 minutes to the good — B&O couldn't have done better.

The *Denver Zephyr,* with which 102 merges in Denver, was awaiting us when we arrived: 4 E units, a flattop coach, 4 dome coaches, a Chuck Wagon buffet-lounge, a diner, a Slumbercoach, and a sleeper. At 6:01 p.m. our 19-car consist was under way, moving out from beneath a large billboard which still promised TO OMAHA–CHICAGO 2 VISTA DOME TRAINS DAILY.

After dinner we settled down for nightcaps in our rooms and talked about what train riders always talk about: trains. Radio exec Weiss, who would be leaving us in Burlington, Ia., next morning to jet back to Augusta, chaired the conversation. We pondered weighty matters, no less absorbing because they were academic — for example, the error so many roads had made in spending money on sections and roomettes when the demand turned out to be for bedrooms and compartments; whether Santa Fe or UP was the better passenger road; why Amtrak didn't route its Chicago-Florida *South Wind* through Atlanta; which held the greatest allure — the legendary trains that ran but briefly (such as the *Forty-Niner*), or the promised ones that never ran at all (such as the *Golden Rocket*).

If we hadn't retired, we would have had one more item on the agenda. For *Pacific Plateau* began to gallop, then to bounce, and finally to sway and bang, metal on metal, side to side, up and down. We were making time, which was all right; but we were aware of it, which was not all right.

Come morning the ride had smoothed out and the *DZ* was in BN's namesake town of Burlington, Ia., making the first of three double stops (to be repeated in Galesburg and Aurora, Ill.) to accommodate its 19-car consist. Those stops were to set the stage for a familiar Burlington drama: a valiant but not quite successful attempt to hold to a fast schedule. I once got into trouble with the late Harry Murphy, then president of the Q, for saying in print that the line's timekeeping needed attention, even if it did have more excuse than most to be tardy. The Q has the power, the plant, and the personality to put away the miles rapidly; the railroad is simply overconfident on occasion.

I made my informal check from the Espee dome and jotted down these start-to-stop findings as we sliced through the cornfields of Illinois: Kewanee-Princeton, 26.77 miles, 24½ minutes; Princeton-Mendota, 21.53 miles, 24 minutes, despite an intermediate M/W slow order; Mendota-Aurora, 44.89 miles, 37 minutes. Running such as that, plus a train crew that managed single stops in 60 seconds and double ones in under 5 minutes, came close to making me regret my minor disagreement with Mr. Murphy years ago. Close, but not quite. The *DZ* due in Chicago Union Station at 11:59 a.m., arrived at 12:05 p.m.

Of course, I date myself by even mentioning a microscopic 6-minute deficit in an 18-hour overnight schedule. No one, I'm sure, took either Amtrak or BN to task for it, assuming anyone besides myself even noticed it. America in our time isn't much on punctuality, and hasn't been since the go-when-you-please automobile replaced the we-leave-on-schedule-whether-you're-on-board-or-not train. Airlines count any arrival of less than 15 minutes late as on time. In 1971 only a B&O or Milwaukee Road veteran would even understand what the discussion is about. Alas.

The inscription on the Statue of Liberty reads in part: "Give me your tired, your poor, Your huddled masses yearning to breathe free." As I looked over the intercity travelers awaiting the calling of their trains that afternoon, I thought that Amtrak might well adopt those words as its slogan. I'm told that Amtrak's p.r. men are seeking a new image (who isn't these days?), one geared to the Now Generation. But the waiting-room benches accommodated those who didn't qualify: mostly old, poor, and/or crippled people, seasoned with a few hippies and a handful of obvious railfans — the rails' unwanted loyalists, the faithful, the dedicated, the do-or-die. There we sat, patiently waiting for our expensive, slow, ancient vehicles, deaf to the siren call of Impalas and 747's, true to the iron horse unto death. Maybe, Amtrak, you can bring back the opinion-makers and the stylesetters. But as of the moment, we're all you have.

I admire to wind up long rail journeys on the Milwaukee Road, particularly on the *Milwaukee Express,* train 23 from Chicago to Milwaukee. Train 23 has been in the timecard since the Year One (well, since 1900 anyway) as a pleasant afternoon exit from The Big City and as a last lap home for wandering Milwaukeeans. Once it made its 85 miles in 80 minutes, and it still manages the job in 92 minutes, two stops included. It has a diner-lounge (Tip Top Tap to us old CMStP&P types) to slake the thirst of the weary, and its conductor still wipes down the handrails before the first passenger ascends to a vestibule.

No. 23's two E9's, four coaches, and diner-lounge got under way on the stroke of their scheduled 4:20 p.m. departure, and the congenial group aboard settled down to conversation, the *Chicago Daily News,* beer, bourbon, and martinis. Pleasantly, very pleasantly, the Express put the miles away, made its appointed stops in Glenview and Sturtevant, indulged a local freight which was tardy in getting off the high iron at Rondout, and arrived in Milwaukee at 5:50 p.m. vs. a scheduled 5:52.

Good old Milwaukee Road. On our 8¼-day, 4793.7-mile safari in search of Mr. Pegler's 4472 the CMStP&P took us out of town on time, brought us back two minutes early. Details, perhaps; yet if you add up enough such details you have found yourself a wonderful way to run a railroad, or an Amtrak. ☙

What was grand about Grand Trunk Western

A photo section special

With all due respect to patrons of Canadian National's U. S. subsidiary, let it be remarked that Grand Trunk Western was a sleeper in steam until the dieselized 1950s. Then suddenly, after Central's Hudsons had vanished and Wabash Mikes no longer rode herd on redballs — suddenly the faithful discovered that the Trunk was still steaming it up, pulling commuters out of Detroit within sight of the General Motors Building, hauling tonnage behind 4-8-4s, sending modest Pacifics to Caseville (where's *that?*), even borrowing Q and IC steam power upon occasion to tide itself over power shortages. So all of us not only "discovered" Grand Trunk Western but were happily surprised by the variety and beauty of its locomotives. They were U. S. with a dash of Dominion influence — or was it vice versa? Regardless, here's a belated but heartfelt salute!

Editor's note: Near the middle of almost every issue of TRAINS was Photo Section, a selection of the best photos submitted by the readers of the magazine. Morgan chose the photos with a theme in mind and wrote the captions from whatever information the photographer provided — and one of the chores of writing captions was filling the last line so the caption would be a neat rectangle.

Northern 6332 cants to a curve about a mile out of Pontiac on the return leg of a Detroit-Richmond (Mich.) fan trip on April 10, 1960, two weeks after the end of regular steam operation. Not apparent in the photo: the 4-8-4 was out of fuel and would have to be towed by a diesel switcher to Pontiac, where coal was available. Photo by John Gruber.

In early evening 4-8-4 No. 6328, just in from Detroit, pauses at the water plug in Pontiac. GTW still had considerable steam in service in July 1958, when this shot was made. Photo by Don Wood.

Years after hood units had shoved steam off most Class 1 branch lines, Grand Trunk Western continued to smoke up its 99.4-mile Pontiac-Caseville (Mich.) branch. Footboarded Pacific 5043 slowly works a Caseville-bound extra around a curve from Pontiac. Photo by John Krave.

It wasn't just that GTW lasted so long in steam but that the road's power was so photogenic — far less severe than, say, the durable engines of IC or N&W. Witness the 5631, a Pacific of USRA design, getting Detroit-bound train 74 away from the Pontiac station on June 11, 1954. Photo by Jim Scribbins.

GTW's Chicago-Port Huron and Detroit-Grand Rapids lines crossed at Durand, 67 miles northwest of Detroit. Late in the afternoon Durand came to life as pairs of Chicago-Toronto and Detroit-Muskegon trains converged on the station. Left to right are Pacific 5629 on Muskegon-Detroit train 56, Northern 6326 on train 17, the *Inter-City Limited,* and Mountain 6037 on train 21 to Muskegon. Photo by George C. Corey.

How pretty in silhouette was the high-mounted Consolidation. Extra 2681 West illustrates the point well as she trundles through St. Johns, Michigan, en route from Durand to Grand Rapids. Can you spot the coal scoop handle? Photo by John Krave.

While riding Pennsy iron from Muskegon to Grand Rapids, an eastbound freight behind a 2-8-2 passes out of the shadow of a PRR water tank and bears down on the frame depot at Ravenna, Michigan, as the faint exhaust stands tall in the blue and the turbogenerator trails just a breath of steam. Photo by Richard Pedler.

It's ten o'clock on a September night in 1952 at Muskegon — and who could the engine be, what with her Elesco feedwater heater, vestibule cab, and Vanderbilt tank, but GTW 4-8-2 6037 on train 56. Photo by Richard Pedler.

The all-American railroad

"We think this is the way to run a railroad"

IN a corporate context, variety was a distinguishing characteristic of the American railroad scene. Whereas government early on tended to monopolize ownership and operation of the iron horse in most other lands with the notable exception of Great Britain, the railroads of America rejoiced in the individualism of sheer numbers. Why, in 1900 there were 1224 railroads in the U. S., and as late as 1957 there were still 635 operating companies, including 116 Class 1's.

Which means that until recently, train-watchers enjoyed carte blanche to indulge in favoritism, even on an intramural basis. There was a choice of New England roads and Anthracite roads, Eastern trunks and Pocahontas coalhaulers, Dixie dynasties and Prairie grangers, Mid-America regionals and Ozark operators . . . and long-legged transcons from Big G to Espee. (There was exclusivity — New Haven between Boston and New York and Rio Grande in the Colorado Rockies. And there was dominance — Illinois Central in Mississippi and Union Pacific in Idaho. But they were exceptions proving the rule.)

Perhaps it is only now, in these 1980's, that it is dawning upon us just how much selection we had in the *Official Guide*. When the holding company whose thoroughbred logo is on the nose of diesels roaming the rails we remember as once the principalities of N&W, VGN, NKP, WAB, P&WV, SR, CG, NS, TAG, G&F, and S&A is bidding for the emblem that covers the onetime entities of PRR, NYC, Erie, DL&W, RDG, CNJ, PRSL, NYNH&H, LV, L&NE, and L&HR over the objections of the camp that enveloped the proprietorships of C&O, B&O, ACL, SAL, L&N, NC&StL, MON, CRR, GA, A&WP, WA, PM, and WM . . . *then* we see how far the last 30 years' worth of mergers have taken us. Shake all these reporting marks well and observe the spinoff in personalities (Bowman, McGinnis, White(s), DeButts, Davis, etc.), shops (Hornell, Macon, Decatur, Mount Clare, Princeton, Scranton, West Albany, Wyoming, etc.), bridges (Starrucca, Rockville, Hell Gate, Scioto, etc.), locomotives (Dixie, Pocono, Allegheny, Niagara, Berkshire, etc.), and train names (*Nelly Bly, Wolverine, Diplomat, Black Diamond, Royal Palm, Cavalier,* etc.). Etcetera. We had endless etcetera in railroading. Timetables and annual reports and rosters and maps' worth of etcetera.

An example, perhaps *the* example: There was a season, a long season too, when the majority of America's population, wealth, gross national product, baseball teams, and electoral college votes were located on a New York–Chicago axis, and along it operated four trunk lines: Pennsy and New York Central, 1 and 2 in that order; Baltimore & Ohio, a distant 3rd; and, last and least, Erie. Daniel Willard notwithstanding, 1 and 2 didn't think too much about 3, and the three of them behaved as if the Erie didn't exist. The Standard Railroad of the World and The Water Level Route were self-evident rationales. You could embrace one or the other or both or, conversely, reject each or both. But you could not ignore PRR or NYC. As for No. 3, Barnard, Roberts & Co., publisher of a series of spiral-bound photo books, perhaps summed up the faith of its followers best a few years ago by claiming that "The serious railfan has two favorite railroads — the B&O and another one . . . " It remained for Professor George W. Hilton to pen the ultimate apologia for the Erie in "The View of the Viaduct from in Front of the Diner" in May 1972 TRAINS by citing its credentials for the coach rider. The point is that in a great transportation market there was choice amongst the great, sublime, historic, and Gould.

In *dimension,* there was no contest among these hundreds of railroads of yesteryear, of course. In February 1979 TRAINS, Robert A. Le Massena's "How Big Was Big?" documented what was universally accepted in terms of size by every index except route-miles — namely that Pennsy was peerless.

Was there a *typical* American railroad, a carrier so unremarked and unremarkable as to serve as the common denominator of all? The same Prof. Hilton nominated the Chicago & Eastern Illinois, a motion subsequently seconded by our Kalmbach Librarian, George H. Drury; I held out for the Missouri-Kansas-Texas.

The 53 nonprofit historical societies devoted to archiving individual carriers [pages 59-60, June 1985 TRAINS] reflect not only the unalloyed *affection* for one railroad vis-a-vis another but the circumstance that adoration is not synonymous with size. Or history or scenery or operating ratio or locomotive roster. For instance, the Gulf, Mobile & Ohio Historical Society numbers more than 700 dues-paying members in behalf of a 2745-mile property whose components were largely Class 1 castoffs, attained a maximum elevation of 749 feet, and never owned a GP7.

Suppose, though, we eschew the criteria of size, commonality, and subjectivity — is it possible to attain a consensus on a railroad so catholic in its appeal as to be worthy of the claim of all-American railroad . . . the people's railroad, if you will, or even the perfect railroad in the sense of being a Class 1 within the memory of the living with a sure claim upon those values we associate with high iron? What mix of history, map, traffic, passenger trains, locomotives, scenery, locale, and people could commend itself to universal endorsement?

(A long time ago, in May 1966 TRAINS, I managed to assemble "The Perfect Passenger Train" without incurring significant dissension, but then I blunted criticism by selecting rolling stock from the consists of a range of limiteds from the *Capitol* to the *Olympian Hi.* My choice of stations was criticized, as was the omission of a name and a routing on Erie's Delaware Division, but these were minor imperfections. Singling out one railroad to represent all those 116 Class 1's of 1957 is infinitely more perilous. Amtrak proved that you can couple cars of diverse origin into a compatible consist. But you can't meld Cajon and the Delaware Water Gap, or make bedfellows of Fairfax Harrison and John Lynch Lancaster, or place a duplex-drive and a cab-forward cheek by jowl in the same roundhouse.)

It is a simpler, more defensible task to list the railroads which on one account or several fall shy of qualifying as all-American. Surely one-man (read lengthened shadow) roads, e.g., Hill's Great Northern, Flagler's Florida East Coast, Rogers' Virginian, are atypical. Single-commodity carriers do not qualify, burdened as their rolling stock inventories are with, most commonly, too many hoppers or ore jennies — or, in Long Island's case, too many cars with seats. Intrastate lines lack the interstate nature of most railroading.

We scarcely need solicit legal opinions of either of the Claytor brothers to establish a prima facie case for elimination of the collossi and the eccentrics. The position-light-signal, Belpaire-boilered, 11,000-volt catenary, Tuscan-red cast of the Pennsylvania would have stamped it as an iconoclast even if its rails had never reached west of Pittsburgh. Ditto, of course, for the steam/electric/diesel, granger-turned-transcon, thrice-bankrupt, orange, 100-mph, Chicago, Milwaukee, St. Paul & Pacific. It is the very nonconformist nature of such properties, is it not, which at once endears them to us and prohibits them from a representative role?

At the risk of enraging the George Harts and Bert Pennypackers of our fraternity, I would similarly disqualify the Reading Company, on grounds that its map looked like a plate of hastily dished up spaghetti and connected communities and crossed rivers only a native could pronounce, as in Perkiomen Junction, Drehersville, and Gwynedd Valley — oh how they make your Milwaukee Road son yearn for the simplicity of Oconomowoc and Wauwatosa and Ixonia! Reading was, well, so very John O'Hara in its affinity with Pennsylvania Dutch mores. Charming, yes, as only a Camelback ride or a ticket to Tamaqua could be, but scratched from candidacy here because of being the only mispronounced word on the Monopoly board.

Well, then, you may ask with understandable asperity, what railroad(s) conceivably merits consideration as an all-American, as the people's choice?

For starters, Wabash, Seaboard Air Line, Chicago, Rock Island & Pacific, and Southern Pacific.

I think of each as an elixir, without which the railroad legend would be immeasurably poorer; I think that . . . but hold the phone! Wabash hasn't been on the scene as a visible entity since 1964, SAL since 1967. Long enough for a person to be born, graduate from high school, and cast his first vote. Funeral services for the Rock were conducted five years ago, and Espee is in financial straits, abjectly awaiting merger orders from its arch rival in distant Chicago. Never mind. There is abundant film on hand to support the memories of those who are eager to swear on a stack of *Official Guides* of . . .

. . . of how Wabash alone spanned the waist of the land from Lake Ontario to the Missouri River, pitching its flag in the Adrians and Albias, Moberlys and Montpeliers of the rich corn country. Wabash and Redball were synonymous, Wabash was sharp enough to relay limiteds to the likes of UP and Pennsy; why, the word "Wabash" is a verb for fast and fancy railroading. Its lacy-limbed Atlantics told you that, as most assuredly did a handsome fleet of look-alike 4-8-2's and 4-8-4's; no B-B hood unit was ever purchased to pull a Wabash named train!

. . . of how America has always pulled for the underdog, and no No. 2 ever tried harder than marginal Seaboard to score points on kingpin Coast Line, laying track into Miami during the flush of the Florida Boom at the expense of solvency, overcoming razor-back grades with fast 2-6-6-4's, ordering up EMC's first 567-powered E's, scheduling the South's first Budd-built streamliner, installing CTC to compensate for single track. SAL (in common with ACL) was a marriage of the New York-Florida tourist trade with the Old South, running an *Orange Blossom Special* but also a *Robert E. Lee,* speeding past Lake Okeechobee for Miami but also steaming gently into Dinwiddie, Va., and Southern Pines, N. C., Savannah and Birmingham.

. . . of how Rock Island graced the land with a larger-than-life presence in 14 states, most notably under the hand of John D. Farrington when the railroad came roaring out of the Depression with *Rockets* and line relocations and the largest roster of 4-8-4's in the land. In its reach, its commuters, its ambitions, the Rock was a penniless, orphaned Burlington. The CRI&P seldom loomed large except in the likes of Liberal, Kans., and El Reno, Okla. (exception: Des Moines), but it registered a presence in most places its nemesis the Q did, and some cities (Little Rock and Memphis) it didn't.

. . . of how Southern Pacific summed up the American West under one Sunset herald in a huge inverted F-shaped system that rolled through snowsheds and tunnels, around the most famous loop in the U. S., through forests and across deserts and down beaches. You name it, Espee had it — in spades: the only major headquarters west of Denver, half of the original transcontinental, a traction empire, Harriman and Huntington, the most beautiful train in the world (by its own admission), an exotic Mexican foray, train ferries, a steamship line, the most scenic of subsidiaries (NWP and SD&AE, not necessarily in that order), narrow gauge, unique cab-forwards . . . *ad infinitum!*

No argument — a list of all-American railroad candidates is, of necessity, arbitrary, though not tenuous.

Working from the same criteria, you might include New England or the East and omit the South. A case could be made for a Frisco here, a North Western there, perhaps a Nashville, Chattanooga & St. Louis. No argument. You may discount Wabash as shy on route-miles, both Rock and Seaboard as overshadowed by their rivals, and Espee as simply too much of a good thing or because its selection would alienate followers of the Santa Fe. Indeed, the more I pondered the thesis, the closer I moved to my preeminent, none-of-the-above choice. To recapitulate, the goal of the exercise is to select one railroad on which most can agree as symbolic of our common concern for what the late Robert S. Henry called this fascinating railroad business, a carrier to engage the camera of a Steinheimer, the pen of a Beebe, the curiosity of a Hilton, the brush of a Fogg.

So the nominee is Northern Pacific. It possessed the name, the heritage, the route, the trains, the scenery, the locomotives, the emblem to underwrite a consensus. A middleman, geographically and physically: older but weaker than Great Northern on the north, stronger than Milwaukee Road on the south. Rich in heritage, following the trail of Lewis and Clark, created by an Act of Congress bearing the signature of A. Lincoln. Traditional as a semaphore blade and T-rail. Long enough at 6700 route-miles to spread across six big states but not so far as to be incomprehensible. And tough: year-round in the summits it fought, every winter in the weather it faced.

Northern Pacific. (Yes, frequently with a period after the name on steam locomotive tenders.) The name neither minimized like Illinois Central nor exaggerated like St. Louis–San Francisco. NP, faithful to its name, bolted rails together from Lake Superior to Puget Sound, period. None of your excursions into alien country (as in CMStP&P down to Indiana, Big G into California, Rock to Louisiana). NP was content to live within its name from incorporation in 1864 until merger in 1970. The Yellowstone Park Line, later the Main Street of the Northwest.

Within the parameters of its name, though, Northern Pacific managed to be several railroads under a common logo, or so it seemed from the pictures in books and magazines. There were, in sequence from east to west, the granger road of elevator-studded wheatlands; the barren yet beautiful Dakota Bad Lands that spawned the world's biggest Z-5's; the mountain-climbing, tunnel-threading main lines of Montana; the backwoods branches of curving trestles in Idaho; the orchard country of the Yakima and Kittitas Valleys; finally the perennially wet district in and west of the Cascades. Examine the range of topography encompassed by all those familiar B's in the railway's timetable: Brainerd, Bismarck, Billings, Bozeman, Butte, and Bellingham. Reflect on a 1964 *Modern Railroads* count of 75 miles' worth of 2598 NP bridges.

NP met the qualification that an all-American railroad must needs be a post–Civil War Western line, born of a united nation, creating states as it laid track as opposed to upgrading communication in a settled region that hadn't yet sorted out its political priorities. Item: North Dakota, Montana, Idaho, and Washington all attained statehood after NP drove its last spike in 1883. This is not to denigrate the pioneers responsible for technological pioneering from T-rails to telegraphic dispatching and for first competing with canals, steamboats, stages, and wagons. It is to say that the railroad came into its own when rails were laid beyond the frontiers of civilization.

You want history with a capital H? Here's a road that fought off Indians to survey its route, was the first line to unilaterally earn the "transcontinental" designation, reused the first spike driven in its main line (near the present town of Carlton, Minn., in 1870) as the last (at Gold Creek, Mont., September 7, 1883), entered bankruptcy twice in the 19th century, became the first railroad to serve a national park, had its stock once quoted at 1000, ran steamships to the Orient, adopted a Monad logo of 11th century Chinese ancestry, introduced a *North Coast Limited* in 1900 that would survive into Amtrak (albeit with the incongruous suffix of *Hiawatha*), began buying Mallets in 1908 and acquired the biggest articulated of all in 1929, and peopled its corporate affairs with President Lincoln, Generals Grant and Sherman and Custer, entrepreneurs Jay Cooke, Henry Villard, J. P. Morgan, James Jerome Hill, and Edward Henry Harriman.

I never met a Northern Pacific man I didn't like, including the hogger who told me, "I wouldn't give one acre of Montana for the whole state of Wisconsin."

Dialogue overheard between an engineer and fireman of a diesel passenger train passing a freight pushed up to Bozeman by a Z-5 2-8-8-2 — Engineer: "Biggest steam engine in the world." Fireman: "Used to be. Union Pacific's got bigger ones now." Engineer: "That so? Well, a 5000's still plenty big."

When April 1941 TRAINS reported that Union Pacific would assume the "world's largest" honors with delivery of its Alco 4-8-8-4's, NP Advertising Manager L. L. Perrin penciled "Tell me it ain't so" across the item and sent it to the mechanical department. For 13 years, he later recalled, the Z-5 had accorded his road one distinction that arch rival Big G could not equal.

Once upon a wintry night in North Dakota, out around Mandan, a December storm had encased the trucks of our *North Coast Limited* cars in ice, and the temperature had sunk to minus 25 . . . and the rail bonds were snapping, turning all the block signals red. There was frost on the inside of the warm coach's windows. After the obligatory halt at one block and we were moving on again, I glimpsed in our car's lights on the snow a signal main-

Northern 2662, an A-3 built by Baldwin in 1938, lifts the *North Coast Limited* up the 1.8 percent grade out of Hoppers Tunnel 10 miles west of Livingston, Montana. Photo by W. R. McGee.

tainer huddled under the tarp of his parked section speeder, waiting for us to clear so he could mend NP's communications.

That same night a deadheading fireman allowed that he was bound for Dickinson, called there for an eastbound freight with eight units. His opinion: "We oughta make it back with 12,000 horsepower."

Recent conversation with retired Conductor Warren R. McGee, dean of NP advocates: "Warren, did you have a favorite NP engine?" "The 2662 and the 5110 [a 4-8-4 and 4-6-6-4, respectively]. Make it the 5110 just after she'd been shopped and was on test with her valves all squared up just right." A national poll would surely convey the popularity award to Z-5 No. 5000.

In company with McGee, retired Dispatcher Ronald V. Nixon was one of the few railroaders and photographers who seemed aware of the implication of the 1940 barnstorming tour of Electro-Motive FT demo 103 and who carefully chronicled the 5400 h.p. diesel's outing on NP. I like to think that by his craft he instinctively realized that if the 103 could so handily best big steam in NP territory, it could acquit itself on any man's railroad.

I liked the verve of the NP publicist who captioned a photo of A-5 4-8-4 2684: "Regarded by many as the most beautiful locomotive on any railroad."

When you examine a Northern Pacific profile, and consider the 1.8 per cent grade to attain Bozeman Pass, and the 2.2 per cent grades over Homestake Pass and Mullan Pass, all in Montana, and Stampede Pass in Washington, and the 4 per cent across Lookout Pass on the Wallace Branch in Idaho — yes, and if you review the enormous distances of its route (out of St. Paul, a westbound *North Coast Limited* had exceeded the end-to-end run of the *20th Century* before it reached the base of the Continental Divide), why then its locomotives begin to come into focus. In its passenger promotion, NP proudly listed 28 mountain ranges from the Absaroka to the Wolf that were visible to its riders in what was termed the "March of the Mountains," but the operating department could have traced the contribution each made to fuel consumption.

Let the record reflect that NP introduced two super-power steam locomotive wheel arrangements (*i.e.,* the Northern 4-8-4 in 1926 and the Yellowstone 2-8-8-4 in 1928), mounted the largest fireboxes ever slung beneath locomotive boilers (up to 182 square feet of grate area, to burn North Dakota lignite) acquired the first all-roller-bearing locomotive (Timken 1111), scheduled the longest coal-burning engine run in the land (1008 miles, St. Paul-Livingston, Mont.), accepted the FT early on (and ran the last of the breed in the U. S.), and accomplished its mission without resort to electrification. If the record also shows that the performance of NP's world's largest articulated initially fell shy of its publicity, that a company beset with mountains never owned a Mountain type, that the road's parsimonious buying habits were the despair of commercial locomotive builders, or that it

Mistake the NP locomotive face? Impossible. Photo by Richard Steinheimer.

acquired only 81 second-generation diesels (vs. 163 for Great Northern), so be it.

Item: NP, credited with the first true Mikado in the sense of carrying its firebox behind the drivers and over the trailing truck, rostered more than 300 Mikes, and once, during March 18–26, 1926, sent one of them — W-5 1844 — through from Seattle to St. Paul, 1897.6 miles, without once uncoupling from its train . . . at an average speed of 17.4 mph, an average terminal time of 19 minutes, and a total consumption of 353 tons of coal and 442,000 gallons of water.

Need I add that nobody *ever* mistook the NP locomotive face — with its above-center headlight incorporating a triangular illuminated number board — for anybody else's smokebox visage?

If an "all-American" appellation in dieselization implies a majority role for Electro-Motive, NP qualifies. The railway's first diesel was an EMC SW switcher in 1938, the last locomotives it ordered were EMD SD45's, and 79 per cent of its all-time diesel roster of 731 units, including all the covered wagons, were 201A/567/645-powered. Item: Regardless of make, from HH660's to U33C's, there was not an idler axle on the roster.

Who could fault Northern Pacific varnish? I don't mean simply the seniority of the *North Coast Limited* (appropriately Nos. 1 and 2 for most of its life) and the splendid way it rode into old age dressed up with Mr. Loewy's styling and Mr. Budd's domes . . . or the absence of extra fare but a brief flirtation with all-Pullman consists . . . or the company's obligation to passengers as long expressed in almost as many passenger train-miles as freight (6.1 million vs. 7.8 million in 1939) . . . or the succession of locals, mixeds, gas-electrics, and RDC's that serviced the Turtle Lakes and Iron Rivers and Big Horns . . . or the reach implicit in the name *Alaskan* (which always reminded me of the international commerce implied in IC's *Panama* and GN's *Oriental*) . . . or the logical lack of commuter trains . . . or the ads which cited each of the 48 rivers NP paced or crossed and blurbed a mid-route window-washing as "Livingston, I presume" . . . or even the diners' famous great big baked potato, yellow sunshine salt, and stewards who wrote up your check.

I mean all of this in concert, because NPs passenger deportment was precisely what one would have expected, or at least hoped, of a Western transcontinental.

As was true of most railroads west of the New Haven and Long Island, certainly for any road proposed as all-American, passengers were only window dressing for the Northern Pacific, earning (in 1939) 61 cents a train-mile. Freight trains took in $6.96 a mile . . . when the tonnage was available. But NP was a granger, dependent on crops subject to the vicissitudes of market and weather; the Panama Canal diverted a lot of the lumber that had sustained the road in its youth; NP carried only a fraction of the ore of rival GN, whose old Mallets patrolled the Mesabi Range;

The diesel-era, Loewy-styled *North Coast Limited* is almost to the top of Homestake Pass, east of Butte, in this 1959 view. Photo by Jim Scribbins.

and NP's traffic was imbalanced — most loads were eastbound. Between its lesser traffic density, mileage handicap (1906 miles from St. Paul to Seattle vs. 1765 on GN), and the necessity to lug its tonnage across those 2.2 per cent mainline grades, NP always trailed rival GN's operating ratio by several points, and without the Burlington dividends and nonrail income NP counted on to cover most and sometimes all of its fixed charges, who can say that it would have survived the Depression intact?

In the final analysis, I suppose the nuances of Northern Pacific commend the railroad to our regard. No recitation of dates and statistics grasp at the soul of the property. Maps and profiles characterize the road topographically, yes, but as for the heart of it, well, I think firstly of the mountains, notably the Rockies, and all the engine-hours expended by that superb forward line of Baldwin A-2 and A-3 Northerns and Alco Z-6 and Z-7 Challengers as chronicled in the photos of McGee and Nixon. Yes, and if you will, the FT's through F9's, and beyond to the U33C's and SD45's that followed in their lignite exhaust. There was a harshness in the early 20th century endeavors of the NP, or such is the reflection cast by the company's ranks of old Mikes and Pacifics and Prairies — engines of spartan mold from inside valves to inboard-bearing trailers. Even the first 4-8-4's seemed to declare that only raw, brutish strength would suffice west of Livingston. But the latter-day steam power of roller bearings and all-weather cabs and Centipede tenders, and assuredly the diesels, appeared to muster the muscle to master the mountains with panache.

A quirk of regulatory history permitted Northern Pacific's finest hour. For if Great Northern Pacific had been born in 1930, when the Interstate Commerce Commission approved unification of GN and NP with the proviso that they divest their common ownership of CB&Q, a condition they could not accept, not only would the old names have disappeared but there would have been less of a need for the titanic struggles of World War II (NP tonnage almost doubled, and its passenger count more than tripled between 1940 and 1944) across Bozeman and Homestake and Mullan and the locomotives that waged them. (GN sampled some NP-design 4-6-6-4's but peddled them off to their joint subsidiary Spokane, Portland & Seattle.)

Lesser folk than NP men would have suffered from an impossible inferiority complex competing head-to-head for 77 years with the Great Northern, which laid a shorter, easier road to the Pacific without resort to land grants or bankruptcy, and bailed its rival out of the Panic of '93. Big G was not one in its advertising to let NP forget its shortcomings: "The Short — Clean — Cinderless — Scenic Route" (that "scenic" claim was, comparatively, untrue, of course, but that still left GN batting .750); "Only National Park on the Main Line of a Transcontinental Railway in the U.S.A." (Yellowstone's gateway was at Gardiner, Mont., 54 miles from NP's main); "Through Marias Pass — Lowest Crossing of the Rockies" (5213 feet vs. 5566 feet at Mullan Pass on the NP); and "1800 Cinderless Miles — Oil-Burning and Electric Locomotives" (NP had no electrics and confined oil-burning steam power to the Pacific Coast). And when the occasion arose for each company to trot out an antique for display at fairs or alongside the newest Northern or diesel, GN fielded rakish 4-4-0 *William Crooks* while NP settled for a thumbnail of a saddletanker, *Minnetonka*. But NP men were resilient, as in a comment by Conductor McGee in a caption in TRAINS for his photo of GN 27, the *Mail*, detouring over NP west of Helena because of a Kootenai River flood: "This was not uncommon — GN running over NP because of washouts or snow blockades. Would you believe that in 40 years of running on the NP, McGee was not detoured once!" That says something about the stability of the NP through Montana.

Some railroads — and I have no intention of naming any of my choice for this category — never matched in person the image they cast in photo or timetable or history book. A publicized canyon was gone in the blink of an eye, a vaunted engine fell shy of its builder photo, a union station proved to be less than august. But not the Northern Pacific. NP exceeded its press. Nothing I'd read had prepared me for the breathtaking descent of No. 1 into Butte. Or the climb of No. 26 out of Auburn to Stampede Pass. I'm still bemused at the audacity of a mechanical department with no larger engine in its inventory than a 541,500-pound USRA 2-8-8-2 ordering up a 717,000-pound Yellowstone. And aerial photos of the hump yard completed at Pasco, Wash., in 1955 always exemplified for me the deep-breath, shoulders-back elbow room in NP territory. Yet withal, NP was traditional, perchance too much so for its own good, but nevertheless traditional in the sense of warming the heart of train-watchers who rejoiced in a railroad conveying its president in an office car worthy of the name, taking its time dieselizing (and then overindulging in F9's), clinging to the notion that people would support a decent passenger train, mounting steam locomotive bells on hood units, and hanging markers on cupola cabooses.

Walter Gustafson, NP manager of advertising and publicity in its final pre-merger season, summed up the case for the all-American railroad in the closing lines he appended to his ads: "We think this is the way to run a railroad. And this is the way we run the Northern Pacific." [1]

Cincinnati Union Terminal: a memoir

"You had to be there, preferably on a soft spring evening"

WHEN I first saw Cincinnati Union Terminal, I was 12 years old, and the structure was the grandest railroad architecture I had ever seen or imagined I ever would. CUT was more than a station. In a sense, its station function was one of its lesser values. The Terminal was the confirmation of everything railroading stood for in my formative, impressionable years. The size and sweep of its masonry symbolized an enduring, self-sustaining, fundamental transportation. For CUT was a built-for-the-ages edifice, fit for the tomb of an Egyptian pharaoh, aptly acclaimed by the local chamber of commerce as a "great temple of transportation." Its very location, 1½ miles west of downtown, expressed its character: the Terminal didn't come to the city; the city came to it.

Imagine, please, the impact of the place upon a boy who had just arrived on the leather cushions of the smoker-combine of B&O 54, a morning train from down-river Louisville. For him, Cincinnati Union Terminal was a ramp leading from the platform up into the train concourse — a 410-foot kaleidoscope of murals and red marble walls and leather waiting-room seats and terrazzo floor — which emptied into an immense (106 feet high, 125 feet deep, 176 feet wide) main-concourse rotunda, which in turn looked down more than a third of a mile of terraced fountains, green park, and dual-roadway plaza.

My recollection is that the Terminal had everything in addition to trains, and research verifies that it did. Everything: a newsreel theater; Western Union; soda fountains; heroic artwork; a time-zoned map of the nation, plus world globes; gift shops; a garage; restaurants; a cocktail lounge; a bank branch; a directors' board room with fireplace; and oh, yes — ticket windows, baggage

rooms, arrivals and departures boards, phone booths, and other facilities of all those other stations in all those other places.

(No wonder, then, that not one of the seven railroads which erected the 41-million-dollar Terminal and which "jointly and severally and unconditionally guaranteed" its bonds was in the hands of receivers; insolvency surely would have been grounds for expulsion from the most august of all railroad associations.)

Cincinnati should and should not have broken ground for a huge rail passenger terminal in August 1929 (a few months before Black Tuesday on Wall Street) and completed it in March 1933 (the month FDR closed the banks). The case can be argued pro and con with equal fervor and fact. In 1928, on the eve of

"Imagine the impact upon a boy . . . of a 410-foot kaleidoscope of murals and red marble walls and leather seats and terrazzo floor." B&O photo.

construction, 108 passenger trains arrived in the city and 108 departed each day. By 1950, half that number were left. Today Amtrak operates one train each way and those soon will leave in search of smaller, less costly facilities. But who could have forecast the ultimate depth of the decline a half century ago, when people still rode trains and when the gateway complexion of Cincinnati traffic (as many as three out of four passengers were changing trains or otherwise passing through) was cursed with no fewer than five different depots, all old? Who was to say that Cincinnati didn't deserve a decent unified station, or that once the banks reopened and the pump was primed, CUT wouldn't make economic as well as esthetic sense?

Regardless, the great work was incorporated on November 12, 1927; stocks and bonds were issued; the first dirt was dug in August 1929; and the builders proceeded with their objective of an 8-platform, 16-track through-type passenger station capable of handling more than 200 trains and 17,000 travelers every 24 hours. This meant 224,534 cubic yards of poured concrete, 45,421 tons of bridge and building steel, 8,250,000 bricks, 94 miles of new track (including 107 switches and 149 signals), and total support

facilities (e.g., mail and express buildings, coachyard, 300,000-gallon water tank, coal dock, power-house, and 20-stall round-house). Depression or not, logic or not, Cincinnati would get a civic wonder of a union terminal on the bank of the Ohio River, just as sister Cleveland had won one earlier within sight of the shore of Lake Erie. As its statistics reveal, Cincinnati's CUT (like Cleveland's) was a complex proposition, and not solely because of its exotic rotunda (the station building itself accounted for only 21 per cent of the total budget). Immense grading was necessary to lift the Terminal out of the reach of a flood-stage Ohio River, and that meant elaborate steel bridges at the south end of the station. Again, CUT's inability to purchase one particular parcel of land meant that the station tracks could not be built at right angles to the train concourse (they're askew by approximately 4 degrees).

The architects and the engineers prevailed, however and at 6 a.m. on Sunday, March 19, 1933, CUT was opened to revenue traffic as Southern 15, an all-day, all-stops local to Chattanooga, puffed out of the station. The first arrival took place at 7:10 a.m., when C&O 5, the *Sportsman,* pulled in. Both trains were premature. CUT had been scheduled to open on April 1, but an unruly river had chased the trains out of their old depots.

Thus did Baltimore & Ohio, Chesapeake & Ohio, Louisville & Nashville, New York Central (Big Four), Norfolk & Western, Pennsylvania, and Southern (CNO&TP) depart the old B&O, Central Union, Court Street, Fourth Street, and PRR-L&N depots to enter the last but two (30th Street, Philadelphia, and Los Angeles Union Passenger Terminal) of the ultimate rail passenger facilities to be built in the land. And thus was created an experience for every sensitive traveler who passed through the Queen City. I know. I was there, first when CUT was a mere six years old; again during the Big War; then on subsequent affairs with steam in twilight; with Mr. Young's X; and with old friends, from the *Cincinnatian* to the *Pan,* that were running out their final miles. If you were ever in CUT, you know the attraction. If not, allow me to tell you about it.

Cincinnati Union Terminal . . . the blueprints, the photographs — they go just so far in describing the place in either its great dimension or its fine detail. You had to be there, preferably on a soft spring evening with a warm shower in progress. You

111

walked outside, across the driveway, down the terrace past the fountains, and then — *then* you turned and looked back up at that huge arch with its illuminated clock, the one with the 16-foot face. I stood there first as a boy with my Dad, I stood there once with the most beautiful girl in the world, I stood there on many occasions alone, absorbed in the fact that something so large, so beautiful could be pure railroad to the last penny of its mortgage. (If you stood inside the rotunda, at one foot of the arch, and talked in normal tones, a person 176 feet across the way at the other foot could hear you.) I don't like to admit it, but it's true: Without the rotunda and the arch, CUT would have been just another nice big station, efficient but forgettable.

It finally has dawned on me what CUT looked like inside. Obvious — a land-locked *Queen Mary.* Bear in mind that the keel of the Cunarder was laid in 1930, little more than a year after work was started on CUT; and that but for a three-year suspension in work caused by the depression the *Mary* would have been launched about the time CUT opened — then compare interiors.

You find the same great halls, the same so-soon-dated decor, the same effect as modernism came to grips with conservatism, the same big-is-best and nothing-is-too-good-for-our-customers. The station and the ship: As a child of their era and as a patron of both, I'm convinced that the comparison isn't coincidental.

In the matter of trains, Cincinnati had much in common with Kansas City. Both were gateways (more people rode through or changed trains than originated or terminated their journeys there), both omitted commuters, both enjoyed a great deal of competing and connecting among tenant roads. There were places you could reach by way of only one road out of Cincinnati (SR's Asheville, N. C., comes to mind), but not many. And to most places you had a choice of at least two daily departures on each of two roads. To tidewater Virginia, for example, there were N&W's *Cavalier* and *Pocahontas* vs. Chessie's *F.F.V.* and *Sportsman;* and to Florida there were L&N's *Southland* and *Flamingo* pitted against SR's *Royal Palm* and *Ponce de Leon.*

I never could make up my mind which trains appealed the most on CUT's Arrivals & Departures board — or why. Louisville & Nashville, which was rural in nature even if it was affluent in coal, hit the big time in Cincinnati as it did in no other town. Its trains crossed the Ohio on Chessie's great bridge, then wound along high over the riverbank on steel trestlework before easing into CUT beside such aristocracy as Central Hudsons. I always felt that L&N looked a bit self-conscious in CUT, with the dwarf signals and electropneumatic turnouts and modernistic rotunda. The *Pan-American* was more one with bluegrass and Gulf bayous, Bowling Green and Montgomery; yet there she was — hey, look me over! We Louisville boys usually rode "our road" up to Cincinnati, but we didn't necessarily tell anyone in the big city how we got there.

If L&N was diffident, Southern was haughty — as any road would be that could field tremendous Ps-4 Pacifics dressed up in green and gold, *and* topped by three-quarter-boiler-length smoke deflectors, and coupled to consists with names such as *Queen* and *Crescent.* But SR went a step further. The system didn't allow its engines or cars to linger in CUT but pulled them back across the river to Ludlow, Ky., for servicing. Even Pennsy didn't try that, and I never found out how SR explained the exclusiveness. Unless, of course, a Ps-4 (6471-6482 series on the CNO&TP) was too regal to find any peers in CUT's roundhouse.

New York Central was right at home in CUT. It should have been. The year work had begun in the Queen City, CUT's architects, Fellheimer and Wagner, had just completed NYC's own Central Station in Buffalo; and allowing for a tower instead of a rotunda as the hallmark, the similarity is apparent. Central was at home in the big time, what with its trains serving Grand Central, Central, and the other CUT. In fact, a mural of a J-1 Hudson hung over the Cincinnati Arrivals board. A J-1 carrying green, at that. My Dad, who is British and therefore is receptive to multiple iron and high speed and graceful design, admired to depart CUT on the likes of the Sycamore, with the hogger of the 4-6-4 up front easing us off the bridgework and down to the riverbank, then screwing up his reverse wheel and allowing that marvelous racer to build up to 60 and 65 and 70 and beyond . . . running wild, running wild.

Rival Pennsylvania loomed large in Cincinnati Union Terminal with, for example, 10 departures between 9:05 a.m. and 11:40 p.m. in the summer of 1939. Of course, CUT was not cut of the cloth of PRR orthodoxy; it had nothing in common with 30th Street, Philadelphia. (Thirtieth Street, although it was newer looked older, yet conversely it may have aged better.) One cannot imagine a GG1 electric nosing into CUT, and heaven forbid speculation on what General Atterbury would have thought of mosaic murals and gray-and-rose terrazzo. PRR owned a shade over 14 per cent of CUT and 50 per cent of Chicago Union Station, and the two structures reflected those statistics.

Baltimore & Ohio, on the other hand, although it was older than Pennsy and scarcely as affluent as Central, and was most celebrated for such venerables as its Mount Royal and Camden stations in Baltimore, appeared to me to mesh with CUT quite well. In those days B&O had to cut corners to maintain the appearance of parity with the Nos. 1 and 2 of Eastern railroading. B&O took you right to the doorstep of your hotel in New York because it didn't have a tunnel; B&O streamstyled old heavy-weight sleepers because it couldn't afford new lightweights; B&O took a plunge on diesels to offset USRA-vintage steam; and B&O welcomed (I thought) a next-generation Cincinnati station for which six other carriers, most of them competitive in some measure, shared the tab. B&O was the only road to run through CUT, was the first with diesels in CUT, and was the owner of the

Cincinnatian, the Terminal's most distinctive streamliner (no, I haven't forgotten about the original *James Whitcomb Riley*).

Of the coal-haulers, Norfolk & Western was Avis to you-know-whose Hertz. N&W came crawling out of the coalfields on a pretty, winding, bridge-punctuated branch, content to play a supporting role in CUT as the least passenger-oriented carrier in the station. But in 1941 N&W changed its image. Roanoke turned out engine 600, prototype of the streamlined J-class 4-8-4's whose bullet-nosed look deserved a modern surrounding. Pound for pound, detail for detail, the J surely was the finest steam locomotive ever to thread the Terminal's doubleslip turnouts. Also, she was an absolute contrast in size and style to the Geeps that pulled N&W out of CUT for the last time.

Which leaves Chesapeake & Ohio . . . and I mean the C&O of Van Sweringen cast, not the latter-day blue-and-yellow invention of Robert R. Young's publicists. Chessie, the old classic Chessie, laid it on for passengers with F-19 Pacifics (remember the stars on the cylinders, and the cameo of the first American president on the Elesco feedwater heater, and the splendid Vanderbilt tank?) and library-lounge sleepers and Imperial Salon Cars ("Individual seats for passengers not desiring Pullman accommodations"). That was eastbound. Westbound C&O scaled everything down to a choice if unremarked little local that a 4-4-2 took out of CUT for an 8-hour, 262-mile journey to, of all places, Hammond, Ind. C&O was a reason, a key reason, we rode the L&N to CUT, for Cincinnati was the one big city where Chessie was to be found in full bloom.

Today Amtrak wants out of Cincinnati Union Terminal. No ticket the agency sells in CUT begins to cover terminal charges, much less contribute anything toward the cost of the train ride itself. Even shorn of many of its support facilities and run by a skeleton staff (321 in 1970, down from 2200 in 1945), the Terminal has turned in an annual deficit of more than 4 million dollars in recent years. The most visionary of Amtrakers can't justify use of a transportation temple at those prices. This will leave the Terminal empty and its owners (the biggest one bankrupt) individually, severally, and unconditionally responsible for 10 million dollars' worth of bonds due in 1974.

I'm sorry about the debt, but I'm happy that Amtrak elected to leave. CUT, my Terminal, wasn't erected for the likes of a quasi-Government agency operating a national system of passenger trains out of a common timetable. CUT was of the railroads, by the railroads, for the railroads — pluralistic, private, posh, a monument to a vanished time of Pullman and Vanderbilt, the Van Sweringens and Willard, Tri-Motors and Model A's, 1½-cent-a-mile fares and 10 per cent reductions on round trips.

Naturally, I'll read about Cincinnati's plans for its empty edifice, if only for material for TRAINS' news columns. But in my heart, the Terminal — the temple, if you will — is secure. Lights wink across the track diagram over its 187-lever interlocking machine. Under the great rotunda tickets are being dated and sleeping-car diagrams inked in. Down the train concourse crowds dutifully assemble at the ramps and stairs leading to the platforms below. And below, at track level, smoke curls from diner galleys, blankets are tucked into lowers and uppers, and enginemen and trainmen compare Hamiltons.

Stepboxes are swung up, a headlight turns bright, a gloved hand tugs at a throttle, and at 6:15 p.m. L&N 1, the Azalean, *moves out of Cincinnati Union Terminal. The rods of its Mountain type revolve above the green dwarfs, and R.P.O. and baggage cars and coaches and Pullmans and diner follow their charge obediently over curving bridgework. From a high-backed green-plush seat a boy of 12, with his face pressed against the window, looks back at that soaring arch of CUT. Dusk is deepening as 69-inch drivers keep couplers taut, as the city and the river fall behind the marker lamps on the rear of the diner, as a waiter makes the first call for dinner. The boy, in his formative years and impressionable, is happy. He has seen the big time and it has lived up to its billing.* **1**

Milwaukee Road . . . Lionel in 1:1 scale

A CMStP&P carol

THE Chicago, Milwaukee, St. Paul & Pacific is my Christmas railroad. For that high purpose, the Milwaukee could not be more my personal possession if I owned all 518,652 outstanding shares of its 5 per cent noncumulative participating preferred series A stock. I found the property in a Lionel Corporation catalog 45 or so winters ago. Ghost of Christmas Past, show me once more: No. 381E. "An exact reproduction [and] a faithful replica" of the electric locomotives that sped the famous *Olympian* over the mountains — an 18-inch-long, 6½-inch-wide, standard-gauge (2¼ inches) model, with two electric headlights, adjustable pantographs, copper journal boxes.

I compared the picture of the prototype in the catalog with that of the tinplate toy and found no discrepancy. Undetected was the fact that the former was a 1-B+D+D+B-1 while the latter was a 2-B-2; nor did I find anything remiss in the *Olympian* train set which included the 381E pulling Pullmans named *Colorado* and *California* and an observation car named *New York*. I just instinctively knew that any model described by the great factory at Irvington, N. J., as "the most elaborate in the Lionel line" must be patterned on the motive power of a great railroad.

A $32.50 381E never saw service in our attic that Christmas, or any Christmas; rather, a $10.75 253E O-gauge electric pulled our unnamed sleeping cars. No matter. A quest had begun. Thanks to Lionel, those initials CMStP&P had assumed a larger meaning than, say, C&NW or CRI&P.

What the Lionel people did for the Milwaukee Road's image in the 1930's, Al Kalmbach doubled in spades in the 1940's. TRAINS mirrored the affection for and awe in which he held the carrier; I think it fair to say that the road's reputation among train-watchers across the land grew in direct proportion to the periodical's press runs. It was Al's little 25-center that pictured the bi-polar genesis of Lionel's 381E; that defined CMStP&P's diversity of power (1194 engines embracing 13 steam wheel arrangements, 8 diesel makes, and those electrics) in a photo roster; that took us into the bay-window caboose of a local freight called a patrol; that announced that John Barriger's super-railroad was in place between Chicago and Milwaukee.

This Pied Piper played a siren song of speed:

Al published a speedometer tape recorded October 6, 1940,

". . . the enginehouse dispatched streamlined 4-6-4 105. 'Still wanta ride?' the engineer asked." Photo by A. W. Johnson.

aboard streamlined Hudson No. 105 on the point of Second 6, the *Morning Hiawatha*. Between Oakwood, Wis., and Edgebrook, Ill., the 4-6-4 maintained an even 100 mph with a few exceptions — one dip to perhaps 98, several spurts to as high as 105.

He told of a railroad with such high track standards that REDUCE SPEED TO 90 M.P.H. signs before curves had been removed.

He passed along the story of "a crotchety old lady who boarded the *Hiawatha* at Milwaukee. After the train was four or five miles out of Milwaukee and was rolling along at about 50 mph, this woman collared the porter in the aisle and complained about the excessive speed. He looked at her for a moment and then broke out into a laugh and said, 'Ma'am, we ain't even started to move yet.' . . . She pulled the shade down and gripped the arm of her seat like a vise. If she had watched the scenery as the train went through Sturtevant at 100 mph, she'd have died!"

Christmas railroad stuff, this. Which is to say, an unseen, far-away line which seemed to realize the imagination that we invested in the straights, curves, switches, tunnels, transformers, and trains of our American Flyer and Lionel empires. A Christmas railroad, in 1:1 scale, would have to be double-track, fast, colorful, passenger-oriented, all beribboned and tinseled — an otherworld property possessed of a magic beyond the grasp of the familiar, which in my case was first Central of Georgia and later Louisville & Nashville.

[Forgive me, L&N, for so grievously underestimating you in those years. Conservative to the core, you resisted such overdrafts as MILW's Puget Sound Extension and 656-mile electrification; rather, you dug coal out of Eastern Kentucky with modest Mikes, seldom strayed out of your region, never defaulted on a bond, and reaffirmed the faith of your shareholders — virtues lost upon the errant young.]

Sometimes a railroad, in whole or in part, doesn't live up to its publicity. If you refilled your coffee cup at the wrong moment on the *Chief*, you could miss Apache Canyon or Canyon Diablo. A. Aubrey Bodone's photo murals cast Western Maryland in a heroic mold that the 872-mile road, seen firsthand, could not possibly sustain. Even Big Boy glimpsed quickly in Cheyenne from a passing Streamliner could scarcely be differentiated from a Challenger.

In the case of the Milwaukee Road, did we distrust Lionel or Al Kalmbach — or our own aspirations? In a secular sense, isn't each Christmas bigger, brighter, and better for every boy than the last one — until that December 25th when anticipation outstrips realization? Suppose one finally attained Mile 0 of the CMStP&P in Chicago and all those shiny memorized quotes of A.C.K. (*Four or six times a day* Hiawathas *sail through at 100 mph, brief bright flashes . . .*) became as sounding brass?

Dad and I finally ventured north to see, among other railroad drama, my Christmas road. I saw CMStP&P initially indoors, from the concourse of Chicago Union Station, darkly as through gate-door glass — splashes of orange cars, gray streamlined boilers, smokeboxes with 45-degree-angle boxes displaying 8-inch-high white road numbers. Milwaukee Road occupied the entire north half of Union, 10 tracks wide — oh, the exclusiveness of our Lionel set, suddenly transformed from 2¼-inch to 4 feet-8½-inch width!

Out of Chicago, we approached the Milwaukee's hometown obliquely, on a diesel-powered, green-and-yellow *400*. There ensued the obligatory courtesy call at 1027 N. 7th; then The Great Experience. I think the year was 1943, I think the train was No. 46; I know the power was an F-3 Pacific and an F-6 Hudson double-headed. I can see them now, framed in my arched coach window, their bells tolling, their rods arcing around the curve out of the depot across St. Paul Avenue. A slow beginning, deceptively so, our "80 Minute train" coiling between brick factories thumping over streetcar rails, crossing a drawbridge climbing toward high ground. Then our Pacific-Hudson tandem began to race . . . and their cinders rained down, peppering our coach, sliding beneath the sealed window and sooting the newspaper in my lap. *If unnamed 46 went this fast,* I thought, *imagine how fast a* Hi *went!*

A Christmas railroad CMStP&P was, as exciting a plant as Lionel 381E and ACK's pictures and prose had promised. Now, the quixotic quality of that 1943 journey aboard No. 46 — indeed, of all the hundreds that followed up and down the old C& M (Chicago & Milwaukee) Division — is that it encompassed just 85 of the railroad's 11,000 route-miles, a mere .77 per cent of the system. Less than 1 per cent of this longer-than-Union Pacific transcontinental was (and is) its showcase and strength. Inside that corridor the Milwaukee was big-time: 100 mph speed limit, 131-pound rail, cab signaling. And the trains: *Hi's,* commuter "Scoots," 5000-ton freights behind bigger-than-GS-or-O5 4-8-4's, the twin-RPO *Fast Mail* ("Does not carry passengers or baggage"), the celebrated *Olympian* and *Pioneer Limited,* the patrols.

Yet all this wasn't the Milwaukee which Wall Street and *Moody's* knew. Item: In steam, the Milwaukee had less than 100 modern engines on its roster, yet these were ample to handle its Chicago–Twin Cities and Chicago-Omaha mains — after which its map diffused into granger country adequately policed by venerable World War I hand-bombers. The vaunted electrification was separated by a "gap" that 2-6-6-2's huffed and puffed to fill until 5400 h.p. FTs came to the rescue. As for its books, the Milwaukee had folded twice in this century, once after completion of its catenary and the Panama Canal coincided, again in the Great Depression. The system had too much track (and still does — 1 out of every 3 miles it operates is too much by a 1977 company estimate); everywhere its rails were bracketed by those of C&NW, CB&Q, NP, and/or RI. Even to this date the ICC has turned a deaf ear on its pleas to be included inside one of the big solvents with which it competes or connects.

Parenthetically, I should allow that *this* Milwaukee, the prairie Milwaukee, the granger Milwaukee, is what the initials CMStP&P connote to many. They insist that the soul of this road lies out on the farms and in the forests which sponsor much of its tonnage. They offer in evidence the facts that the two states with the most Milwaukee mileage are Iowa and South Dakota; and that once upon a time the Milwaukee's motor and mixed train miles alone equaled the total train-miles of the Minneapolis & St. Louis. The Milwaukee to them is a squad of SW's crawling along on light iron forbidden to an SD7, in Willa Cather country whose grain elevators were once smudged by the smoke of all-purpose 4-6-0's and 2-6-2's. The problem with this contention is that the more remote one finds the Milwaukee from its old super-railroad C&M Division, the more the road blurs into the likes of a North Western or a Rock. Granted, only 1 route-mile in 10 of MILW was laid with rail weighing 130 pounds a yard or more; still, that heavy steel is what bore the fast-rolling wheels which gave the road its individuality.

My point, then, is that the Milwaukee's adversities gave it a built-in excuse to be a colorless also-ran, a cop-out which the road never exercised. That is why the Milwaukee apologist enjoys his work.

Expunge the record of all the eccentricities of the Milwaukee and you have a railroad industry demonstrably less fascinating than Col. Robert S. Henry's book declared it to be. I mean, economic or not, the Milwaukee did string copper, albeit from wooden poles, across two mountain ranges while Pennsy, with umpteen times MILW's traffic density, conceded the Alleghenies to 2-10-0's. What is the saga of streamlining without a chapter on the road that resurrected a wheel arrangement which hadn't been in production for 21 years and employed it to haul home-made welded cars in a successful contest with Electro-Motive and Budd? Imagine the consternation of the operating department witnesses who testified that the Burlington Northern merger would reduce Chicago-Seattle freight transit time from 76 to 65 hours when the Milwaukee simultaneously offered its shippers a 55½-hour XL *Special* between the same cities.

Oh, the curious, delightful turns taken by the Milwaukee with sleight of hand . . . as when an electrical genius in its ranks contrived to multiple electrics and diesels, even to blending their regenerative and dynamic brakes; as when the Milwaukee took over not only Union Pacific's *City* Streamliners for Chicago delivery but also appropriated their Armour yellow and their red sans-serif lettering for its *Hi's;* as when CMStP&P so adroitly petitioned for protection from surrounding mergers that it emerged from the hearings with a 2686-mile single-system main from Louisville, Ky. to Portland, Ore.

Now, if the Ghost of Christmas Past were to call upon me on the stroke of 1 on the morning of December 25, 1977, even as he visited Ebenezer Scrooge, and rend the veil which lies across bygone years on my Christmas railroad, I would ask to journey again behind Nos. 2 and 15A&B and aboard the 105, as well as in any consist which includes a Skytop and a Tip Top Tap.

No. 2, that huge Atlantic, shrouded to her knees, driving on her first coupled axle, her great oil-fired boiler generating steam at 300 pounds pressure per square inch to propel driving wheels 84 inches in diameter. I went to Chicago once (again on train 46 out of Milwaukee) in a nonairconditioned, red-plush, 12-wheeler only a baggage car removed from the tender of No. 2, *i.e.,* in

"Fast Fifteen? The records say she was simply two E6 cabs." Photo by Robert Wietzke.

superb quarters to hear that machine at work. Once she had put the .67 per cent climb to Lake behind her, she accelerated steadily up to 90 mph, there slipping into what I can only describe as a rising/falling rhythm, a pulsating melody in metal, a sort of deep-pitched *zing . . . zing zing, zing, zing zing/zing/zing*, making memorable the miles down through Sturtevant and Wadsworth and West Lake Forest on a lazy September afternoon 30 years ago.

The 15 — rather, Fast Fifteen? The records say she was simply two E6 cabs, a pair of 2000 h.p. A1A-A1A's, an assembly of four 567-series V-12 engines turning over four D-4 generators feeding eight D-7 traction motors . . . from the same mold as the other 90 E6A's sold by GM during 1939–1942. Maybe. For eight years plus, night after night, these units took *Fast Mail* No. 57 out of Chicago to Minneapolis, all 15 to 25 or more cars of that prestigious schedule; then, day after day, they doubled back on the *Morning Hiawatha,* No. 6. For Milwaukeeans, No. 6 was vital; it was one's entry to Chicago to connect with the *Broadway* east, the *Panama* south, the *Denver Zephyr* west. Now, the genius and guts of Fast Fifteen was that she could uncannily carve minutes out of her

75-minute allowance for the 85-mile C&M; thus when No. 6 got away a few minutes off the mark, her intimates relaxed. Speed logs indicate she once touched 106.2 mph; and on another occasion, she ran off those 85 miles start to stop in 64½ minutes, including a quarter-mile slow order of 30 mph. As the years passed, the Milwaukee returned to the builders' catalogs — for E7's, Erie-builts, FP7's, E9's, FP45's — but the road never found an in-kind replacement for 15A&B.

Hudson 105, the engine on the speed tapes published by Al Kalmbach: how beholden I am to her. On March 24, 1950, I had a pass to ride a Fairbanks-Morse C-Line, demonstrator from Milwaukee to Chicago — on No. 46 (what else?). But instead of FM's newest, the enginehouse dispatched streamlined 4-6-4 105. "Still wanta ride?" the engineer asked. My penciled notes read: *Little more than 7 minutes late, 300 lbs. pressure, go. Slipping on [Menomonee River] bridge, 20 mph, loud exhaust. S-2 [4-8-4] 214 south. 45 mph past C&NW [Chase Street] roundhouse. Then red light on nose 4-unit FT from Savanna — broke in two — fireman out with fusee to stop us. Right by Heil [Company] No. 3 plant on curve. Opening up under North Shore. Under beltline at 45 mph. 55-60 at Lake. Comforting heat from fire. Fireman shakes grates. Machine gun vibration at 60-75. 80 at Signal 73.4. 80-85 to Sturtevant, slow to 20 there as another train is stopped. Engr.-fireman shout — hard to understand. 60 mph by 6.02 signal. 83 at Truesdell. Curve: Engr. looks back for train check. Russell 88. 90. Rondout 92 (X). "Will hold 90 all the way — long time to get it" — Engr. 85 Edgebrook for yellow, then up. X's at Mayfair 80. Healy — 85. 16 mph Western Ave. for outbound C&NW commuters. 7 cars. Arrive 5:27 p.m.*

What I am saying is that what the Lionel Corporation and Al Kalmbach had so grandly promised, the Chicago, Milwaukee, St. Paul & Pacific delivered.

Ah, the conversations enjoyed over VO and L&M's in the basement (or bomb bay, as we dubbed it) lounges of Super Domes, never mind how rough-riding and hard-to-see-out-of those monsters were . . .

. . . And the diners with wallpaper up their walls; how inviting. As the years passed, and I acquired credit cards and titles and three-week-vacation seniority at TRAINS, I could slide behind a table with as much aplomb as the next guy — but I never

"... the diners with wallpaper up their walls; how inviting." CMStP&P photo.

"... the snow swirling up in the wake of the Skytop observation ..." — as enjoyed by Margaret and David Morgan. Photo by George G. Weiss.

really got over the wonder of whooshing through those through-girder, steel-decked bridges over Chicago streets, of feeling the trucks beneath the carpet groove the diamond at Tower A-20 at 95 per, of knowing the E7's up front were in Run 8 and bound for three digits on their Chicago Pneumatic speedometers . . .

. . . Finally, the snow swirling up in the wake of the Skytop observation, then eddying about in the ballast between cold steel rails. Passengers up ahead, snugged down in their swivel parlor chairs, *Chicago Tribunes* unfolded across their paunches, would be dozing. Not me. For the thousandth time I was untying the ribbon and tearing the shiny paper off my present, my 1:1 scale Lionel, my Christmas railroad. ⚊

Gee whiz

THE places his little hand in yours and holds on tight as you walk about the engine terminal, which is just as well for he's so engrossed in the power on the ready track that you must guide him over the rails and around the standing pools of muddy oil. He waves to the hostler filling the slope-back tank of an ancient 0-6-0 and asks you which way a four-unit freight diesel with a cab on each end is headed. He is intrigued by a pair of men cleaning the firebox of a Mike on the ash pit.

For seconds he is awed and standing very close to you as a passenger engine backs past with its cylinder cocks open. He studies the white clouds of steam shooting forth from the Pacific and curling about his feet, then he glances up at you with a small uncertain grin.

Beyond the coal tower he releases your hand and runs to where a black, dirty 4-8-4 is standing alone. He scurries alongside the bulk of its boiler, then squats down to make his own examination of its eight-coupled disc drivers.

"Gee whiz."

Then, "How fast will she go, Dad?"

"About seventy-five or eighty."

He asks about sand pipes and domes and air pumps and power reverse, and your answers recall the spring when the S-2's were new and you pedaled out past Highway 100 to watch them come fighting up the grade through Elm Grove to Brookfield. The Baldwins came in 1938 — before the university and the Army and Margaret. And before the diesels. The sight of Rod getting his hands all black and grimy on the main rod of an S-2 makes 1938 seem far away and not quite real.

"Dad, is this better than a diesel?"

"No."

"Why not?"

"A diesel pulls more cars," you hear yourself saying, "and it doesn't go to the shops so often. Nobody builds steam engines anymore."

"I like steam best," he says flatly. "Don't you, Dad?"

He searches your face intently for a moment, then grins because he knows that you know that nothing on wheels is better than an S-2.

1938? Not so long ago.

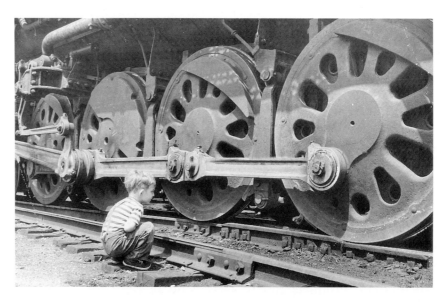

Milwaukee Road 4-8-4 and friend. Photo by C. P. Fox.

My kind of town?

Concerning *a, b, c, d, e, f, g,* and *h*

WHAT is Amtrak's greatest claim to fame? Reclaiming the name and most of the route of the *California Zephyr?* Appointing W. Graham Claytor Jr. president? Eliminating steam heat? Covering more than half of operating expenses out of passenger receipts? Bringing back the upper berth window?

None of the above.

Amtrak has done what all the king's men and all the iron horses couldn't do: originate and terminate all intercity passenger trains serving Chicago in one station. Everything else from Metroliners to All Aboard America fares to Auto Train to the New River Gorge in daylight to 800-USA-RAIL pales into warm ginger ale.

Chicago was, in a passenger station context, America's London, i.e., competitive rather than complementary. Except that a higher percentage of travelers disembarking at Charing Cross, Euston, Kings Cross, Liverpool Street, Marylebone, Paddington, St. Pancras, Victoria, and Waterloo had attained their final destination than was the case 3958 miles west. Chicago was divisible in the *Official Guide* index by eight: (*a*) Dearborn; (*b*) Grand Central; (*c*) Union, (*d*) Central; (*e*) La Salle Street; (*f*) C&NW; (*g*) Wells Street; and (*h*) CNS&M. Distances between these terminals required 3½ column inches of 5-point type to compute, the range being from ⅛ mile (*c* to *f*) to 1¾ miles (*f* to *d*).

There were really only two decent structures in the lot to sort out passengers. Oh, the rest possessed a charm of sorts for those of us with architectural or railroad leanings. In TRAINS' all-Chicago August 1948 issue, Frank P. Donovan Jr. summarized the steam-road terminals thusly — "a kind of railroad barony set apart from the Loop" (Central), "friendly informality" (Dearborn), "leisurely atmosphere" (Grand Central), "could easily pass for an office building or hotel" (La Salle), "almost a city within a city" (North Western), and "business-like and austere" (Union).

Poet Conrad Winski was moved in our November 1981 TRAINS to declare: "Call once more the roll/As did the Parm'lee coachmen:/Central, Lay-sal, Union deepo/Gran' Central, Nort' Western, Dearborn." Touching, but I'm talking Stations with a capital S . . . as in 30th Street, Philadelphia. I'm talking about places where you'd already been somewhere before you hit the taxi rank, facilities that impartially mixed commuters and long-distance travelers, plants that lifted the soul without debasing the body.

Union Station and Chicago & North Western Passenger Terminal — in that order.

Union united only 4 of the 24 line-haul passenger carriers (in 1941) entering Chicago, but you could board a train for New York, Seattle, San Francisco, or Miami . . . or La Grange or Lemont or Libertyville. Its consists mixed reds and oranges, greens and silver. Fred Harvey served meals, and there was a box to post a letter for the RPO of the *Broadway Limited.* Union fielded the fastest trains of any station in Chicago, as in 16 hours to either Gotham or the Rockies. Union *looked* as if it should host and be part owned by the Pennsylvania. It was really two buildings, one a waiting room, one a place to catch trains — both all stone and high ceilings and arches and fit for pharaohs.

The anomaly that a sometimes bankrupt Chicago, Milwaukee, St. Paul & Pacific should occupy half the tracks and concourse of Union could perchance be excused on grounds that the

Union: looked as if it should host and be part owned by the Pennsylvania. Photo by John Gruber.

Milwaukee was the second longest railroad in the city and one of only two in the town that reached the Pacific Ocean. Burlington, of course, had the history and the solvency to warrant space in Union, particularly in the sense that it was the Chicago anchor of

Dearborn: dear, dreary, dilapidated — so how did Santa Fe streamliners get in? Photo by William A. Wight.

its Hill Lines parents. And as for Alton, its demeanor was orthodox, it was the majority carrier to St. Louis — and its trains didn't take up that much room.

Just an eighth of a mile away, on Canal Street, stood Union's only rival as a structure: the North Western Terminal. The only major station in the city exclusively occupied by one railroad. A fitting Mile 0 for the Overland Route, if really a touch grandiose for C&NW's own trains to Ashland, Deadwood, Eau Claire, and the like. Naturally, Mr. Harriman's trains couldn't dock just anywhere in Chicago — the *Citys, Overland, Challengers, Portland Rose:* limiteds of that cut. And they looked just fine, bracketed by rows of green-and-yellow *400's* and shiny black commuter Pacifics. I derive some satisfaction from the fact that the station was Chicago's last to survive in its originality.

Still, C&NW Terminal sat in lonely splendor. A pity.

Dearborn, dear, dreary, dilapidated old Dearborn. One could explain all but one of its tenants. Monon hardly had a choice of terminals. Ditto for Erie. Yes, and CN's Grand Trunk Western. (I was about to say that if Canadian Pacific had sent its red trains to Chicago, they would never have pulled up to the bumper posts in Dearborn, but thinking back to the ancient edifices that CPR called home in Montreal and Vancouver, I will discard that thought.) Also Chicago & Eastern Illinois. (C&EI, per se, was scarcely more than a Monon, but thanks to its Evansville connection with L&N, the marginal carrier was Mile 0 of the Dixie Route, hence the majority carrier to Florida — which says something, if not as much as the Overland Route said for C&NW at Canal and Clinton.) Finally, Wabash, read Gould first, Pennsy stepchild later.

It was emblematic of Dearborn that owner Chicago & Western Indiana's minor-league commutation service consisted of 2-6-0's and Stillwell coaches.

But incongruously, Santa Fe also occupied Dearborn, for reasons no one will ever satisfactorily explain to prejet luxury passengers. Never. The clientele of the *Chiefs* and, earlier, the *California Limited,* had no more business shining their markers in Dearborn than the *Mauretania* would have had tying up in Hoboken. Imagine the Hollywood set attempting the considerable feat of not getting their high heels caught between the boards of those narrow wooden platforms cluttered with baggage trucks and all steamy with the breath of Grand Trunk 4-8-4's! (But better westbound than eastbound, for patrons of AT&SF inbound streamliners had to allow for 195 feet of F units at the head end of their consists.) No higher praise can be bestowed upon the quality of Santa Fe service than that its patrons condoned Dearborn and Polk Streets. After all, *Super* passengers destined for MGM expected more amenities than a patron of the *Erie Limited* bound for Youngstown Sheet & Tube. Think on it — six railroads jamming their trains into fewer tracks (8) at Dearborn than one railroad occupied (10) on one side of Union. In a weak moment I once defined Dearborn as cosmopolitan, but let me hasten to add that the adjective applied to its trains rather than the terminal itself.

La Salle had, well, location: adjacency to the Wall Street of Chicago. And there was a certain ethereal quality about rising from street level to track level on an escalator that befitted embarkation on the *Century* or the *Commodore Vanderbilt.* Smallish and elderly by Union standards, true, still La Salle didn't condone the unthinkable, that is, risk offending the sensibilities of the Commodore's customers.

Rock Island, by virtue of commuters, ran the most trains in and out of La Salle, but CRI&P never quite tipped its hand about how little was in its till upstairs in headquarters. A *Rocket* resembled a *Zephyr* to the uninitiated, and a *Golden State Limited* could look an *Overland* right in the headlight without blinking. Nickel Plate? Did patrons of the adjacent NYC No. 90, the *Forest City* departing at 11:40 p.m. (in 1941), know that they could have

departed 20 minutes earlier in a through sleeper on unnamed NKP 6 and arrived in New York (well, Hoboken) only 10 hours after they did? Would they have cared?

Central was something else again. Central only by virtue of its owner's second name, the station looked just inside its street-level door like a commuter ticket office, but up above there was an enormous waiting room under a great arched ceiling which — here's the horrid part — fed through three gates down one impossibly steep stairway to the platforms below. Why the elderly didn't plummet daily to their demise down that 17-foot stair I do not know. (One consolation: only outbound passengers had to make that trek; inbound passengers simply cut across the tracks to the cab stand.)

Central meant Illinois Central, which in turn meant that if you were bound for an Illini education or business in Memphis or fun in New Orleans (especially on the depot's one indisputably class train, the all-Pullman *Panama Limited*), you were in Central, stairway or not. Or Cincinnati on the Big Four. Or Detroit on Michigan Central, save for the elite aboard the *Twilight Limited,* which graciously departed from La Salle Street instead because it exceeded the quota of Big Four/MC trains allowed in Central — making MC one of the few roads to originate name trains in two stations in one city. Item: the *Guide* credited South Shore's orange

M.U.'s to Central, but they really didn't enter that station proper and should have been accorded an (*i*) in the index.

Which leaves Grand Central — more central than grand, as serene as London's Marylebone, a home for also-rans: proprietor Baltimore & Ohio (if you were at home in Mount Royal and Camden in B&O's hometown, you took Grand Central, Chicago, in stride) and tenants Chicago Great Western, Pere Marquette, and Soo Line. In the ultimate paean to the building, George W. Hilton argued in September 1969 TRAINS that it combined "the function and the esthetic about as well as any piece of railroad architecture." In the same edition I termed it "the quiet place, very much the church of Chicago railroad passenger terminals." If you were eastbound on the B&O, Grand Central also gave you the most leisurely exit from the city, for its trains required 33.3 miles and 60 minutes to attain the Gary, Ind., that the Pennsy reached in 25 miles and 30 minutes.

The remaining Chicago railroad stations served the Insull traction trio, either along the elevated (Chicago Aurora & Elgin and Chicago North Shore & Milwaukee) or on the same high-level platforms that served IC electric suburban service adjacent to Central, but these facilities were rapid-transit in nature and beyond the scope of this critique save in the context of being three more reasons to change stations.

I spent a lot of hours and blocks transferring between these stations in Chicago, first in the limos of Parmelee and later in the scruffy blue-and-white mini-buses of Railroad Transfer if I availed myself of the free service for interline passengers, or by cab if connections were close. *Super*-to-*Afternoon Hi, Morning Hi* to *Seminole,* Milwaukee 58 to *Shenandoah,* and the like. And each time I pondered how the rivalry of the railroad age had come back to haunt the industry when it had to face intermodal competition.

There was a negativism about all the station changing, something equivalent to throwing on all the coach lights at 3:25 a.m. in Evansville for a ticket check, or that blue sign DINING CAR IN THE OPPOSITE DIRECTION at the end of the Pullman aisle, or that admonition in every timetable: "In event of any disagreement with Conductors or Agents relative to ticket conditions, privileges allowed, etc., passengers should pay the fare required, take receipt, and refer case for adjustment to the General Passenger Agent."

How I envied the patrons of the true union stations in Cincinnati, Denver, Jacksonville, Kansas City, Los Angeles, New Orleans (eventually), Tampa, St. Louis, and St. Paul — yes, and Washington, D.C. Chicago was the railroad capital of the world (to quote TRAINS), but just try transporting self and luggage from *a* to *g* or *b* to *f*! Especially in a snowstorm. Logically, one of the Interstate Commerce Commission's first directives in 1887 should have been the restriction of separated passenger stations to those communities with clement climes say, like New Orleans.

Interline passengers passing through Chicago were blessed or damned by origin and/or destination. Pity the soul arriving from Dyersburg, Tenn., on IC's *Creole* and ticketed through to Benton Harbor, Mich., on PM No. 2; nothing to do about it but Parmelee 4752 feet from *b* to *d.* Conversely, Milwaukeeans tended to take the Union Station concourse of least resistance, taking the Milwaukee into Chicago and Pennsy to New York or Alton to St. Louis or the Q to Denver — or if bound for southern California, North Western to Chicago, connecting in its station there for the *City of Los Angeles* or the *Challenger.*

The show (call it vaudeville) is over now. What Frank Donovan thought would await "until the millennium when a real union station is built" came about after the railroads skeletonized their passenger service . . . and Amtrak picked up just half the bones . . . and — this was the tricky part — found a way to get IC's trains across town. A new union wasn't needed. The existing one, even with its concourse side squashed into contours of a Trailways terminal, managed the mission.

So now you can go from Memphis to St. Paul, if not St. Joe, from Gaithersburg to Gallup, and from Toledo to Tomah without riding rubber from, respectively, *d* to *c, b* to *a,* or *e* to *c.* Of course, all the intercity trains in and out of Chicago are red, white, and blue, most of the domes are gone, the name PULLMAN only appears on one sleeper (honoring a man rather than a company), and there're no more F's and E's, much less any K4's and O-5's. Franklin Parmelee, the work you began in 1863 is done. The trains are united in Union at last, just like the planes in O'Hare but a lot closer together. ɪ

The mystique of electrification

When we regarded electric traction as noncontagious — hence safe

I IN the innocence of youth I once asked my father if the railroad would ever electrify its line through our town. We lived in a small Georgia county seat, Monticello, on a mixed-train branch of the Central of Georgia — just up the pike from Hillsboro and not far from Shady Dale. Not being one to depreciate the imagination of a son who had just finished *Tom Swift and His Electric Locomotive,* Dad weighed the question carefully and replied that he didn't think so but that possibly instead the CofG might purchase one of those gas-electric cars he'd read about. Satisfied, I went back to watching our 2-8-0's and left electrification in the capable hands of Tom and Mr. Damon.

Unbeknownst to me, the railroads had reached the same conclusion. The industry had dabbled with the idea of steamless operation since 1895, when the Baltimore & Ohio laid third rail inside its Baltimore tunnels. And even before. As early as 1883 President Henry Villard of the Northern Pacific politely ushered out of his office a man who wanted to discuss a better design of steam locomotive. The proposal was academic, Villard said; the future belonged to electric power.

Villard had company. In 1912 Edward Hungerford wrote of a Chicago traffic manager who said, "The first railroad that electrifies for the thousand or less miles between this town and New York is going to get all the rich passenger business. Not a big portion of it, mind you, but every single blessed bit of it!"

So convinced of the efficacy of electric traction was James J. Hill that he contemplated wires over his new Spokane, Portland & Seattle in 1906. In 1912 Rio Grande announced that work would be started soon on electrifying its entire line. In 1916 Great Northern was figuring the cost of catenary for its Spokane-Seattle main. In 1923 Santa Fe was thinking of eliminating its desert water problems once and for all with electric power. In 1924 Canadian Pacific was leaning toward the proposition that the way to conquer the Rockies was with pantographs.

Yet the U. S. peaked out with only 3100 of its steam-road route-miles — or 1.23 per cent — under catenary or beside third-rail; that figure had declined to 2061 miles by 1957, and is below 1900 today — no more than Poland or Spain possesses.

Some never bought the electrification pitch. Wrote L. F. Loree: "By looking with optimism upon all phases of electrical working and predicating the most efficient installation, and looking with pessimism upon steam operation, and taking for contrast a line poorly equipped and badly worked, a very favorable case may be drawn up for the use of electricity." Many who did subscribe to the Edison ethic couldn't come up with the money or were confused by the A.C. vs. D.C. debate — or both. Any chance that catenary had in my youth was killed by the depression (except on the Pennsy, which strung wire down to Washington and out to Harrisburg on the strength of RFC and WPA loans) and by the diesel. In the indexes of aging volumes of the trade press one finds that ELECTRIFICATION immediately precedes ELECTRO-MOTIVE COMPANY, and the two listings tell of dreams realized and unrealized.

The scarcity of electric traction in America gave it an allure for us train-watchers. Many of us made the mistake of dismissing the diesel as a novelty, only to focus upon it our resentment as steam departed. Not so with the electric. Electrification was something fixed, noncontagious, safe. Only the Pennsy really took it seriously, and The Standard Railroad of the World did

Prototype for Tom Swift's invention: Milwaukee Road's first GE boxcabs. Photo by Fred Matthews.

many nonstandard things. We could recite the endless advantages of electrification with impunity because we knew that its one disadvantage — cost — canceled them all out. That didn't explain how one notoriously weak road, the Milwaukee, owned the longest electrified routes on the continent; but then, nobody has yet explained how the Milwaukee has lived with a line out to Seattle (of which 662 miles are under wire) anyway. We simply knew that electrification occurred only where there was extraordinary, passenger-oriented schedule frequency (New Haven and Pennsy), a mountain that even a Triplex couldn't master (Virginian), a station that disapproved of cinders (Cleveland Union Terminal), a tunnel susceptible to smoke (Great Northern), or a public-spirited commuter operation (Illinois Central).

Romantically, Milwaukee Road topped them all. The St. Paul always employed the words of Thomas Edison by way of preamble: "... *No grinding, no jerking, no puffing, no pulling, no straining, no disturbed slumbers — just a keen sense of moving swiftly, of being propelled by power vastly in excess of requirements. You ride with ease — you are at ease — it is the very last word in transportation.*" Those italicized words, strung poemlike beneath a portrait of the *Olympian* ascending the Cascades behind a bipolar, mesmerized one for the hard sell that followed.

"Cinders that blind, and sparks that fall in red-hot showers, and gases that fill the tunnels and tight-sealed cars with suffocating fumes — all these are a memory of less progressive ways, forgotten now except for the contrast of unalloyed delight made possible by this newer, better way." So shouted the St. Paul of "the wonder of 'White Coal'" (read hydroelectric power) propelling "the world's mightiest locomotives" (also "Kings of the Rails") over "the world's longest electrified railroad."

CMStP&P had everything going for it: orange passenger trains with herculean names; a complete catalog of power from steeple-cab B-B switchers to articulated 28-wheeled, 521,200-pound passenger haulers; regenerative braking ("The restored current automatically sets back the power company's meters and credits the Railway with the amount. Electricity keeping its own books, forsooth!"); scenery (the Rockies and the Cascades under trolley); and longevity (where else did one encounter World War I–era motors helping — even M.U.'d with — GP9's?). Milwaukee's electrification had everything but side rods.

Pennsy, conversely, began with side rods — with the DD1. It was the first electric I ever saw. One came clanking past my Pullman window at Manhattan Transfer, N. Y., after having propelled us out of Penn Station, under the Hudson, and up into sunlight where a K4 waited to relay us to Washington. I didn't know it then, in the early 1930's, but PRR was embarking upon electrification minus Milwaukee's romanticism, with the cool detachment of a trunk line which needed something more than steam to keep its traffic tide fluid. PRR was as close as we got in the U. S. to European-style electrification: multiple-track, high-level platforms, flying junctions, expresses and commuter rushes and tonnage — all under 11,000-volt catenary. And after a shaky, steam-inspired start with the likes of O1 4-4-4's and P5 4-6-4's, the system came on us with the GG1 — the ultimate machine, the timeless machine, the beautiful machine.

Everything that PRR-under-wires was and is is summed up below the concourse of 30th Street Station, Philadelphia. One stands there on the crowded platform, and the announcer begins calling the train, and one rechecks his car number and goes to the appointed platform location, and the hole of daylight in the distance is suddenly occupied by this cyclops creature which comes humming past, a wizened engineer hanging on its barred cab window, the air full of the rush of wind and the smell of warm brake shoes — and, just like that, one is aboard, just sitting down, and with a slight lurch the GG1 is off again. *That* is big-time electric railroading to me, and I'm not so sure I've ever seen anything across the Atlantic as moving, if only because of the discrepancy between our clearance diagrams and those of BR, DB, SNCF, FS, and SBB.

It's a pity PRR never electrified across the Alleghenies. Horse Shoe was definitely not P5 or GG1 territory. Broad Street HQ would have had to come up with something more brutish to cope with the mountains, something more along the lines of the "Big Liz" FF1 experiment of 1917; and all enthusiasts are the poorer because such plans did not come to pass.

I mean no affront to New Haven by all this emphasis on CMStP&P and PRR. NH was stringing wire in 1895, amassed a parallel traction empire, operated a short but very intensive electric network (in 1957 the road had 127 route-miles but 453 track-miles electrified), thought nothing about running by third-rail into Grand Central and under catenary across Hell Gate to reach Penn Station, sponsored some of the grandest motors in the business, and ordered the last passenger units.

New Haven, Conn., itself was surely one of the most interesting train-watching sites in the land (and still is not bad today). There was a season when ultragraceful GE-built 2-C+C2's of class EP-4 were spelled there either by back-to-back Alco DL-109 diesel cabs or by beetle-browed Pacifics and streamlined 4-6-4's in steam. A shrewd observer might have predicted then that this contest of wills would be settled by electrification remaining inviolate and steam giving way to diesel. But no soothsayer, however blessed, could have predicted diesel-electric-electric FL9's passing right through New Haven without change and, ultimately, GG1's showing up in the dress of a new owner.

Elsewhere, U. S. electrification was rather less than Edison had extolled it. Water-level, passenger-minded, PRR-contending New York Central had a wealth of electric traction experience — but all confined to third rails in and near New York, Cleveland, and Detroit. It was as if electric propulsion was fine for GCT's and CUT's and commuters and tunnels. But once open countryside was reached at Harmon or Linndale, the romance was rent by the mighty Hudson. Imagine a Walter L. Greene calendar of Centuries passing in the night behind 2-C+C-2's . . . I can't, can you? "Social electrification" is what John W. Barriger termed Central's kind of juice. Electricity was there for essentially a nontraction purpose. The same was true of the wires strung through Hoosac and Cascade tunnels, and the diesel proved the point when it eclipsed the motors employed through both bores.

Virginian: now there was a he-man, no-nonsense electrification. Patterned on an older system of neighbor N&W, VGN's excursion in catenary was designed to do what Mallets couldn't do — move coal in 6000-ton trainloads up 14 miles' worth of 2.07 per cent at a steady 14 mph. The power employed, one on the point and one shoving, were three semipermanently coupled side-rodded 1-D-1's which, in triumvirate, weighed almost a million pounds on drivers and exerted 231,000 pounds tractive effort. I can see them now, churning their way downgrade under regenerative braking ("Electricity keeping its own books, forsooth!") through a bucolic Virginia, 9000 tons on the drawbar (trains were filled out at the summit where the helper cut off), mass transportation personified . . . and I tell you, those were locomotives.

Locomotives and electrics are not compatible. So says John W. Barriger. "Let it be remembered that the derivation of the word 'locomotive' implies the capacity of self movement,' he opines. "It is therefore an inaccuracy of terminology to call one drawing its power from an overhead wire or third rail, a locomotive. The first syllable of the word then becomes incorrect when the machine does not produce the power by which it moves itself. What is commonly called an electric locomotive is actually an electromotive."

Well, now — General Motors would never have stood still for that; the alternative terms such as motor and juice jack are either less than adequate or flip; and the authorities from GE to Westinghouse unabashedly termed electrics locomotives.

It hurts me to part company with Mr. B on the matter, because he is Mr. B, and because, technically and semantically, he is right. But when you saw a brace of VGN "Jugheads" bringing tidewaterbound coal toward you, or when you wait today at 30th Street for the *Congressional* to show, that's just got to be a locomotive on the point — never mind that catenary which is the true source of its seemingly limitless energy.

John W. Barriger won't agree, but he'll understand. ℐ

Nobody else's RR

I THE artist can shrug off the limitations of the lens, even of the eye, and record what intrigues the mind and the imagination. For instance, if you must be specific, we're looking beyond the end of the high-level platforms at Newark, N. J., and into the maw of the lift bridges across the Passaic River as an eastbound train starts to reel in the last 10 miles to Manhattan. But the brush has swept more (and less) than detail onto French watercolor paper. For what we have here is a cameo, a glimpse, a 10,000-words-in-one-picture of urban Pennsylvania Railroad railroading: multiple-track main line (155 pounds to the yard per rail?), position-light signal, taut catenary, soaring steelwork, Loewyized GG1. This is the diametric opposite of Soo in Thief River Falls, SP in San Luis Obispo, SR in Meridian. This is Pennsy full strength, undiluted by density or distance (is it possible that this same railroad reaches all the way out to Lake Michigan and the Mississippi?). And this is Pennsy when passengers equaled prestige.

The eye is anchored by that striped and blurred 2-C+C-2 mechanism, is it not, inhaling 11,000 volts of alternating current and spreading the energy through insulated innards so that the wizened guy in the cap behind cab window bars can notch back on a lever causing a dozen great spoked driving wheels to rotate with a force that 880 or 1000 tons behind cannot resist? And then the eye is drawn inexorably skyward through the wire-webbed, signal-studded superstructure and . . .

. . . why it's just PRR and nobody else's RR.

But Land of Goshen, I-n-d.: don't look for a keystone birthmark on me. I was as awed an alien in Newark, N. J., as was Alan Pegler's LNER 4472 in Cut Bank, Montana. Newark wasn't my kind of USRA/semaphore/bay window/take-water-in-Worthville country.

But it was a place to see and feel and hear Pennsy . . . and for TRAINS Art Director George Gloff, an artist from streetcar-and-interurban Wisconsin, to grasp its singularity. I

129

Tractive effort of the adjective

By Wake Hoagland

HISTORY has sung the praises of the brave engineer, stirred us with accounts of the builders who spiked rails to the Pacific in spite of snow and Sioux, and paid homage to the daring of those who stole and recaptured the *General* on a misty day in 1862. All this is well and good, but history is partial and plays favorites. She has shamefully neglected a man among men, a profession of the high iron that has too long gone unsung.

Isn't it time someone extolled the nerve and imagination and utter lack of modesty of the railroad advertising agent, the man who prepared copy in the era before agencies and account executives and charcoal suits? Specifically, honors are due those hardy souls who enlivened the pages of the *Official Guide*. Armed with nothing more than ink and a dictionary, they strode into a jungle of uniform equipment, a cinder for every eye, and dog-eat-dog competition. And with the somber realization that their words would reach only ticket agents at best and were destined to gather dust in countless flagstop depots on the lone prairie — which is where all good and dog-eared *Guides* end their days.

Hardly inspiration for great writing — no chance of Pulitzers or letters-to-the-editor or political reverberations. And yet the ad men of old acquitted themselves nobly. Hark to the persuasive prose of 1883:

"The Chicago and North-western Railway is the *oldest, best equipped, and best constructed* road in the West."

Nice handling of italic, that, and not a bit too liberal either, in view of the fact that Burlington viewed itself as THE PEOPLE'S FAVORITE LINE BETWEEN ALL POINTS (what a wonderfully democratic point of view for a young America!) and was ready to document its case with these obviously uncontroversial points: "Their track is steel. Their trains are rolling palaces. They wait for their connections and always arrive on time."

Pity the railroad that was sparing in its use of superlatives — at least, west of Chicago. No claim was too big, no opinion too lavish. The alert ticket agent no doubt looked askance at the road which pulled its punches. How much better to specify the GREAT ROCK ISLAND ROUTE, secure in the knowledge that it offered "smooth track, safe bridges, Union Depots at all connecting points, Fast Express Trains, composed of COMMODIOUS, WELL VENTILATED, WELL HEATED, FINELY UPHOLSTERED and ELEGANT DAY COACHES, a line of the MOST MAGNIFICENT HORTON RECLINING CHAIR CARS ever built; PULLMAN'S latest designed and handsomest PALACE SLEEPING CARS, and DINING CARS that are acknowledged by press and people to be the FINEST RUN UPON ANY ROAD IN THE COUNTRY, and in which superior meals are served to travelers at the low rate of SEVENTY-FIVE CENTS EACH.

At this distance it is difficult to believe that such impressive prose described banging along through Iowa on open-platform cars behind a 4-4-0, even though those meals probably wouldn't require an apologist — even in 1956.

But the years moved on and no men were more alert to the stepped-up pace in reading intelligence than the railroad ad writers. By 1890 the Pennsylvania could express an observation car in terms of how "broad plate windows admit a wide expanse of light, and the broad platform at the rear makes a pleasant open-air observatory in fair weather." Pennsy was even ready for woman suffrage with such solicitous comment for the fair sex as this: "Ladies could never before travel in such comfort. For their convenience a waiting-maid is assigned to each train, whose duty it is to serve as ladies' maid in all that the term implies. Ladies without escort, ladies with children, and invalids, are the particular objects of their care." And the observation naturally "forms a magnificent sitting-room for ladies." Quite obviously the *New York & Chicago Limited* was the only train on which little Nell could safely ride out to Aunt Maud's in Fort Wayne.

By the turn of the century the boys had been separated from the men in the ad game and certain fundamentals were in the rulebook. For example, you had to have A Slogan or be A Route. Just being a plain railroad wasn't enough. To illustrate:

The Maple Leaf Route — Chicago Great Western.

America's Most Popular Railway — Alton.

Natural Gas Route — Lake Erie & Western.

The Great Four-Track Trunk Line of the United States — New York Central.

35th Parallel Route — Choctaw, Oklahoma & Gulf.

The Rhine, the Alps, and the Battlefield Line — Chesapeake & Ohio.

Best Line to Texas — Frisco.

The Lookout Mountain Route — Nashville, Chattanooga & St. Louis.

Such banners were merely a good starter. There was a pressing need for young men who could lift a quill pen and dash off a sales message with impact. Colorado & Southern ("The Colorado Road") had such a man: "You know when traveling one's meals are either an abomination or a delight. OURS ARE IN THE LATTER CLASS."

Baltimore & Ohio managed to be reasonably clever in promoting the Finest Daylight Train in the World — the New York-Washington *Royal Limited*. "Five states in five hours," it said in a count that included the ferry across the Hudson. Nice play on symmetry. Delaware & Hudson even got its Camelbacks into the act by pointing up the fact of "Anthracite Coal exclusively, insuring freedom from dust and smoke." Talk like that was asking for it, sort of a pioneer version of the recent controversy about which cigarette had the least nicotine. Erie quickly pointed out that it was the only Chicago–New York line without tunnels, while Soo and Great Northern prided themselves on the operation of vacuum-cleaned equipment. Santa Fe and Southern Pacific were quick to allay the fears of the ladies with the words "oil-sprinkled roadbed" and, eventually, with the magic, enviable stamp of cleanliness: "Oil-burning locomotives." Who wouldn't like a nickel for every time those words have appeared in the *Guide*!

The coal-burners just looked the other way and shouted all the louder about the virtues of wide vestibules, electric lights, high-speed brakes, paddle fans, and all-steel consists.

The reputation of a railroad's top varnish continued to be the ad man's priority assignment. Frisco, for instance, ran a full-pager headed by a sketch of a mustachioed conductor standing beside his train at a lonely telegraph office and reading flimsies by lantern light:

"Take siding at Hillsdale for No. 105," ran the headline. Then this: "All along the route from Kansas City to Jacksonville train dispatchers are sending train orders to clear the track ahead of No. 105, the 'KANSAS CITY–FLORIDA SPECIAL.' Not merely a Through Sleeper, but a complete, independent train . . . No changes en route, except for fresh engines and freshly stocked Diners. No missed connections — no missed meals. A continuous ride all the way from Kansas City to Jacksonville."

Was there a shoe drummer in 1911 with soul so dead that he didn't yearn to ride aboard such a train of trains. How satisfying to lie abed in your "Electric-Lighted D. R. Sleeper" and know that green-eyeshaded dispatchers were clearing the track for No. 105.

Illinois Central vouchsafed that there was "no safer or finer train" than its 1913-model *Seminole Limited.* Not a bad effort, but what less could be said in defense of the *Santa Fe deLuxe's* $25 extra fare than "America's finest train," even if the slogan did somewhat conflict with the same road's *California Limited,* which, as every smart traveler knew, was the "King of the limiteds"? That one sort of conjures up MGM's lion.

San Antonio & Aransas Pass — which unabashedly labeled itself the SAP route — was perhaps nearer the heart of the businessman when it ballyhooed the *Davy Crockett* as "the train that always runs on time." A glance at its schedule and you could see why, but then, *Davy* wasn't extra fare.

Judging from the *Guide's* exhortations, the way to a man's purse was via his stomach. Long before the Spanish-American War, the Chicago & North Western felt the issue strong enough to label itself The Dining Car Line. Of course, in those days many a road — Santa Fe, for one — was still herding its passengers into lunchrooms while the engine took water, and the concept of filets at 50 miles an hour was akin to a 42-inch center of gravity in our time. A generation and more later, everybody had diners, so advertising had to draw a distinction between excellent and merely adequate fare. "Famously good" meals were to be had aboard Northern Pacific while Milwaukee served "meals by Rector of Broadway fame." Come 1929 and the brand-new *Erie Limited* had dining car service "extraordinary," and the *Chief* boasted menus "without a parallel in American railroading."

Came the depression and science handed the ad man a new challenge: air conditioning. Milwaukee Road went medic with the advice that "filtered air renewed every five minutes" flowed through its new coaches; Pennsy, as you might expect, boasted The Largest Fleet of Air-Conditioned Trains in the World; and Chessie insinuated something or other by saying its cars were "genuinely" A.C.

The diesel brought out the old-line ad writer in his last no-holds-barred effort. Baltimore & Ohio was typical. Diesels, said B&O, assured "a smooth, comfortable ride; eliminating the need for frequent changes of engines on long runs." Which was an unkind but rather accurate dig at its rival's elderly K4's. Seaboard was more specific. Gloriously aware that it had made *the* choice buying 6000-horsepower EMD's while rival Coast Line put its money on Baldwin 4-8-4's, SAL termed its engines the "world's largest-mightiest" and for the benefit of the uninformed ticket stamper pointed out that "in the event that any of the six engines should develop trouble, it can be cut out and repaired en route, while the train continues without delay."

Peace really pulled the rug out from under the old railroad advertising agent. No longer was there a need to come through with adjectives on what a railroad could not fulfill in technology. With every railroad possessing sootless, cinderless, jerkless, non-change trains protected by "the newest type electrically operated safety signals," why what could a man do but hang up his black sleeve protectors and take his pension?

Our world is a more honest but somber place since he departed. ⫯

Editor's note: Occasionally errors slipped through the editing and proofreading processes. Usually alert readers wrote in. If they didn't and Morgan felt it was necessary put the correction in print, he'd write a letter to the editor from Wake Hoagland. Through the years Hoagland also wrote a few short essays for Trains *on subjects less weighty than Morgan's usual fare.*

Before drive-ins and convertibles

JUST before Victoria died, before there was such a catastrophe as a world war and when railroads competed only with each other for passengers, there waltzed onto the scene Phoebe Snow — that mythical maiden in white who was "wont to go by train to Buffalo." By Lackawanna train, that is, because white gowns were never smudged by the Camelbacks that burned anthracite. But, bless us, here we espy Phoebe neglecting her commercial to flirt with a pair of young swains on the open platform of the *Lackawanna Limited*'s parlor-observation. The straw-hatted chaps are making a brave show of indifference, but our money is on that artful stance in the doorway to win. Say, if there's any slack in No. 3, that boy in the jacket is going to be sitting on the track when the engineer's finished taking water.

As for you, Phoebe — cut that out and get back to selling your "bright and snowy white on the Road of Anthracite." ⌶

Photo from the collection of George A. Moffitt.

Nominating the New Haven

For connoisseurs of the curious

CAUTION: This critique is intended solely for the information and enjoyment of those readers for whom the New York, New Haven & Hartford has until now been as remote as the London, Tilbury & Southend or the North Western Railway of India, and its dissemination to, and any perusal by, members of the New Haven Railroad Historical & Technical Association without the express written consent of the author is discouraged. Which is to say, the NHRH&TA has, with British tenacity and thoroughness, documented the why and wherefore of every locomotive of its namesake from electric 01 to 3-cylinder steam switcher 3615; and the society patently could, if asked, count every crosstie between Provincetown, Mass., and Campbell Hall, N.Y. Thus, the data hereinafter discussed would be redundant to subscribers of the society's Shoreliner, *although the thrust of its presentation could generate bemusement. For what these Shoreliners take for granted will, I submit, confound the unwashed amongst us.*

Now, if NHRH&TA members have left the room, let us begin. Geographically, the New Haven was compact. The entire system would have fit inside Florida without so much as a bumper post touching the waters of the Atlantic Ocean or the Gulf of Mexico. Indeed, the old Atlantic Coast Line had more route-miles in Florida than New Haven owned in total. Or, the New Haven could have been placed inside central Nevada without its rails intersecting those of any other carrier.

Thirty years ago, the New Haven compared favorably in length with the Texas & Pacific. Otherwise, their disparity was all but total, exemplified by the fact that T&P's 1166-mile New Orleans–El Paso sleeper haul took two nights and a day, whereas NH's 231-mile Boston–New York *Owl* barely qualified for Mr. Pullman's services. Consider this 1953 comparison:

	NH	T&P
Route-miles	1778	1833
Track-miles	3812	2697
Passenger train-miles	10,127,591	2,368,186
Freight train-miles	3,597,653	4,114,134
Average freight haul (miles)	157	236
Freight to all traffic (%)	58	87
Railway operating revenues (millions)	$165	$86.4
Net income (millions)	$6	$11
Employees	18,948	7,946
Locomotives	430	202
Switchers (included in above)	137	66

These figures tell us that (1) route-miles are no index of a railroad's character; (2) New Haven was, for better or for worse, wedded to the passenger; (3) short hauls imply many terminals, i.e., yard engines; (4) NH's *modus operandi* resulted in an outsize payroll and number of track-miles; (5) NH was peculiarly susceptible to highway competition; and (6) it can be easier to turn a buck in railroading in Texas than in Connecticut. What the statistics do not say is that almost two-thirds of the New Haven's passenger business was commutation or that the road terminated most of its freight traffic or that it was one of few carriers to simultaneously operate mainline steam, diesel, and electric motive power. Or that New Haven fielded, for its size, the most diverse diesel locomotive roster in the land. T&P, incidentally, was true-blue GM, buying every last one of its own diesels with a La Grange imprint.

Now, now we're getting to the point of an identifiable fascination of the New York, New Haven & Hartford for outlanders . . . its dieseldom. Which is not to denigrate, you understand, the railroad's pre-internal-combustion locomotive stance.

New Haven in steam was, if not ordinary, scarcely extraordinary. Glancing across its post-1900 roster, one is attracted to its excursions into the Alco-inspired three-cylinder extravaganza of the 1920's, a net of 13 4-8-2's and 16 0-8-0's. Only the Pennsylvania's K4's come readily to mind as equals of New Haven's I-4's as Pacifics in the sense of holding down for 30 years what the British would term top-link express duties. Who could fault the streamlining of the I-5 Hudsons (or their performance, once their counterbalancing problems were contained)? And, if mundane in point of specification, the road's 2-10-2's in four subclasses will remain synonymous with the ridge-ridden Maybrook, N.Y.–New Haven, Conn., bridge line. NH had no articulateds, no experimentals (if you exclude McClellon boilers with water-tube fileboxes), no Super-Power other than the 10 I-5's — small granger Chicago Great Western possessed as much, perhaps more, intrigue for the steam student. And yet New Haven's engines were a distinctive lot, perchance rendered a trifle odd by the scarcity of those all-American wheel arrangements, the 2-8-0 and 2-8-2, with a mere 15 of the former and 38 of the latter on the roster by 1939.

In electrification, New Haven excelled in both time and technology. NH was the first (1907) steam road to install a major passenger/freight mainline electrification, one automatically rendered complex by the necessity for its motors to employ both 11,000-volt catenary-fed A.C. and 660-volt third-rail D.C. power (the latter for entry into Grand Central Terminal, New York). What a lovely line of locomotives rolled beneath NH's distinctive triangular cross-section catenary, the gamut from side-rodded box-cabs to the 1-C-1+1-C-1 EP-2's (which shared builder, quill drive, and appearance with Milwaukee Road's EP-3's) to the grand EP-3 and EP-4 77-footers (in both orthodox and streamlined contours) to the striped-beast C-C rectifiers. Item: Those zero-prefixed numbers New Haven used on its non-steam motive power to differentiate it from the coalburning breed intrigue;

Denver & Intermountain's narrow-gauge traction, albeit anchored by a decimal (as in .01), comes to mind, as do Detroit Edison's unit-train C-C diesels — but what else? A book could be written about, and an engineering landmark award has been accorded, a railroad propulsion system whose great loss was that it was stymied in New Haven instead of achieving its natural eastern terminal of South Station, Boston. The sole consolation we may draw from this arbitrary halt is that the aforementioned I-5 4-6-4's, as well as the balance of this report, would have been largely negated by an all-electric New York–Boston Shore Line.

Dieselization on the New Haven began innocently, indeed logically, enough — with purchase of an Alco demonstrator in 1931. A railroad which had to import every ton of coal it burned, a railroad for which traction motors were second nature, a railroad for which switching was "a very real and important problem," and a railroad with an Alco-majority roster, could have been expected to have been an early employer of Schenectady's answer to the 0-6-0. There was every reason to assume that New Haven would remain faithful to Alco forever (in 1931, the word "forever" seemed synonymous with both builder and carrier). In terms of internal combustion, that assumption held for almost two decades — if one forgives the single aberration of Nos. 0901-0910, customized 600 h.p. General Electrics, half with Ingersoll-Rand engines, half with Cooper-Bessemer engines, both power-plants interchangeable. One need not forgive the 19 little GE 380 h.p. 44-tonners that entered the roster during 1941–1945 . . . for in those years, Alco-GE jointly merchandised diesels and the former had no equivalent lightweight in its catalog.

Ultimately, New Haven rostered 117 Alco yard engines with McIntosh & Seymour inline 6-cylinder engines — in models HH600, HH660, S1, and S2, and in 600, 630, 660, and 1000 h.p. sizes.

Enter the DL109 . . . and in its wake the question: Have any production road diesels in the Western World been accorded so much acclaim relative to their numbers and range of operation? Consider that only 74 units' worth of these Otto Kuhler-styled AlA-AlA's with "low-speed" engines* were constructed, of which

---

* The discrepancy was marginal, i.e., 740 rpm for the 4-cycle, 6-cylinder, 12½ x 13-inch M&S 539 vs. 800 rpm for an equivalently rated GM 2-cycle, V-12, 8½ x 10-inch 567.

New Haven's 81 per cent worked out their lives in a thumbnail corner of the country. Yet is there a train-watcher alive who is not familiar with the legend of the dual-service diesels which hauled passengers by day and tonnage by night?

(Why New Haven and Alco-GE were allowed to claim the first mainline dual-service diesels is a mystery, for Great Northern installed Nos. 5700A&B and 5701A&B, a pair of 2700 h.p. EMD A-B FT's, in joint passenger-freight service between the Twin Cities and Duluth in the summer of 1941, following a successful test of two units of FT demonstrator 103 on such schedules. NH's first DL109 operation, on the other hand, occurred December 13, 1941, when the original pair replaced steam on train 175, the *Colonial,* out of Boston. Nevertheless, GN's boiler-fitted, 89-mph FT's soldiered unsung while the world worshipped at the Shore Line shrine of the 4000 h.p. "0700's" that could take the place of a streamlined 4-6-4 on the *Yankee Clipper* or a 4-8-2 on symbol freight OB-2.)

The DL109, tolerated by the handful of other roads that acquired it, was so warmly embraced by the New Haven that the War Production Board exempted it from a ban on non-EMD diesel road locomotive production during WWII, and NH's 60 units nearly attained a normal 15-year diesel depreciation lifespan, the final survivor not ending revenue service until 1959.

If the DL109's initiated New Haven's penchant for a difference in dieseldom, the railroad resumed orthodoxy after World War II with a textbook replacement of steam on its 124-mile Maybrook line in 1947. In one fell swoop, 45 Alco-GE FA and FB 1500 h.p. B-B's, marshalled in 15 4500 h.p. A-B-A sets, displaced 46 2-10-2's, eliminated an eastbound 1.15-per-cent helper district, reduced running time on trains of perishables by an hour, and exceeded estimated annual savings of 1.3 million dollars. Item: In 1947, NH had the seventh largest diesel fleet in the U. S. And the railroad simultaneously enlarged the hold of Alco's 244-model V12's on its operations by building a roster of 17 RS2 road-switchers, all fitted with boilers for optional passenger duties, and by adding (what else?) 27 units' worth of the DL109's successor, the great PA-1 passenger cab. A dozen little 1000 h.p. RS1 road-switchers fleshed out the all-Alco content of New Haven's postwar diesel purchases through 1949.

DL109s, shown at Canton Junction, Massachusetts, were the first evidence of New Haven's tendency toward the unorthodox. Left-handed semaphores testify to NH's intention to extend its electrification to Boston. NH photo.

New Haven at this juncture was a siren Schenectady success story, one to count with nearby Delaware & Hudson and faraway Spokane, Portland & Seattle.

The diesel disparity of New Haven began innocuously enough in 1950. Nationally, diesel orders were peaking, NH was driving hard to drop the fires on its elderly and worn-out steam roster (the only modern members of which were the 12-year-old I-5 Hudsons), the builders were backlogged with orders. Thus, installation of 10 Loewy-styled Fairbanks-Morse H16-44 road-switchers and 10 Lima-Hamilton 1000 h.p. yard units, in a year when the road was simultaneously assembling a fleet of 44 Alco RS3's, was surely understandable. Other roads of greater, lesser and equal route mileage — Rock Island, Western Maryland, and Central of Georgia come to mind — also purchased an assortment of makes and models in their eagerness to eliminate steam.

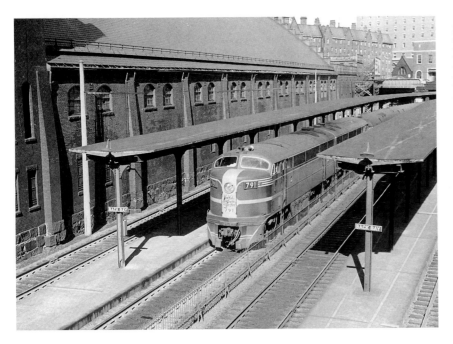

Fairbanks-Morse CPA24-5s packed more power into less length and less weight than a PA. Photo by Lewis A. Harlow.

The appearance on the New Haven of 10 FM 2400 h.p. C-Line passenger B-A1A's in 1951–1952 strikes one as odd — until allowance is made for the facts that FM was hard-selling its new line, the first two of NH's C-Liners were demonstrators, and FM's CPA24-5's packed more power into less length and weight than a PA. In 1952, when New Haven became officially steamless, its non-Alco diesel population totaled just 30 units in the 600 h.p.-plus range, a mere 8 per cent minority.

It is the post-dieselization, pre-second-bankruptcy locomotive record of the New Haven, then, that beggars the imagination, a baker's dozen of years in which this uncommon carrier contrived to field unique diesel-electric-electric and diesel-hydraulic-electrics, add the products of three more builders to its roster, return existing diesels to the builder for upgrading, and de-electrify and re-electrify line-haul freight operations west of New Haven, all without severing its traditional Alco alliance. All this

may be credited to a brew of the strong personalities of the Messrs. Dumaines, McGinnis, and Alpert, a proxy fight, a flyer in low-center-of-gravity single-axle lightweights, a contraction in maintenance facilities, and a preoccupation with eliminating the engine change in New Haven.

During the years 1956–1965 the railroad added 209 diesels in 9 models and 5 makes, as follows: Alco — 15 RS-11's and 10 C-425's, Baldwin-Lima-Hamilton — 2 RP-210's; Electro-Motive — 20 SW1200's, 30 GP9's, and 60 FL9's; Fairbanks-Morse — 2 P12-42's and 15 H16-44's; General Electric — 25 U25B's.

Let us discuss passengers first. If one excludes the Long Island on grounds of its almost total preoccupation with commuters, no American railroad was so identifiable with passengers as the New Haven. Consider its high percentage of bidirectional equipment, named trains, parlor cars, multiple track, hood units with steam generators, customized cars, passenger-to-freight revenues and train-miles, self-propelled rolling stock, and varied color schemes. (The fact that one is compelled to regard the omission from its steam heritage of a double-ended tank engine equivalent to South Station neighbor Boston & Albany's 4-6-6T as a curiosity tells us something.)

Without passengers, New Haven's incidence of iconoclasm would have declined to manageable proportions. Because of passengers, NH was obliged to electrify to gain access to Grand Central Terminal as well as cope with high traffic density. Passengers obliged its dual-power locomotives to cope with both GCT and Penn Station. Passengers caused its search for low-slung trains that could speed through the Shore Line's constant curvature. Passengers necessitated purchase of EMD's unique FL9 when the road sought a diesel which could become a straight electric at speed to cope with New York City's anti-smoke ordinance.

Passengers, however, do not explain all those makes and models on the New Haven during its last years of independence. The presence of non-Alco power was scarcely token in nature. Simultaneous acquisition of stock models from Alco (15), EMD (30) and FM (15) in 1956, then Alco and GE (10 each) in 1964, bemused as it amused us outlanders, and we found ourselves rereading Sy Reich's invaluable rosters in *Railroad* Magazine to be sure his curio counts were correct. The obvious omission of Baldwin, excepting

The FL9s looked liked everyone else's diesels to the general public, but inspection showed only the nose and cab were orthodox EMD. Photo by Don Wood.

a pair of Maybach-engined lightweights, is perhaps explained by the fact that trials of Eddystone's original road passenger cabs Nos. 2000-2001 and prototype A1A-A1A 1500 h.p. hood No. 1500 were conducted on the New Haven during or soon after the war, i.e., in the years of Alco dominance; and that the builder was exiting the trade during the road's second-generation diesel-buying spree.

What strains the mind is the proposition that theoretically a New Haven shopman or foreman could have, across his career, become familiar with inline, vee, and opposed-piston engine blocks in 2- and 4-cycle designs, normally aspirated and turbocharged, 6-, 8-, 12, and 16-cylinder sizes, and 160 to 2400 h.p. ratings, all attended by a similar complication of controls, generators, traction motors, and running gear. And, presumably, an equal disparity in windshield wipers, cab heaters, gauges, and whatever. Perhaps he could have found someone in Altoona or Silvis to talk his language, but the relative size of either Pennsylvania or Rock Island presumes more specialization of employment in terms of who worked on what.

The drama is over now, and the program is of concern only to connoisseurs of the curious. Poor old New Haven in the years since 1968 has been merged into Penn Central, divided up between Conrail and Amtrak, and/or spun off to lessors such as Providence & Worcester and neighbors like Boston & Maine. A fire on the great 210-foot-high bridge across the Hudson at Poughkeepsie, N.Y., severed the Maybrook line, and western connections Erie, Lehigh & Hudson River, Lehigh & New England, and New York, Ontario & Western have joined the New Haven in history.

Only a few Budd cars live on from the lineage of nonelectric self-propelled cars and trains that began in 1897 with a steam motor-nee-diner and embraced the Comet, railbuses, gas-electrics, a company-built steam train, and RDC-1's through -4's, including a pair with locomotive-style cabs.

The locomotive roster that will long engage historians has been largely scrapped . . . no more Alco cabs (excepting a pair of Long Island power cars), or any FM's or Limas, of course. Where the older NH diesels do exist, they're few in number and are scattered — the GE 44-tonners to industry, Canada, and Trinidad, for example. Amtrak still has two or three ex-NH RS3's active in the Northeast Corridor for switching and work trains, and some ex-NH U25B's are intact, but stored, on Conrail. Most of EMD's influence survives, though, notably in the rebuilt FL9's but also amongst the GP9's (one, oddly enough, chants away in orange-striped silver on SEMTA commuter trains out of Detroit after a Paducah upgrading; most of the remainder are on CR and ICG, but one may be in Liberia!), and SW1200's, all still on CR's roster and held in high regard.

Amtrak has a *Yankee Clipper* in its timetable, but you can't ride it (or any other Shore Line Amtrak train) out of Boston to Grand Central Terminal.

In 1983, the New York, New Haven & Hartford, per se, is spiritually the province of the historical and technical association which bears its name, devotes its energies to preserving and promulgating its imprint upon the railroad scene, and lists 9 Shady Lane, Oxford, MA 01540 as its membership address. Which is appropriate. For any railroad with so few route-miles yet so many legends was not "born to blush unseen and waste its sweetness on the desert air" . . . even in liquidation. I

Southern in the streets

WE are in Augusta, Ga., in the spring of 1942. Paddling toward us down the brick street is a Southern Railway accommodation in the charge of Ps-2 Pacific 1321. The full foliage and the fact that the brakeman riding the pilot has doffed his coat tell us that the weather is warm, that the sun glinting off the engine's green domes and the roof of the Chevy at the curb is also raising the temperature. We would submit this idyllic scene to those who might say that the world of Norman Rockwell's paintings never existed off his canvases. But exist it did. Just look at the couple walking along the sidewalk (is he a G.I. from Camp Gordon?), absorbed in each other, oblivious to the train. Rockwell posed people for his paintings. He could have posed that girl and boy. The brakeman, too.

I like to think that the photographer, whose name, alas, is unknown, snapped this picture on a Sunday. My Uncle Frank presided over the pulpit of the First Presbyterian Church in Augusta in the 1930's, and the Southern strolled down a street nearby. He told me how on a Sunday morning the enginemen would exercise uncommon restraint over their charges lest the sermon be disturbed. See here how the stack is clear, the bell stationary. Only a flutter of steam from the turbogenerator tells us that the 1321 is alive.

I'll tell you this. If I had a time machine, I'd wind it back 37 springs to this day and place, and I'd get me one of Hoagy's old rocking chairs on the front porch of one of those big frame houses on this tree-lined brick street, and I'd just watch the Southern in that street. Lovely.

Photo from the collection of Don Wirth.

O Canada! oh yes!

I WHAT can an American write about the railway scene in Canada that a Canadian has not already said? He can set forth what railroading in that land means to us in the U. S. For it is what the Canadian assumes that awes us. Immensity, to begin with. More than 4000 route-miles, and a Sunday-to-Friday train trip's worth of immensity from Sydney, Nova Scotia, out to Vancouver, British Columbia, excluding the off-shore railways of New-foundland and Vancouver Island. To equal that journey here, you'd have to travel diagonally across the nation from northeast to southwest, say from Van Buren, Me., to San Diego via Memphis.

And the Canadians crowned their achievement by unfurling a common banner over a true transcontinental line, as their anthem has it, *From East to Western sea!* Imagine! One name — CANADIAN PACIFIC RAILWAY — on letterboards, locomotive tenders, conductors' hats, tickets, from the St. Lawrence River to the Pacific Ocean . . . as of 9:30 a.m., November 7, 1885, when the final spike was driven home at Craigellachie, B. C. And they repeated the feat in 1923 when they welded all of their other trunk lines ("the polyglot inheritance") into another and even longer coast-to-coast property, Canadian National. None of your interchanges and gateways, rate-making regions and territorial fiefdoms, and run-throughs and "East is East, and West is West, and never the twain shall meet" for the Canadians. Item: Toronto and Winnipeg have no TRRA's, no Union Railroads, no EJ&E's. What *Official Guide* reader wasn't impressed by the fact that CP and CN each required four pages' worth of maps to document lines and stations whereas the longest U. S. roads could cover theirs in two?

Canada's climate lends itself to latitude. The depth of Minnesota is sufficient to cover the maximum distance between the Canadian transcons (it occurs in Alberta) as they parallel one another from the Maritimes to Vancouver. As if our Great Northern and Northern Pacific had begun in Boston instead of St. Paul . . . and we'd left the rest of our land to the Mohawks and Seminoles and Navajos.

Of all lands, is there one more indebted to the mass-transportation, bulk-commodity nature of railroading for realizing natural resources than Canada? Ore, coal, grain, potash, sulfur, lumber — the nouns summon up panoramas of SD40's and M-636's in full cry with box cars, covered hoppers, gons, bulkhead flats, open hoppers. Again the anthem: *Where pine and maples grow, Great prairies spread and lordly rivers flow, How dear to us thy broad domain . . .*

In a railway context, now, what does Canada connote to you? The disparateness between a three-piece-suit commuter swinging

Engineering landmark: the Quebec Bridge across the St. Lawrence River. Photo by William D. Middleton.

aboard an every-20-minute GO Transit bilevel into Toronto and an Indian with arm raised at the Mile 278.6, Manitoba, flag stop for the triweekly *Hudson Bay* in adjacent provinces? Perhaps the Quebec Bridge or the structure over the Saskatchewan River at Edmonton or the viaduct at Lethbridge, Alberta, or the arch at Stoney Creek, B. C.? Uncountable nonrevenue miles of flangers bucking snowdrifts that send enough Canadians south each winter for Florida motels to fly the maple leaf on their flagpoles? Prairies punctuated by grain elevator exclamation marks? All the pleasant names, past and present — the Esquimalt & Nanaimos, Pacific Great Easterns, Dominion Atlantics, and Temiscouatas? Or the Spiral Tunnels, which is to say an underground Tehachapi in spades?

Give my generation the Elesco closed-type feedwater heater. Carried ahead of the stack on the smokebox of everything worth a trailing truck and a few that were not, this tube-filled vessel was surely the locomotive signature of Canada. What better locale to preheat boiler water? And what other auxiliary could have added so much authority to the helm of wheat extras and pool trains and the *Dominion*? I delighted in these bundle-type heaters, whether frowning on the prototypes of the largest fleet of 4-8-4's in the Western Hemisphere, or countersunk on streamlined Selkirks, or worn like a bonnet on dainty Pacifics. They must have made Erie and T&P folk feel at home!

And after the Elesco, give me Frank L. Packard's memorable, CP-influenced fiction about turn-of-the-century railroading in the mountains. Do you remember Superintendent Carleton and Master Mechanic Regan — and Spitzer, and the 1601? When I arrived in Field, B. C., in the cab of Selkirk 5927 in May 1950, their ghosts were there on the platform. The idiosyncrasies intrigue. The two ingenious if inconclusive splurges on lightweight, low center-of-gravity passenger equipment, TurboTrain and LRC. The fact that CN fielded a two-unit road diesel in 1928 that could displace a 4-8-2 on an intercity limited. The intermodal mentality which enveloped telegraph and steamship and aircraft and truck and express and hotel under the same logo. (Try training, sailing, and flying Santa Fe, as thousands have CP.) The discrepancy, in their favor, between the mileage of U. S.-owned track in Canada and vice versa. Only three A1A-A1A passenger cab units in a country with just as much flat land as we've got. The international oddity of a nation crossed by parallel railways, one privately

Can you imagine Canada sans grain elevators, as on CP Rail at Rivercourse, Alberta? Photo by Charles Bohi.

Symbol of Canada: Elesco feedwater heater. Photo by Don Wood.

owned, the other public property. (How the Canadians must have smiled as we wrestled with the creation of Conrail and may now grin as we debate its disposition! Of course, we have had our moments, too, as VIA Rail put on swaddling clothes.) The noble experiment of a high-pressure (up to 1750 pounds *per square inch*) 2-10-4, Angus-built CP T4a 8000. All that post–World War II railway building, without parallel south of the border, in Labrador and up to Great Slave Lake and throughout British Columbia. CN 4-6-4's with awesome, asymmetric beer-barrel tenders. And yes, CP Ten-Wheelers imported from Scotland and Germany.

Royalty. One cannot discuss Canada absent royalty. The British Empire is gone, Canada is no longer a dominion, there is

CP's *Dominion* alongside the Bow River west of Calgary — a streamlined 2-10-4 built for passenger service. CP photo.

CP 4-6-2 and steamship *Princess Helene* under common ownership at Digby, Nova Scotia. Photo by Philip R. Hastings.

CN's brief flirtation with the TurboTrain at Dorval, Quebec. Photo by Hugh Strobel.

Barrel-tendered 4-6-4 and ex-Grand Trunk Mikado at Bayview, Ontario. Photo by W. H. N. Rossiter.

the Quebec issue, but the monarch still comes and is still conveyed by Royal Train even as her father and uncle were, as attested by those crowns on 4-6-4 running boards and by a photo of the then princess climbing into the cab of CN U-1-e 4-8-2 6057.

O Canada! Oh yes! We Americans go and we keep going back across that frontier ("Guarded only by neighborly respect and honorable obligations," as Churchill said) because Canadian trains are just like ours, only as different as Saskatoon and Spartanburg. Perhaps we traveled north at first because the Canadians were slower to discard steam, mixeds, branch lines, Morse, limiteds, and cabooses, but now we return to watch 'em

haul herculean loads across the Rockies, operate a passenger train 2887 miles between origin and destination, dispatch freights up to the 61st parallel in the Northwest Territories, and customize SD40-2's with safety cabs and SD50's with Draper tapers. We can touch the FM's — C-Liner and Train Master — that we were too blind to preserve. We can schedule ourselves behind F's to a dock on Hudson Bay where one can board a ship for Europe, and into Montreal behind electrics so venerable (1914) that they were around a year after Rudolf Diesel drowned. And we can wait in waiting rooms of stations that look like stations.

O Canada! . . . keep thee steadfast thro' the years. ⅃

There's a spot in my heart . . .

. . . which no other railroad may own,
There's a depth in my soul never sounded nor known,
There's a place in my memory, my life, that you fill,
No other can take it, no one ever will*

* Verse from "Mother Machree" (Chauncey Olcott-Ernest R. Ball). © 1910 M. Witmark & Sons. Copyright Renewed. All Rights Reserved. Used and partly paraphrased as title by permission of Warner Bros. Music.

IN his eminently readable *The Trains We Loved* [George Allen & Unwin Ltd., 1947], English railway writer, historian, and artist C. Hamilton Ellis wrote of the passion that schoolboys possessed for their favorite rail lines in pre-Grouping Britain. His preoccupation as a youth was the London & South Western and whatever the L&SWR's shortcomings, he would not be swayed from that conviction by the crimson compounds of the Midland or by the Premier Line imperviousness of the London & North Western.

Whenever I've read his words I've wished I could reimburse my own favorite among railroads with a measure of the affection Ellis paid his. Singer John Gary, of all men, showed the way. Last fall I was listening for what must have been the hundredth time to an LP of Irish songs he cut, getting moist in my eye as usual, when he stroked through the verse of "Mother Machree." I picked up the tone arm and replayed the lyrics. Why, that's it, I thought; it's perfect. Simply substitute the: words "other railroad" for "colleen" and the lines speak for all of us who hold dear one road — Louisville & Nashville, in my instance — above all other roads.

Thus the title of this piece.

Pacific 274 exemplifies the USRA look that L&N adopted in 1918. In common with all good Old Reliable engines, she wears her number boldly on her headlight glass. Photo by Robert Holly.

Now for the rationale: L&N, as I knew it from ages 10 to 18 during 1937–1945, was an experience which should be shared. And I hope that in the accounting of that experience the Old Reliable may become less of an enigma to outsiders and will remind you of the debt owed to your favorite carrier, be it Western Maryland or Western Pacific. Think, if you will, of the enduring enjoyment that the railroad of your formative years imprinted upon mind and soul . . . of how you committed to memory the classes, numbers, and wheel arrangements of its roster, of how its colors shone brighter than those of the competition; of how you rejoiced in whatever were its claims to repute, were they a larger-than-anybody-else's 2-8-2 and a James J. Hill founder or a Thomas Viaduct and a *Capitol Limited.* For your indebtedness and mine both are nonetheless real for having eluded the audits of Price Waterhouse and the tabular totals of the ICC. I know that there is no way I could earn or borrow enough dollars to repay L&N's owners for a train known as the *Pan,* a branch that wound through Limestone Springs and Nazareth, and an engine numbered Nineteen Ninety-Nine.

Railroads come in many guises. They can be imperial, endless, cosmopolitan, old-shoe, heroic, runner-up, heart-breaking. Louisville & Nashville was — well, comfortable. L&N didn't awe or stun one with 100 mph speed limits or four-track mains or Virginia green paint. L&N was cautious and conservative, content to let others brag and experiment. L&N lived by its slogan: Old Reliable. L&N never saw fit to change its name even though the system expanded from the 187 miles between Louisville and Nashville to more than 5000 route-miles in 13 states from the Ohio River to the Gulf of Mexico. L&N was so deferential, in fact, that when it finally fielded a flagship passenger train of its very own, the *Pan-American,* in 1921, the limited — in the words of the company's authorized history — "was looked at askance in some quarters, it being felt that a coal-hauling railroad had better stick to its last." L&N surrendered a motive-power image of its own between world wars. The standardized engines allocated to the system by the United States Railroad Administration during 1918–1919 proved so satisfactory that L&N ceased building power of its own design in its own shops and ordered 0-8-0's, 4-6-2's, 4-8-2's, and 2-8-2's of Federal stamp through the year 1930.

It is important that you understand that Louisville &

Nashville's unpretentiousness belied its books. The Great Depression sounded L&N's strength and did not find it wanting. During that terrible time of bank failures, crop failures, and factory closings, no other major road in the South came close to equaling L&N's record of covering fixed charges with earnings in all but one year (1932) and paying a dividend in all but one year (1933). L&N stayed out of the courts and in the good graces of its owners and creditors for two reasons: coal and conservatism.

Coal — good, fragrant bituminous mined in Eastern Kentucky in such quantities as to cause one out of three freight cars to be a hopper; to fill out 8500-ton trains; to necessitate double track and a retarder hump to contain and classify; and to account for 57 per cent of all company tonnage and 40 per cent of total revenues. Was any railroad west of the Pocahontas Region so blessed by on-line fossil fuel? All that coal might have bred profligacy on a less responsible road. But hardly on L&N. J. B. Hill, who occupied the president's chair from 1934 to 1950, explained the corporate creed in monthly messages in the *L&N Employees' Magazine.* He recalled, "The first job I had with a railroad almost 45 years ago was in a branchline agency where the agent paid me $15 per month and board. I got up at 4:40 a.m. to get off the first passenger train at 5:20. The last duty of the day was to report the consist of a coal train anywhere from six to eight o'clock in the evening. Long hours, yes, but it was willing service and I was learning." Once Hill reminded employees that the company had to haul 1887 pounds of freight a mile to pay for one lead pencil; and with coal costing $2.10 a ton, or a penny a scoopful, he observed, "As the fireman reaches for a scoopful or operates a stoker he is handling money as surely as if a suction pipe were operating directly to the firebox from the Company's cash drawer."

In the innocence of youth I once wrote to Mr. Hill suggesting that L&N paint its top-line K-5 passenger Pacifics blue, citing Frisco and Wabash engines as precedents. I received a cordial reply, thanking me for my idea but deferring it on grounds of cost.

I must admit to mixed emotions as I grew up in a manse one house short of a block away from L&N's main line in the road's birthplace and headquarters city of Louisville, Ky. In the years from knee britches to long pants and from grade school to high school, one is possessive and prejudiced about his railroad *(No*

10th and Broadway in Louisville: L&N HQ, where the decisions were made; Union Station, where good times began. L&N photo.

other can take it, no one ever will), and for better or for worse, L&N was my line. Louisville's catholic array of eight line-haul railroads and two terminal companies made comparisons inevitable and ofttimes painful. We L&N devotees could cope with a Monon or a branch of B&O. We reckoned that beneath their green paint Southern's low-slung Ps-2 Pacifics were no match for our built-in-South-Louisville-Shops K-3's and K-4's. But there was no getting around our admiration for Chessie's Mikes, with their smokeboxes smothered by air pumps and feedwater heaters, their Delta trailing trucks, and their Vanderbilt tanks. Those New York Central H-10 Super-Power 2-8-2's lurking across the Ohio River in Jeffersonville, Ind., haunted us too. And Illinois Central was a sinister quality, pumping those square-sandboxed Paducah rebuilds into our city.

Pennsy was our nemesis, though. PRR came screaming down through Indiana with those 80-inch-drivered K4's making 80 per, piloted by nerveless crews with goggles over their eyes and bicycle clips around their pant legs. A tall, red-haired member of the old Louisville Railfans Club, at whose sessions we consulted on

these comparisons, had the habit of stressing Pennsy's superiority to us. Our rebuttals were fervent, made all the more emotional because we knew he was right.

Those members who had traveled east to the Promised Land and had returned to tell us of giant green Pacifics under smoke hoods propelling trains named *Ponce de Leon* and *Royal Palm* over a Southern subsidiary lettered CNO&TP — those members we didn't even argue with.

Never mind. L&N was home, native, our own; the others, however glamorous, were foreigners. L&N permeated Louisville as the city's largest taxpayer should. The company's landmarks were, properly, a classic old stone Union Station on Broadway; an immense (368 feet wide, 60 feet deep, 11 stories high) brick general-office building beside the station; and a South Louisville Shops complex so large that in its first 10 years of existence (1905–1915) it built new 282 locomotives, 184 passenger-train cars, and 14,009 pieces of freight equipment (do you read, Paducah and Mount Clare and Citico?). Add three classification yards, a mile-long elevated grade-separation project, and a 25-stall roundhouse; weave with main lines and industrial spurs; and gently soot with the fussings of 0-6-0's and 0-8-0's — and you have L&N's Louisville. Never mind those other lines headquartered in faraway Philadelphia, New York, Baltimore, Cleveland, Washington, and Chicago; they were simply connections, ribs not to be confused with the spine.

How does one romance a railroad? Through constant courtship, unswerving adoration, unblinking affection. Vital statistics were gleaned from the L&N roster published in the January 1936 *Railroad Stories,* from employee magazines and timecards begged from brakemen, and from passenger timetables cribbed off the racks in the Starks Building Arcade ticket office. The school librarian was cajoled into subscribing to the *Official Guide.* And the frame depot in suburban St. Matthews, Ky., gave access to the dispatcher's phone, a train register, freight tariffs, and agency gossip.

What a wondrous dawning! I learned that the reason No. 8 shot off to Cincinnati as if fired from a cannon was that Pennsy wouldn't hold there for the New York-bound 10-section, 3-double-bedroom red Pullman which brought up No. 8's markers if L&N

145

Fast No. 8 charges at the mail crane at Anchorage, Kentucky, while making time to Cincinnati behind Pacific 264. Pennsy will not tarry for the red Pullman that brings up the rear. L&N photo.

didn't show on time. I learned that employees dispensed with proper division names in favor of "Short Line" and "Texas" and referred to the *Azalean* as 1 and 4. I learned that whereas a heavy Mike could lug 1725 tons from Louisville to Cincinnati, she was allowed only 1460 tons *from* that city; yet in between, the profile permitted the 2-8-2 up to 4200 tons.

Intimacy was born of knowing that No. 1824 mounted the only Worthington BL-type feedwater heater on the railroad. An understanding of the system's low-key character was derived from the knowledge that its ultimate authority rested in Wilmington, N.C., headquarters of the Atlantic Coast Line — which owned 51 per cent of L&N's stock, all pledged to 4 per cent collateral bonds (whatever that meant). Pride was taken in the fact that the road had not suffered a passenger fatality since 1917 (a record destined to be broken in 1944 when Mountain No. 418 led a troop train into an out-of-gauge 35 mph curve at 45 mph).

I wonder if steam locomotive designers knew how the tangents, circles, arcs, and angles which their pens laid down were — in finished metal — to mesmerize youths. Did those designers

dream of the consternation their blueprints would cause for boys trying to make up their minds on whether an H-29A or a K-4 was entitled to greater respect? For in looking back to those lineside years with the Old Reliable I realize that it was the work of those draftsmen that infatuated me with the railroad. Yes, and that fueled an irresolvable debate about company vs. USRA engines.

The 400 Pacifics, eight-wheel switchers, Consolidations, and Mikados constructed by South Louisville Shops during 1905–1923 were, if I must tell the truth, ordinary power — in the main a continuation or enlargement of classes previously obtained from commercial builders. But in keeping with their owner, the company power was comfortable — characterized by high-mounted boilers, generous cabs, and congenial smokeboxes. And their large rectangular builder plates identified these K's, C's, H's, and J's as *ours*. Some of the shopmen who overhauled 'em had built 'em to begin with — and South Louisville had that in common with Altoona and Roanoke and how many other shops?

My favorite locomotive of the lot was 235, a Johnson-bar Pacific regularly assigned to Cincinnati local 104 whose flag stop in my suburb coincided with my trek to junior high school and made the task a bit more palatable. I can see her now, swinging out of a curve into view; coming furiously to a stop with pops raised in response to a patron's lifted hand; champing at the bit while a brakeman lifted trap and lowered stepbox; then charging off for St. Matthews, Worthville, Zion, Latonia, and all the other stops en route to CUT. Two Thirty-Five — South Louisville serial 313, born in 1917 — was then living the lazy local life an engine might expect in middle age. But before she and I would part company, the war of wars would return her to the point of named trains, double-heading with a Mountain on the *Azalean's* 16 cars, working her heart out across 1.56 per cent hills.

The Government engines were a different breed, not only superior in performance but unqualifiedly handsome. L&N rostered USRA's in vast quantities: 16 0-8-0's 22 light 4-8-2's, 26 light 4-6-2's, 93 light 2-8-2's, and 165 heavy 2-8-2's. If a word had to suffice as a description, mine would be adaptability. The heavy Mikes, for instance: They would handle the hottest hotshot and coal drags with equal aplomb *and,* when asked, would keep an *Azalean* on time. The Pacifics performed over their heads, taking the streamlined age in stride and subbing more than once for

EMD's. L&Ners loved the USRA's, for the way they rode and steamed and moved out; yes, and for their power reverses and mechanical stokers — qualities and components not always synonymous with the homemades.

This happy affair with the Feds put me in good stead for my post-Louisville years. I mean, a Pennsy man removed from Belpaire boilers and high headlights was a man bereft. But a man raised within sight and sound of squadrons of USRA's, as I was, could find solace later beside the iron of faraway Grand Trunk, Milwaukee Road, Omaha Road, or Pere Marquette — any road which ran such power.

As J. B. Hill, rest his soul, would have been the first to caution, locomotives alone do not a railroad make, however consuming is their imprint upon impressionable youth. Trains were what put money into the company's cash drawer to pay for the coal the locomotives burned at the rate of a penny a shovelful. The L&N trains of my acquaintance bore labels: named passenger, local passenger, mixed, hotshot, local freight, and work extra. In Louisville we were far removed from the coal fields and hence from drags. My recollection of the prediesel days is that 8 cars made a *Pan*, 12 a mixed, and 35 a freight. (Lucius Beebe's *High Iron* depicted Chesapeake & Ohio 3003 on a 210-car test train, but to me the count was incomprehensible — as was the big 2-10-4.)

The fun trains were the mixeds. My buddy and I mowed and clipped lawns until we hated the sight of grass in order to raise the quarters and the dollars necessary to ride the Bloomfield, Bardstown, and Greensburg branches. Our rewards were deluxe. We could dangle our legs off the steps of the open-platform wooden coach if the conductor consented or could occupy the cupola if a caboose brought up the rear. There were switching moves to observe, forbidden Twenty Grands to smoke, 2-8-0's and 4-6-0's to help turn on armstrong tables. The Bardstown Branch, which really terminated beyond there in Springfield, was our hands-down favorite. Its *raison d'etre* was Kentucky bourbon, as was implied by such station names as Limestone Springs, Bourbon Springs, and Early Times. Mixed No. 35 brought coal to the distilleries; No. 36 hauled away their whiskey. Daily except Sunday, year in and year out, No. 1237, a 2-8-0, would collect the mixed's mail-baggage car and coach in Louisville Union Station

at seven o'clock in the morning, fill out with freight cars in South Louisville Yard, paddle down the main line to Bardstown Junction, and then spend the day on the branch. In the afternoon the process was reversed. The highlight of the 118-mile round trip began at Bardstown Junction on the return journey. As 1237 steamed quietly, her fireman would ring up the dispatcher for clearance onto the main. This took time because No. 36 was never on time and a mixed seldom is superior to anything in a timecard. But ultimately sanction came, we eased onto high iron, the flagman realigned and locked the switch off the branch, and then — shorn of all pickup and setout obligations — we were off to the races. You might be surprised at how many rpm's an engineer could coax out of 57-inch drivers, or at how balmy the breeze could be sweeping through open windows and across green walk-over plush.

The named trains went farther and faster. An italicized *"Flamingo"* entry lent one's notebook substance. The big-time runs were assigned the newest and largest passenger engines — the USRA Pacifics and Mountains. For me the trouble with the limiteds was that I seldom rode them. If one multiplied L&N's coach fare of 1½ cents a mile by the hundreds of miles a proper journey on the *Pan-American* called for, one arrived at a figure that lawnmowing wouldn't cover, even allowing for a 10 per cent reduction on a round-trip ticket. So for the most part I simply watched Nos. 1 and 4 and 98 and 99. The sight of the dining cars almost diluted the joy prompted by the engines that preceded them. Visible through the diners' broad windows were people seated at tables, being waited upon, dining off linen, supping from china and silverware, bound for far-off places . . . and here was I riding a trolley bus toward an algebra exam I surely would flunk. There was no justice, only envy.

Slowly, then suddenly, the Louisville & Nashville changed. Remember that the system as I came to know it was in a somnolent season, rendered so by the economic depression which blighted the land. The long line of engines stored serviceable (many of them USRA's) alongside South Louisville Shops had told the story. In consequence there had been no new trains, no new engines, no new signals, no new anything. It never occurred to me that there would be. L&N simply would roll into the year 2000 "as is." Definitions would remain frozen: "new" always would connote piston valves and Walschaerts, and "old" would mean slide valves and Stephenson.

An economic upturn and then a war intervened. The former shifted the local freight from a triweekly schedule to daily except Sunday (its Mike carried white flags on the unscheduled days until the timecard could catch up with the good times), reduced the length of South Louisville's dead line, and introduced a super freight as well as a streamliner. The latter made doubleheading SOP and passenger trains SRO, introduced road dieselization and centralized traffic control, and inked the class "M-1" into engine diagram books. Both eras transfixed train-watchers.

Silver Bullet and *South Wind:* I wouldn't care to choose between them for surprise and excitement. *Silver Bullet* was a Cincinnati (Covington, Ky., technically)–New Orleans truck-competitive merchandiser. The *Bullet* was undistinguished in appearance, being simply a burly black 2-8-2, a line of box cars, and a red caboose. The professional eye of a trainmaster would have noticed that the cars were sealed and that the consist was conspicuously devoid of empties, open-top cars, and junkers. What impressed me, though, was its *modus operandi* and punctuality. The train came out of Covington as Second 101, sandwiched in the train sheet between that local and No. 1, the *Azalean*. On the last lap into Louisville, downgrade through our suburb of Crescent Hill, evening after evening the scenario was this: 101 by at 8:30; the *Silver Bullet* by at 8:35; No. 1 by at nine o'clock. Imagine, a Mike pacing 4-6-2's and 4-8-2's! A freight train you could predict, whose headlight shone while the fragrant smoke of 101 still scented the soft, humid July night. Imagine.

In one fell swoop, *South Wind* impressed upon Louisville streamlining, speed, full-width diaphragms, budget meals (dinner cost 75 cents), Budd, and reserved coach seats. I was among the spectators lined up beyond Union Station's trainshed on December 19, 1940, to see the first run. A Loewyized, bullet-nosed Pennsy K4 which depended upon her chromed cylinder-head covers for accents uncoiled a caterpillarlike consist of low-slung, tuscan-red streamlined cars. The all-coach, every-third-day speedster had departed Chicago at breakfast time and would be in Miami soon after lunch the next day. The Old Reliable was so taken by the *Wind* that it had shucked all inhibi-

tion, fielding as power a great cone-nosed, skyline-encased, silver-flanked, Chinese-red-trimmed Pacific trailing a 27½-ton, 20,000-gallon-capacity, 12-wheel tender bearing the numerals 295. Oh, my gosh, the legendary experiment of 1925 was back among the living.

You see, L&N, of all roads, had caught the three-cylinder fever of the Twenties and had indulged itself in two such Alcos: 4-6-2 295 and 2-8-2 1999. Neither survived the economies of the Thirties; both had been shoved onto the dead line and there had been stripped of components that would fit their close-kin USRA brethren. Inauguration of the *Wind* saved the Pacific from scrap. South Louisville Shops recycled her as a two-cylinder engine, draped her in semi-*Daylight* dress, and pinned her rear drawbar to the system's first (and only) large tender. Paint did the rest. But for the company's emblem mounted beneath her cab windows and the engine number painted on her headlight glass, I never would have credited the 295 to our roster.

Yet there she was; and as the audience waved, there she went, thundering south to Nashville. She hit 75 mph according to the *Courier-Journal*'s reporter, but the best was yet to come. After pausing in Nashville just 7 timetable minutes to slake her thirst, the big Pacific set out to hang a record in the annals of American railroading by running off the 205¼ miles to Birmingham nonstop — a peerless achievement for a regularly scheduled, coalburning operation. Two Ninety-Five, you did it — you straightened the shoulders of all of us beholden to the L&N . . . There's a place in my memory, my life, that you fill.

"Our country is now at war," President Hill told his employees in a message dated January 1942 which capitalized Country

President Hill (third from left) poses with the crew of L&N's first road diesels on May 18, 1942. L&N photo.

as well as Company. "Somehow," he said, "I feel that we of the 'Old Reliable' will not be found wanting." They were not. If I had to settle on a single emblematic impression of those years, it would be of doubleheaded heavy USRA Mikes inbound through St. Matthews, 16 63-inch drivers trying to straighten out an S-curve, 60 or more cars rolling in their smoky wake, fireman and head brakeman of the lead 1800 hanging onto the cab sash as they pounded home. A solidly solvent property simply leaned into it. All its engines went to war. Its employees labored long. But I never sensed that L&N neared the breaking point, that it might be forced to beg Q 2-6-2's or to cancel midday diner meals in order to survive, as another road did.

Cameos from the war: Three-cylinder Mikado 1999 — retrieved from the dead and overhauled with inner piston intact — dispatched north on the local freight to DeCoursey Yard across the river from Cincinnati, there to exert her 65,700 pounds tractive force as a hump engine . . . Passenger trains so packed that entraining riders found vestibules to be impassable and had to be let aboard by the baggageman or the chef . . . Slide-valve Moguls

working South Louisville Yard in the company of 0-8-0's 20 years their junior . . . A *Pan* in sections — one running to New Orleans, the other to Memphis . . . The searchlight signals and power switches that denoted CTC creating the strangeness of taking siding without stopping and of dispensing with "19" and "31" flimsies plus the order hoops that lofted them to the outstretched arms of firemen.

In 1942 new road locomotives were added to L&N's roster for the first time since 1930, neither class of newcomers reflected the company's conservative cut. Ironically the passenger diesels arrived first. Understandably, coal-conscious L&N had settled on the 4-8-4 as its next-generation passenger power, but the company discovered that the size and axle loadings of the design precluded use of the contemplated 4-8-4 south of Nashville — to say nothing of across Gulf bayous — because of bridge restrictions. Instead, Electro-Motive was called upon to furnish eight 4000 h.p. locomotives (i.e., sixteen 2000 h.p. E6 cab units operated back to back). Eventually their air horns, gyrating headlights, and traction that was contemptuous of any-length limited penetrated Crescent Hill. *L&N what have you done?* The E's were among the last of their model, for the War Production Board curtailed passenger-locomotive construction; and VE-Day or VJ-Day seemed light years in the future. Still, the E's worked relentlessly between Cincinnati and New Orleans without change or complaint, 922 miles each way, day after day after day. The lesson was not lost upon Mr. Hill and his associates.

The other new engines, 14 M-1 class 2-8-4's from Baldwin, were something else. Unhappily, they were out of my sight, allocated exclusively to the high-density coal lines in Eastern Kentucky. Still, their description in the company magazine both awed and confounded me, even as it implied that L&N would forever entrust tonnage to steam. Obviously expense had been the least consideration in their acquisition. They boasted roller bearings on all engine and tender axles; high-speed boosters; air pumps with aftercoolers; lightweight rods; clasp brakes . . . it would have been easier to list the accessories the M-1's did not have. The twin yellow stripes across their large tenders, previously an honor accorded to only a few passenger engines, proclaimed what the company though of the engines. *L&N, what you have done!*

The Berkshires, L&N's biggest steam locomotives, spent their lives pulling coal out of eastern Kentucky. Photo by John Krave.

And then, as suddenly as it had begun in the spring of 1937, my association with Louisville & Nashville ended. In a gloomy armory I became Army serial 45011641 and was whisked off to Camp Atterbury, Indiana, in a red-plush P70 behind a tired K4. In retrospect, the timing of the draft board was appropriate. The L&N I knew had attained the peak of its war efforts in 1944 and Mr. Hill already was addressing himself to the future: "We should strive to excel our competitors." Neither he nor I knew that the future would sweep steam from the system by 1956, and all but one passenger train by 1971. Hill might have been able to prophesy the presence of L&N in Chattanooga, having once presided over the Nashville, Chattanooga & St. Louis, whose absorption made it possible. But L&N in Chicago? And a Family Lines?

I never returned to the L&N as a lineside resident, which was providential. I wasn't around when they razed the station in Bardstown Junction, scrapped 235, and italicized and simplified the company logo. Out of my sight they took down Union Station's trainshed, annulled the *Azalean,* and ceased stopping at Worthville, Ky., for water. I experienced altogether too many of those sadnesses on railroads which didn't have the hold on my heart that L&N did. My memory of the Old Reliable is clean, in focus, not blurred or sullied by having been witness of such dreadful if inevitable happenings.

Conversely, the passage of more than three decades between the old L&N (Old Reliable if you will) and myself has softened recall. I can't seem to remember the cinders that 1237's stack lodged in my eye. The heartbreak has gone from the Saturday I glimpsed the mighty 1999 pass by on the local freight and ran all the way to St. Matthews to see that cylinder tucked beneath her smokebox, only to find her gone. I have even forgiven Dad for making me go to school the day an H-29A 2-8-0 showed up in Crescent Hill with a work extra to dump new ballast. When I got out of school and ran to the tracks, the fresh white rock was there but the H-29A was not. Even the sense of inferiority I felt when I finally came upon a CNO&TP Ps-4 over in Danville, Ky. — the huge machine all green and gold and smoke-deflectored and blowing off — is something with which I've learned to live.

What remains, and ever will, are bright visions. I see Pacific 245 (her brass number plate is a book stop in my living room) charging toward Cincinnati on fast No. 8, with red Pullman *Villa Ideal* toting the marker lamps. I see a column of black rising over the slip track behind the fence at South Louisville Shops as a newly overhauled 2-8-2 inches over oiled rails at 5 mph, her drivers furiously turning at 45 mph (the procedure eliminated the need for break-in runs on local freights). I see the *Pan* and mixeds and strawberry extras — all steam, all on time, all judiciously burning the cent-a-shovelful coal banked in tenders lettered "L. & N." on their shoulders.

Postscript: As I tried to put these reminiscences down on paper with some measure of fidelity, young men of the firm were wandering in. They would look over the mound of books and timetables on my desk (including *Messages and Addresses* of James B. Hill; Kincaid Herr's L&N history, *Louisville & Nashville Railroad 1950–1959;* Richard E. Prince's *Louisville & Nashville Steam Locomotives; Moody's Steam Railroads 1940;* and timetable No. 475, October 1, 1941), and they would tactfully ask about the article in progress. I'm too old to show mercy in these matters. "You want action, you should have seen an L-1 climbing

Muldraugh Hill. You know, there never was in steam anything prettier, more symmetrical, than a USRA. Now look at these photos in Prince's book . . ." The young men would grow restive, remember deadlines and phone calls to make, and would excuse themselves. For them the answer is the 11:45 a.m. Amtrak Turboliner to Detroit, a last look at a Baldwin S12, a slide of a brand-new MP15AC, a map of Conrail. None of these attractions is to be equated with the fading snapshots in my little 7 x 10-inch brown L&N album. Just as my friend C. Hamilton Ellis in England will read these lines and will reflect upon the wonder of a Drummond T9 in Waterloo, all filmy in oily green and impatient to be off with a West of England express, in those splendid times before that Serb terrorist Gavrilo Princip shot the Archduke of Austria in 1914 and ruined everything. But the young men do not know that, of course.

Thus are the wonders of memories — old ones deserving of print, new ones abuilding. Fresh depths of soul never sounded or known. For instance, down in Louisville, out on River Road, some sensitive souls are striving mightily to breathe life into a metal hulk numbered 152 and classified K-2A, Rogers serial 6256. There is reason to believe, I am informed, that one morning a fire will burn on her grates and the needle on her steam-pressure gauge will lift toward 200. Conceivably, the veteran Pacific could walk out of Union Station, whistle an acknowledgment to waving South Louisville shopmen, bang across the Salt River bridge at Shepherdsville at 45 or 50 mph, and lean into the curve at Bardstown Junction. If so, she will impress upon a new generation the images of L&N that her long-scrapped sisters imparted to me. That would — let us hope *will* — be a worthwhile endeavor. So sing on, John Gary; the verse is right . . . there is a spot in my heart which no other railroad may own. ⌐

151

Early on one frosty mornin'

Look away, look away

ONCE upon a time, to borrow a phrase, New York Central's 13-syllable subsidiary Cleveland, Cincinnati, Chicago & St. Louis scheduled mainline passenger service with almost interurban, if not streetcar, frequency. For example, out of its Indianapolis Union Station hub to its namesake cities, the Big Four offered the traveler daily trains to Cleveland at 6:30 a.m., 11:30 a.m, 1:45 p.m., 5:10 p.m., 6 p.m., 10:55 p.m., and 11:30 p.m.; to Cincinnati at 2:55 a.m., 4:40 a.m., 7:45 a.m., noon, 2 p.m., 3:05 p.m., and 6 p.m.; to Chicago at 12:10 a.m., 1:55 a.m., noon, 12:05 p.m., 2:45 p.m., and 5 p.m.; and to St. Louis at 12:35 a.m., 3:20 a.m., 8 a.m., 8:10 a.m., 11:55 a.m., noon, 2:45 p.m., and 6:30 p.m.

In June 1931, in Schenectady, N. Y., the American Locomotive Company completed CCC&StL 4-6-4 No. 6628 to help shoulder that load of limited and not-so-limited varnish. Numbered and sublettered for the Big Four, she was the next to the last of 205 J-1 class New York Central Hudsons.

The 205 total explains much. No other U. S. railroad bought so many copies of a single class of a modern (read post-1925) wheel arrangement in steam. And Central's 4-6-4 count grows to 275 if you add the 20 J-2 variations of Boston & Albany and the 50 J-3 Super Hudsons produced a decade after the prototype of 1927. This unique domination of a two-cylinder, nonarticulated type caused many to write off non-NYC Hudsons as caricatures. For these folk the only comparison was intramural: J-1 vs. J-3. And pray not mention those aberrations of the same axle count flawed by being bigger or rebuilds or Baldwins or boorish.

Hudson! The word is synonymous with color calendars and publicity photos of the machine racing along the river whose name it bore . . . with the world's most famous train . . . with designer Paul W. Kiefer (most American engines were uncredited, whereas British mechanical officers signed their works) . . . with Lionel's landmark O-scale 5344 (whose $75 pricetag exceeded what most boys' fathers possessed for discretionary spending) . . . with grace forged into metal . . . with one engine when the competition required two . . . with Harmon and Elkhart and Utica, Battle Creek and Bellefontaine and Mattoon . . . with "The Water Level Route" and "You Can Sleep."

The 6628? She became the 5403, which was just as well because I don't know if I could ever have felt at ease with a J-1 prefaced by anything other than a 52, or a 53, or a 54. (That may put too fine a point on it; Southern's contemporary Ps-4 Pacifics in the disparate numberings of two subsidiaries never troubled us.) One assumes 5403 received her class repairs at Beech Grove. Perhaps she spent most of her life working out to St. Louis, the westernmost reach of the system. (Cairo, Ill., was geographically closer to NYC's New York City heart even if more route-miles distant from Grand Central Terminal.) I know I caught up with her on a chilly November 24, 1944, cycling past the tower of St. Louis Union Station, as viewed from the 18th Street viaduct. Sages of those years referred to NYC's Hudsons as feline and handsome. They also wore an aura of the aristocrat, and it was hard to erase, though Central tried by appending Centipede tenders and unmasking the ruler-straight edge of inner smokebox doors on destreamlined J-3's.

Of course, age and circumstance took a toll on the 5403. By 1954, the railroad was deep in a dieselization program that would be expedited by a fiery proxy fight. And on Saturday, September

17 of that year, the 5403 became the only active steam engine on the main line west of Indianapolis simply by virtue of a diesel failure at Mattoon, Ill. Her assignment: the eight head-end cars and rider coach of unnamed train 473 — as much of a nonentity as one could imagine shy of a caboose.

What mattered was the fire on her grates, as opposed to the cold and white-lined U-3 switchers, H-5 Mikes, and L-2 Mohawks that encircled her on the turntable at Mattoon. What also mattered was that photographer Phil Hastings and I chanced upon the engine terminal in time to record the event for our "Smoke over the Prairies" steam farewell series for TRAINS.

Mention has been made here of the aura of a J-1. Would you believe that 5403's was so compelling that I failed to notice her missing cylinder head cover, unshielded and/or blocked off sander pipes, and a trailing truck bereft of booster? True.

Well now, for those who missed the June 1955 issue — and you must be in a majority — here is what took place: I drove my 1954 Ford west from Mattoon on Illinois Highway 16, which paralleled the Big Four. Phil and his Rollei took up position in the back seat, understanding motorists hung back, and No. 5403 appeared in the distance. She played out that familiar role of all the Central Hudsons I'd watched or ridden behind, first that deceptive lope of 30 to 35 mph, just flexing her alligator crossheads and Baker gear and main and side rods (and there was a slight knock in this old J-le's machinery); then that explosive wham of unbridled horsepower, winding the speedometer needle rapidly past 40 and 50 mph to sweep beyond to 60, 65, 70 . . . Omigosh, she didn't look 23 summers old, and her crew didn't

look like they'd be wearing sport shirts to work next week for a ride between armrests and behind split windshields with wipers and sun visors. The 5403 was making like she had the *Southwestern Limited* or *Missourian* in tow, and she was cruising past 75 to 80 and leaving us behind at 85 and — well, the doctor's photo at left tells you all that can be said or needs to be known. To recall what Lucius Beebe wrote about photographing the *Chief* in Cajon for this magazine's first issue, "to know that one has it, cold turkey, is one of the great delights of the business of living." Phil had the 5403, cold turkey.

Subsequently my boss, publisher Al Kalmbach, penned (in his round, legible, railroad operator-like longhand) a congratulatory note on the receipt flap of the check we mailed Phil for the 5403 photos. Al was not given to unearned praise.

As for us, we broke off the chase and headed west for a rendezvous with doubleheaded Wabash 2-6-0's. Phil delighted in little engines. He looked forward to the Moguls with as much enthusiasm as I had accorded the Hudson. Which was awesome.

During the three decades and more after such searches for steam, I never felt compelled to retrace our routes . . . to climb again the knoll where we watched four Pennsy I1's lose their footing in the rain, to return to the building where we witnessed a Missabe Road articulated severed from its forward engine for repairs, to stand where we observed a small CB&Q engineer wrestle a large 4-8-4 into motion. It's not that I have any Thomas Wolfe qualms about the present obscuring the past. Hey, I toured that stone palace of a Union Station in Louisville, Ky., after they razed its trainshed and took up its tracks, sandblasted the structure and made it the HQ of the local transit authority. (I was caught up in an NRHS Convention tour and it would have been impolite to turn down an inspection of what I had proclaimed to be a city shrine.) But do you know, once I walked out of the place, I could hear once more the thud of ticket daters, the nonstereo call of the train announcer for the *Pan-American,* and the high-born sigh of a Pennsy K4 at the bumper post.

Yet why revisit Hurricane, Renovo, and Two Harbors when Phil and I had been there only yesterday? Suddenly, of course, Phil's untimely death in 1987 made our journeys together seem what in fact they had long been, ages ago. That melancholia was deepened by an awareness that Conrail, having no use for two main lines into St. Louis, had abandoned almost a hundred miles' worth of the old Big Four from Paris, Ill., just west of Terre Haute, Ind., through Mattoon to Pana, Ill. (and would have farther west, except that MoPac needed it and so bought it). One could rationalize that circumstance by the thought that the rails that bore Hudson No. 5403 would have been figuratively gone by the 1980's in any event. If not retained as a secondary main, the affected track's only recourse would have been sale as a short line. And no matter what, Amtrak, having given up on any direct service between the East and St. Louis, would not have reconstituted the *Southwestern.* Thus a Big Four by any other name would not have been a Big Four.

Yet withal, I had Mattoon on my mind and perhaps only Hoagy Carmichael could have put my thoughts on paper. Ultimately, Margaret and I pointed the T-Bird south in the autumn of 1988, ostensibly in quest of a few sunny days along the Gulf and perhaps the Atlantic. My 3 x 5-inch trip cards avoided the Interstates in favor of the undivided two-laners through the Yazoo Citys, and I included a few locomotive-linked locations, among them Waycross, Paducah, Vaughan, Norris City, and Mattoon.

Waycross, Ga., elev. 135 ft., pop. 19,371, enter U.S. 84, exit U.S. 84: The gods of megamerger, conglomerate high iron, who seem often to frown, have smiled upon this junction, dispensing a new retarder yard and diesel shop, and it flexes a muscle like unto the Atlantic Coast Line in the best of times. We passed through the town twice, and there were always freights leaving and others waiting to follow. One of them took me back half a century. Three units in an appropriate mix of Chessie and Seaboard System colors led a unit train of round-bottom coal gondolas. As we paced them out of town I thought of a family trip to Florida in 1937 on which we overtook an ACL Vanderbilt-tank 2-10-2 in Georgia (or was it Alabama?). I'd never seen so many driving wheels in unison, nor a caboose tucked in behind the tender. (Whether there was another hack on the rear I recall not.) I bet I wouldn't have had to knock on too many doors in zip code 31502 to find someone who remembered those handsome Baldwin 2000's.

Paducah, Ky., elev. 339 ft., pop. 29,315, enter on U.S. 60, exit U.S. 45: I am awed by locomotive shops, and I've spent a lifetime walking through their halls. But of course there are omissions, large and small, e.g., Angus, St. Augustine, Princeton(s), Crewe, Morris Park, Topeka, West Albany, Paducah. I particularly regret not having visited Paducah when that Illinois Central complex was in the midst of recycling a steam roster of more than a thousand engines. This unique program, in which boilers and frames were shuffled with abandon, squeezed more than 18 million pounds of additional tractive force from existing power (the exact figure depends on your acceptance of the road's generous formula for computing same) and enabled IC to survive World War II with only 20 new freight locomotives. The rebuilds were not fancy — no roller bearings or feedwater heaters or state-of-the-art wheel arrangements (excluding one 4-6-4); few one-piece frames. Just your basic steamers with the bark on. But they got the job done. And, blessed by easy grades and good water and on-line coal, they held off EMD longer than most. (Hastings and I had a splendid day chasing hard-charging plain-Jane, ex-2-10-2, 2500-series 4-8-2's in 1954.) The Paducah Story may be the most overdue book on the railroad shelf. And make that two volumes if diesels are covered too. The man at the gas station directed us to the buildings where a private company now remanufactures diesels. But the name chiseled in stone over the door of the office building read ILLINOIS CENTRAL RAILROAD, and the establishment looked its heritage, i.e., built as a unit in 1925–1927. I was impressed. I wished I wasn't 50 years late. I didn't knock on the door.

Vaughan, Miss., elev. 215 ft., pop. 40, enter on State 432, exit same: John Luther Jones, the ballast-scorching Illinois Central engineer who became a synonym for his trade after perishing in a rear-end collision here April 30, 1900, is remembered in two places. Most tourists apparently prefer Casey Jones Village in Jackson, Tenn., but the tour-bus-oriented park of onetime Jones home, unrelated rail equipment, general store, country music museum, and motel intimidated us. We settled for the wreck site itself. Vaughan isn't easy to find. And when you get there, the state-operated depot that houses the museum turns out to be from nearby Pickens, where it's depicted in Gil Reid's painting of Jones making time with Ten-Wheeler 382 just minutes before eternity. Again, the Espee-ish 0-6-0 parked outside would intrigue Casey with its electric headlight, piston valves, and Walschaerts gear, but he wouldn't be impressed by its diminutive drivers and footboards. Still, the quiet setting of the place (we were the only visitors near noon on an early December Friday), its rudimentary artifacts, and its diagrams of the accident struck us as the memorial Mrs. Jones might have preferred.

Norris City, Ill., elev. 421 ft., pop. 1515, enter on U.S. 45, exit same: My sole contact with New York Central's remote, single-track coal line to Cairo, Ill., was watching its Pacific-powered *Egyptian* arrive in Chicago, where it was La Salle Street Station's only acknowledgment of the Big Four and perhaps its least pretentious name train. But I knew its story. S. Kip Farrington Jr., popular railroad book author of the 1940's, said it deserved to be "burned on brass in the railroad hall of fame." Briefly, when German subs invalidated coastal tankers in World War II, the Government rushed completion of a 24-inch-diameter pipeline between Texas and the East — the "Big Inch." When its construction was temporarily halted at Norris City, Ill., NYC was asked to fill the gap with tank trains. During 6½ months in 1943, a pool of 10,000 tank cars moved more than 1650 trains' worth of oil (at 75 cars per train) east to B&O, PRR, DL&W, LV, B&M, CNJ, RDG, and Erie connections. On a single day, Norris City loaded 982 tanks. You can look it up — as Casey Stengel would say — on pages 98–105 of Farrington's *Railroads at War* (Coward-McCann, 1944). Did some of the whitelined engines Phil and I had seen around the pit at Mattoon in 1954 help to marshal and move this tidal wave of petroleum? I wondered, recently if not at the time. Today, CCC&StL's old Cairo Division is no more between Paris and Mount Carmel, Ill., and from there south the track now belongs to the Southern. We paused in Norris City for soft drinks at a general store. I found an oldster who recalled the oil trains and said the yard had just been ripped out. The last H-5 and the final *Egyptian* had pulled out long before. Still, I'm glad I set foot in a place whose name should be burned on brass.

Yes, in our 8½-day, 3195-mile circuit of the South, we saw the Gulf (I pretended the whistles of CSX were those of the L&N) and the Atlantic, and a considerable length of the Mississippi. But

"How temporal is transportation. Here the Illinois prairie was erasing the Big Four just as surely as the North Atlantic had smoothed over the wake of the *Mauretania* and *Rex* and *Ile de France.*" Photo by John Fuller.

what will linger in the mind was, in railroad parlance, our first scheduled stop.

Mattoon, Ill., elev. 735 ft., pop. 19,300, enter on U.S. 45, exit on State 16: We arose in the motel early on the frosty morning of Thursday, December 1, 1988. In the blue-black of dawn the thick frost only reluctantly loosened its grip to heater vents and scraper blade. Margaret drove as we negotiated downtown Mattoon and turned west on Illinois 16. I picked out the Big Four roadbed . . . no rail, no ties, no ballast, no signals, no grade-crossing crossbucks: simply a level, ruler-straight roadbed between farmlands and highway. And one culvert. Or rather two concrete culverts, one atop the other, bearing the: dates 1894 and 1922. No, no. I didn't glimpse or expect any apparition of the 5403 and train 473. Rather, I felt as if I were a relative of the Cleveland, Cincinnati, Chicago & St. Louis, summoned by the authorities to identify its remains and certify the institution as extinct.

How temporal is transportation. Here the Illinois prairie was erasing the Big Four just as surely as the North Atlantic had smoothed over the wake of the *Mauretania* and *Rex* and *Ile de France.* Transportation may be built for the ages, but more than most agencies and works of man, it had best be enjoyed at the moment, never assumed, ever considered an expendable experience. Look away, look away. ⫶

David P. Morgan, 1927–1990

By J. David Ingles

A GUIDING LIGHT in railroading has been extinguished. David P. Morgan, Editor Emeritus of TRAINS who led this publication as its editor from 1953 until he retired in 1987, died on January 10, 1990, of complications resulting from emphysema. He was 62. Unquestionably the top U. S. railroad writer for over three decades, Morgan led this monthly from the status of being just a money-losing pet project of Publisher A. C. Kalmbach to a profitable magazine that had long since become *the* independent voice for the railroad industry and hobby. During Morgan's 34½-year tenure as Editor, TRAINS' monthly circulation climbed from 39,000 to 88,000, and his writings made an indelible mark on thousands of us who still read these pages. Many say he helped shape their careers as railroaders or writers.

Those who have read TRAINS for sufficient time and can recite David's favorite railroads can thus also trace his life. (For 16 years around this office, incidentally, it was always "David" for the Editor, and "Dave" for this new kid on the block who came on board in 1971.) Chronologically, if not in rank in David's heart:

1) Central of Georgia. David Page Morgan was born to a British-born Presbyterian minister and his wife, the Rev. Klingsley John and Juliet Freda Morgan, in Monticello, Ga., on March 17, 1927, the second of three sons. Monticello was on CofG's Athens branch, 45 miles northeast of Macon, and although David never really took to true short lines, he retained his fondness for the down-home, branch-line railroading provided by the daily mixed trains that called at Monticello's country depot. David inherited his interest in railroads from his father (also the son of a clergyman), and the accessibility of the depot enhanced the bond.

2) Louisville & Nashville. When his father took the Crescent Hill Presbyterian Church in that eastern Louisville, Ky., neighborhood, David was in his formative years, and the L&N put the heaviest stamp of any single carrier on the future editor. Often in the company of chum Charlie Castner, David would watch action on L&N's "Short Line" main to Cincinnati down the block on Hillcrest Avenue or at the suburban St. Matthews depot 1¼ miles away, and visit the South Louisville locomotive backshop down the road a piece. After David graduated from Louisville Male High School, he enlisted in the service.

3) Florida East Coast. David was first exposed to the oil-burning steam locomotives on FEC's double-track passenger speedway on family vacations in 1936, 1937, and 1944, and again at a U. S. Army Air Force base in Boca Raton in 1946. FEC's Key West extension, devastated by a hurricane in 1935, also fascinated him, being perhaps the most significant piece of U. S. rail mileage he could not put on his travel map.

4) Southern Pacific. By 1946, when David left the service, the church had called Rev. Morgan to tiny Taft in south Texas, and David was able to enjoy the Espee (as he usually abbreviated it) in an unremarked corner of the Texas & New Orleans portion of the Golden Empire. Later on, SP's often misunderstood stance on passenger trains struck the right chord with TRAINS' editor, helping solidify its reputation in his eyes. David's times in Taft were also marked by his only college attendance (Del Mar) and by his taking a few locomotive photographs. This latter fact might surprise many of you who — as this writer did — envied David his ability to devote all his energy to observing and making entries in his reporter's notebook, while leaving the burdens of photography to others.

5) Chicago, Milwaukee, St. Paul & Pacific. While serving as a reporter for the Taft Tribune in 1948, David was offered an associate editor job by Al Kalmbach on his "little magazine" about full-size railroads. David accepted — at $37.50 a week and in June brought his wonderful God-given writing talent north to a city that, while served by six Class 1's (three by water) and two interurbans, really took only one steam road to its heart, the one whose home shops were here.

6) Southern Railway. From perhaps his favorite single class of steam locomotive, the Virginia green Ps-4 (seen on the CNO&TP not far east of Louisville), through the progressive D. W. Brosnan years and into the W. Graham Claytor Jr. era of fond recall, this system repeatedly touched David. *Locomotive 4501* of 1968, the fifth of his 10 books, told the story of the rebirth of steam as a public relations tool by the Southern, and for the next decade-plus he, wife Margaret, and other Kalmbachers (often including Art Director George Gloff) would range far with this most traveled of excursion engines.

Also, the railways of England. David never ignored his British heritage, which of course is also that of railroading itself. He seasoned TRAINS with as much overseas material as he dared without alienating its largely North American readership, and GWR, LMS, LNER, and Southern (and, yes, British Rail) became familiar to readers.

David's 39-year Kalmbach career was spent entirely at the company's previous building at 1027 N. 7th Street in downtown Milwaukee. Promoted to editor in 1963, David remained a Company man from the old tradition. He considered this "the only job in the world, with the best employer," and made it his life's work. Marriage to Margaret Blumer, a fellow Kalmbach employee, on October 20, 1961, gave him a faithful traveling companion a year too late to go along on his only round-the-world sojourn (February–November 1961 TRAINS) but one who would trek many a North American mile with him, in regular service and on excursions.

Never nonplussed by men of importance, David made it a point to interview and ride with railroad chiefs when invited, and tell the railroad story without apology when the world wasn't all rosy. His landmark 38-page issue-length "Who Shot the Passenger Train?" of April 1959 bared the handwriting on the wall, but he and TRAINS were ready to weather the storm of subscription cancellations that resulted when that analysis wasn't what many wanted to hear. A private-enterpriser, David really never accepted Amtrak in principle but did come to realize what many readers did, that Amtrak passenger trains are better than no passenger trains.

Similarly, although a steam man by age, he jumped on the diesel bandwagon and nurtured the magazine back from a slump incurred in the 1960's when many readers abandoned TRAINS as their favorite road abandoned steam.

TRAINS became a unique fence-straddler, a combination trade and hobby magazine. A champion of seers as well as doubters, David made these pages an available outlet for anyone with a sound idea that would promote the concept of flanged wheel on steel rail. Two examples: RoadRailer, and the integral-train concept espoused by John G. Kneiling, who signed on in January 1966 as author of the based-on-optimism-for-railroading "Professional Iconoclast" column that would run for over two decades, through March 1986. David's editorial door was open for photographers, too. Despite the long-ago perception by some that TRAINS' photo credits were only for a clique, perhaps nothing pleased David more than to introduce a new credit line under quality photographs.

A gentle and private person, basically shy and sensitive, David talked with his typewriter. One of the best kept secrets in railroading, though, is that this most prolific rail writer did it all with only his right-hand index finger (and his left thumb ready for the space bar and shift key)! No hunt-and-peck typist, he did this with amazing speed.

As one might expect, David was a walking index of TRAINS, before as well as during his tenure. When did that Quanah, Acme & Pacific article run, and who wrote it? Chances are, he'd shoot right back with, "Don Sims, I think it was, maybe 1960 or 1961." (For the record, it was February 1961.) "A mind like a steel trap," he'd boast, kiddingly, around the office. What was, say, the first diesel he saw at Denver Union Station when he was at Lowry Air Force Base? Out would come the *original notebook* from his desk drawer with the on-the-spot answer.

Despite working with computerized editorial tools late in his career, he had a knack for composing right-the-first-time prose, of making his first draft his final one. And, he could create a major story in a hurry. When things didn't work out at the last minute with an author of a nice going-home-for-Christmas piece for December 1977 TRAINS (the story was in layout stage), the Editor sat down at his Royal and pounded out the five-page "Milwaukee Road: Lionel in 1:1 Scale" . . . in less than two days! [It begins on page 116 of this book.]

He boasted there wasn't a story he couldn't cut (or flesh out) by any given amount of lines if it didn't quite fit the layout or if a late ad came in, and there wasn't a caption he couldn't fill out to "square" in a space. It was all in the tradition of newspaper and magazine editors everywhere, fighting the never-ending war of "man vs. white space." And in filling that white space, David set the standard for the kind of railroad accuracy that is getting tougher every month to champion as the world shies away from the written word . . . it's Chicago & North Western, not Northwestern; Horse Shoe Curve, not Horseshoe; and Southern (and AT&SF and the others) Railway, not Railroad. Item: in 34½ years, for 415 issues beginning with January 1953, David never missed writing his monthly "Railroad News & Editorial Comment." Not once. How about that 40,000-mile, 37-day, round-the-world trip? He wrote two before he left.

David's attention to detail and tradition also were evident beyond the magazine. In 1976, when his good friend Graham Claytor was at Southern's throttle and operating a singular Washington–New Orleans passenger train outside Amtrak, David prevailed upon him to reinstitute a tradition that had died in the 1940's, when the universality of diesels came to be realized: adorning the bulldog nose of Southern's 17 E8's with the name of the only varnish on the system, *Southern Crescent,* in script.

Ever the apartment dweller, David strove mightily to locate in view of the tracks, and even in retirement he kept us up-to-date on the goings-by — e.g., Soo Line's new wide-nose red SD60M's — on the double track outside his third-floor Elm Grove vantage point . . . a double track that in his heart, of course, was still the Milwaukee Road.

In the notice of his passing we prepared for local newspapers and other rail trade and hobby publications, we dutifully listed his books: *True Adventures of Railroaders* (1954), *Steam's Finest Hour* (1959), *Canadian Steam!* (1961), *Diesels West!* (1963), *Locomotive 4501* (1968), *Fasten Seat Belts* (1969), *Our GM Scrapbook* (1971), *The Mohawk That Refused to Abdicate, and Other Tales* (1975), and *I Like Trains* (1980). We also must not forget Kalmbach's quarterly AIRLINERS INTERNATIONAL MAGAZINE, an extension of his interest in commercial aviation. Its 1974 discontinuance after four issues was a wound that David never showed.

But as laudable and memorable as those works are, it's the now-sometimes-yellowed pages of this publication that will remain his legacy. Whether they're loose copies in piles or maroon bound volumes neatly lined on a shelf, TRAINS from 1948 to 1987 (and as occasionally thereafter as we could coax him) stands as testimony to the insight, knowledge, and fun brought to the faithful by the man arguably most deeply versed in U. S. railroading. Although he wrote about a relatively small industry in a large world, he shaped more opinions and careers than scores of statesmen. As a husband, brother, uncle; writer, story-teller, mentor, boss, consultant, friend; David P. Morgan will be sorely missed. ⊥

Editor's Note: Dave Ingles is Senior Editor of TRAINS. *His obituary of David P. Morgan ran in the March 1990 issue.*

Morgan's brother Len wrote the following article, which first appeared in the June 1990 issue of Flying *magazine.*

Trains, planes, and ships

By Len Morgan

AFTER THE MEMORIAL SERVICE Mick said, "I wish I could say I really knew him, but I cannot. He was both strange and brilliant. He was our brother, and a good brother, and we shall miss him."

My earliest recollections of him are of a carrottop who loved trains. The Central of Georgia Railroad linked our rural town with the outside world; in fact, it provided the only reasonable travel when rains turned red clay to slippery mud. There were no paved roads in Jasper County in those Depression days. Everything from coal to coffins came in by rail; cotton and peaches went to market on daily mixed trains.

I shared David's awe of steam locomotives and wanted to be an engineer, a notion quickly forgotten when a barnstorming OX-5 Travel Air landed in a pasture near town. Even after I said I didn't have $3 and wouldn't have been allowed to ride anyway, the pilot let me look at the cockpit. My interest in trains waned. The glorious aroma of leather, dope, and gasoline was too much. David watched from a distance, unmoved.

We moved to Louisville and lived near the Louisville & Nashville main line. David camped by the tracks, jotting down engine and Pullman numbers, and prowled the stations downtown. There was more for him to watch by the tracks than for me at Bowman Field, where hours passed with little action. To show him the light, I bought us a hop in a slab-wing Stinson Reliant, unknown to our parents, who would not have appreciated my missionary zeal. He agreed that flying was fun, then resumed his trackside research. "You've inhaled too much coal smoke," I said. Boys who ached to sit in cabs or cockpits were expected to "grow up" and find respectable work. Railroading would do if it

meant working at L&N headquarters — but flying? Oh, my dear!

David was 13 when I enlisted. In the half century that followed we rarely saw each other. We spent perhaps a month together all told, but we kept in touch and were closer than some brothers who live on the same street. In another sense I hardly knew him.

We considered ourselves hugely successful in being paid to do exactly what we wanted to do. Robert Louis Stevenson wrote in 1878, "I travel not to go anywhere, but to go. I travel for travel's sake. The great affair is to move." That's how we felt.

My interest was narrow: I wanted to fly airplanes, period. A larger picture intrigued David. He wanted to know everything about railroading — its history, its contributions to civilization worldwide, its impact on modern life. He was hired at $37.50 a week by a small Milwaukee magazine, TRAINS, circulation 39,000. Within five years he was editor, and he remained so for 34 years. I was hired by Braniff at $47.50, with $10 deducted for a uniform. Neither of us doubted that grand years lay ahead.

We agreed that public transportation is by far the most fascinating of businesses but disagreed on its management. He deplored taxpayer funding of airports and airmail subsidies, while railroads paid for their tracks and stations. I reminded him of the land grants that encouraged early rail expansion and that the global air transport network so vital in World War II was based on airline expertise. The fawning service accorded fares in DC-3 days amused him. "You won't be able to keep this up if and when you attract the mass market," he said, and we couldn't. After watching a P-80 fly in 1945 he wrote, "You'll be able to buy a jet ticket in seven years." I guessed 15, but he was right. We watched and discussed dramatic changes — from steam to diesel power in his corner, from pistons to turbines in mine. The growth of air travel and shrinking of rail passenger service revolutionized our industries.

"David was the leading writer in the railroad field for more than three decades," said a friend. He was more, being an astute student of transportation in all its forms. His research took him and his wife around the globe and led to a hobby of collecting airlines, airliners, and places, all of them meticulously recorded in pocket notebooks.

From Nairobi and Nome and Sydney came picture postcards of foreign trains with teasing notes. "We rode an Alaska Coastal Grumman Goose today: Skagway-Juneau." Or, "Add the Viscount to my roster: Zambia-Kenya on Central African." If a trunk or feeder flew it, David and Margaret probably rode it, from the Ford Trimotor ("Oh, but it's a fine thing to experience.") to Concorde ("You've got to try this one, Len!"). He could get more on a postcard than most people can in a two-page letter.

Getting there the quickest way was secondary to adding another airliner or baggage tag to his collection; itineraries were planned accordingly. He and Margaret were aboard the ancient Sandringham flying boat Charlie Blair flew to England in 1976. That publicized trip took 20 hours; they returned supersonically in three. Their logs eventually included more than 50 airliner types, as many airlines and hundreds of destinations.

After every trip came questions. If flaps decrease landing speed, why are they dropped for takeoff? Is Concorde's cabin as wide as the Convair 340's? What's a step climb, a VOR, a PRT, a check valve? How many Electras were built? Was there a DC-5? I often had to dig for the answers, yet I never once stumped him. His knowledge of railroads was encyclopedic.

In 1969 David compiled his impressions under the title, *Fasten Seat Belts: The Confessions of a Reluctant Airline Passenger,* an insight into what passengers thought. What a shame that delightful little volume was not updated after his later travel adventures. He founded an excellent magazine for airline enthusiasts; it died from lack of promotion.

We discussed writing. He had the uncanny knack of putting his thoughts on paper exactly right the first time. No revisions, no corrections. He made it look so easy. He was the pro, I the hack.

He loved ships. The passenger lists of the *Queen Mary, Queen Elizabeth,* and *France* on their sad farewell crossings included the Milwaukee couple. Typically, he wanted to be there when the curtain fell. I envied him those voyages. Travel left him unjaded. He never lost his rapture for locomotives that snaked 120-car freights up mountain grades, great ships that rivaled grand hotels, choosing dinner wine while moving at rifle-bullet speed 11 miles up. It was not his nature to become blasé about such wonders.

Railroading was his life. He learned it hands-on, in steam and diesel cabs, cabooses, switch towers, presidents' private cars, at the same time maintaining a lively interest in flying and sea travel. A postcard from Long Beach of a restored steam locomotive read, "We stayed another day to see Howard Hughes' flying boat. Amazing!" He never missed an air show or TV documentary, and he sent a check to help finance Rutan's *Voyager.* Whenever his paper carried an aviation item, he clipped it for me, adding questions in the margin.

A stickler for detail and accuracy in what he wrote, his work reflected the drama and importance he saw in railroading. He appeared on network television, gave talks, and was invited to the White House to watch President Johnson sign a railroad bill. But he was a quiet, sensitive, private person who avoided attention. He spoke with his typewriter. Under his editorship TRAINS' circulation grew, and today it approaches 100,000.

Among other things he kept the overall picture in perspective for me with his kidding ("Can't you guys stay away from those volcanoes?" when a 747 lost all power, or, "I thought 737s had brakes," when one overshot and stopped on railroad tracks). We in aviation have tunnel vision. Highly visible, we think we occupy the center of the travel universe, whereas we own but a corner of it. David never let me forget it.

Illness forced his early retirement. He wanted to spend the winter here in our warmer climate. We would talk trains and airplanes and faraway places and catch up on the years gone by since we were kid brothers in a little Georgia town. We would get to know each other a little better. I think I looked forward to that more than he. But it was not to be. His condition worsened; a few days after Christmas he was gone and with him that wonderful chance. I never knew anyone like him. ⊥